THE
SALVAGERS

Hervey Benham

Published by
ESSEX COUNTY NEWSPAPERS LTD
COLCHESTER

1980

DEDICATION

For my daughter Jane, who now knows the salvagers' cruising grounds better than I do, and who has helped and encouraged me with this book from conception to completion, splicing together many disjointed passages and putting whippings on many untidy loose ends, as well as drawing the end paper maps.

OTHER BOOKS BY HERVEY BENHAM

Last Stronghold of Sail (Harrap 1947). Stories of the Colne and Blackwater.

Down Tops'l (Harrap 1951, reprint 1971). The story of the East Coast sailing barges.

Once Upon a Tide (Harrap 1955, reprint 1971). East Coast shipping in the 18th and 19th centuries.

Two Cheers for the Town Hall (Hutchinson 1964). A study of the structure of local public affairs before reorganisation, based on Colchester.

Some Essex Watermills (Essex County Newspapers 1976). An account of the mills, past and present, of the Rivers Chelmer, Blackwater and Colne, and of the Essex coastal tidemills.

The Stowboaters (Essex County Newspapers 1977). The story of the Thames Estuary sprat and whitebait fishermen.

The Codbangers (Essex County Newspapers 1979). The story of the Icelandic and North Sea cod fishermen in the days of sail.

© Hervey Benham 1980

First published 1980 by Essex County Newspapers Limited, Colchester
Designed by Keith Mirams, Colchester
Printed by The Anchor Press Ltd, Tiptree
Bound by William Brendon & Son Ltd, Tiptree
ISBN 0 950944 2 3

CONTENTS

ILLUSTRATIONS

ACKNOWLEDGEMENTS

Photos: Nautical Photo Agency (6 and 12), John Leather (3), Aldeburgh Moot Hall Museum (4), Ford Jenkins (6), Essex Record Office (7 and 10), Roger Finch (8 and 10), Librarian of the Royal Society (8), Mrs Winifred Cooper (9 and 10), N R Omell (11), Royal National Lifeboat Institution (13), Ray Wood (16).

In text: Wreck of the *Floridian* and ss *Adelaide* are by courtesy of Essex Record Office. Plate 2 was first published in *The Tidal Thames*, the view of Harwich Navy Yard in *A Season at Harwich*, and the Ramsgate lifeboat approaching the *Indian Chief* in *Heroes of the Goodwin Sands*.

Preface

I have chosen to tell the story of the Essex salvagers in three sections.

Book One, The Salvagers' Century, offers an introductory background.

Book Two, Memories of a Scroper's Son, recreates the story of wreck and rescue as it might have been recalled by one who remembered brave men and gallant deeds, and cherished a proud tradition instilled in him from his boyhood.

Book Three, Who, What, When and Where, provides references for those interested in closer detail, including dates, names and particulars of salvage claims and payments, as well as the sources of the material. It also lists many further incidents for which there was no space in the main narrative.

Readers unconcerned with local history who prefer to confine their interest to Book Two will incur no reproach from me.

The anonymous old Harwichman who recalls the Memories of a Scroper's Son never lived – or did he? I can only say that he has become just as real to me as many people I have to meet every day of my life, and twice as interesting as most of them. I have found him a delightful companion, and at times a great nuisance, for he has insisted on taking this book over and telling the story in his own way, quite contrary to my original intentions and expectations.

He is in fact a compound of many of the old fishermen and bargemen I have listened to over the past fifty years. I hear their voices still, though most, alas, have now passed on, or in the charming Brightlingsea euphemism 'gone round to Pin Mill'. Because I hear them so clearly I have told these tales in their language, which I hope will not be too daunting to readers less familiar with East Coast lingo and phraseology. I have often been aware of the debilitating effect of translating into conventional English subtleties of outlook and expression which that language cannot fully convey, and for once have determined to be free of such restraints.

Of course I have had to credit my old friend with a capacity for instant recall beyond that to be expected even from an ancient mariner, even allowing that the memories of these old-timers often put more sophisticated intelligences to shame. Nor is it in fact probable that he read and could quote from *The Times*, which took a lively interest in such affairs. I must therefore crave from the reader a certain suspension of disbelief, though I would at the same time assure him I have often found yarns which I could hardly believe confirmed and corroborated in the local paper reports on which I have in fact relied.

In keeping with this style I have not loaded my narrative with dates. An old East Coaster will preface a tale by stating the month it occurred, and the day of the week and often the time of the day, while the year seems irrelevant.

But to set the period I have assumed that my old friend was born around 1860, and that he relied on his father's memories and knowledge for the events of the first half of the century. I have observed this broad differentiation of period in Chapter Two, and indicated it now and again throughout the narrative. From time to time I have assembled incidents remote from each in time; those seeking a more precise historical perspective must refer to Book Three.

My narrator would thus have left school and grown up in the late 1870s, a time when many long-established ways of life were beginning to disappear in Harwich. In particular the arrival of the steam tugs and lifeboats was starting to transform the ancient calling of the salvagers who are the subject of this book. Thus he might well have lived to set down these memories as an octogenarian during the early years of the Second World War – another reminder that a centuries-old way of life vanished without trace and almost without memory all in a single lifetime.

I have also accepted the limitation of my imaginary old friend's memories and interests to Harwich and its immediate neighbourhood, with only such excursions further afield as might be expected in the way of East Coast knowledge and gossip. A wider detailed coverage had its attractions, but there is a limit to the sagas of wreck and rescue which can be digested at a sitting. I have therefore preferred to offer a representative selection of incidents, and to sketch in the background against which they occurred.

I have also welcomed the opportunity to continue a task I began in my last book, *The Codbangers*, in recalling the traditions of this fascinating and neglected seaport.

Harwich had to suffer another three-quarters of a century of the depression my old friend could see descending on it in his youth. In the past decade, with the revival of European trade, it has attained a new prosperity, or at any rate a new activity, as a container port. Its streets and quay, long idle and deserted, are today jammed with juggernaut lorries loading crates on to North Sea ferries of unprecedented ugliness at the new Continental piers which occupy the site of the old Navy Yard where John Vaux built his paddle tug. Plans to develop the Bathside have continued to be discussed to the present day, but as my old friend would have said, 'still nothing never come of them'. The lifeboat station, discontinued after the First World War, was, however, restored in 1967 with the forty-four-foot steel lifeboat *Margaret Graham*, replaced in 1980 by the *John Fison*, lying in the Pound where the second *Springwell* and the steam lifeboats once lay. An inshore rescue boat was also established in 1965.

A fuller account of salvaging in Suffolk and Norfolk will be found in Robert Malster's *Saved From The Sea*. The same author's *Wreck and Rescue on the Essex Coast* supplies the lifeboatmen's view of the story, while John Leather's *The Northseamen* has further information about the Colne smacks. I am indebted to all these books, and also to Roger Finch's *A Cross in the Topsail* (the history of R & W Paul, the Ipswich malsters), Ernest Cooper's *Storm Warriors of the Suffolk Coast*, and Frank Hussey's *Old Fitz*, which records Ablet Passiful's connection with the translator of Omar Khayyam.

Since some of the subject matter of this book has already been touched on by these authors, and also in my own *Last Stronghold of Sail* and *Once Upon a Tide*, I have, in selecting my stories, sought to find unpublished alternative material, though certain incidents of outstanding importance must find a place in any account. This particularly applies to two of the most unforgettable wrecks of the nineteenth century – the German emigrant liner *Deutschland* in 1875 and the sailing ship *Indian Chief* in 1881.

In the case of the former[1] I have sought to show the impact of the violent criticism in press and Parliament which contributed to the provision of a lifeboat at Harwich.

The story of the latter was superbly told by Clark Russell, who published interviews with the cox'n of the Ramsgate lifeboat and with the mate of the *Indian Chief* in the *Daily Telegraph*. These great pieces of journalism were reprinted in the *Lifeboat Journal* of February, 1881, and have since

---

1. Readers who compare my account with that in *The Northseamen* will note that that book associates the *Aquiline* with the *Deutschland*, which was a family tradition as reported to John Leather. Contemporary accounts show, however, that it was the *Indian Chief* she sailed in to report.

appeared in many books, including Achilles Daunt's *Our Sea Coast Heroes* (Nelson), *The World of Adventure, A Collection of Stirring Stories* and *Moving Accidents* (Cassell 1889), Rev P Stanley Treanor's *Heroes of the Goodwin Sands* (Religious Tract Society, 1904) and Major A J Dawson's *Britain's Lifeboats* (Hodder and Stoughton, 1923). I have been content to summarise these two stories and to merge them into one narrative, but I have also contrasted them with the far less glorious but equally fascinating story of the fiasco of the Harwich rescue attempt, led in person by the Mayor of Harwich, standing on the open bridge of a paddle tug that was his pride and joy. This seems to me to give a new dimension to one of the epic stories of the North Sea.

For the wreck of the *Berlin* I have made use of an article by F G E Moll of Voorburg, Holland, in *Sea Breezes*, February, 1962, and I have allowed myself the dramatic licence of permitting my narrator to borrow the identity of a steward named W C Carter who was, in fact, saved in the manner recounted and must, I think, have seen the events much as described.

Local newspapers, particularly the *Essex Standard* (now *Essex County Standard*) and the *Harwich and Dovercourt Free Press* (now *Harwich and Manningtree Standard*) have in fact provided most of the material which I have credited to my old narrator's memory. I only hope I have succeeded in conveying the vivid immediacy which emerges from the contemporary reports and advertisements, along with some unfamiliar terms such as one usually encounters in charting hitherto unexplored waters. What was the 'boat called a centipede', captured full of contraband in 1834? What was the Whitby collier's 'pan boat' sold in 1838 or the 'paddle box lifeboat' borrowed from a Naval vessel (and not returned) in 1855? A sale in 1833 included 'three steering sails' and cable 'in junks'.

I have also been particularly helped by two unpublished collections of information. The late Dr Jack Groom devoted much of his life to recording conversations with Harwich mariners who were veterans in the 1930s. He was particularly concerned with the cod smacks and sailing barges owned by his family, and extracts from his notebooks formed part of my last book, *The Codbangers*, in which a fuller note about him and his family will be found. But there was also much general maritime gossip, and many stories of the scropers and stone dredgers which find their place here. I have made my imaginary narrator contemporary with many of the men Jack Groom knew so well, and particularly with Frank Goodey, who also features in *The Codbangers* and who was often in my mind as I wrote. I must again express my thanks to Mr Tom Groom for allowing me access to his brother's notes and papers, which include a letterbook used by Cooper in *Storm Warriors*. The letters in this from and to the Harwich Receiver of Wreck (J W Wood) have been used for Chapter Five.

The Brightlingsea Parish Magazine has provided much of the Colneside material, and I have also dipped freely into the unpublished memories of a former Brightlingsea Lloyd's agent, A A Jefferies (who also appears in *The Stowboaters*). For both these my gratitude is due to Mr John Fieldgate, who himself succeeded his father in the office Jefferies once filled. Further details will be found in Book Three.

The Protection Against Impressment Certificates issued during the Napoleonic wars are in the Public Record Office (Admiralty 7). The registers in the Customs Houses at Colchester and Harwich have filled in the details of the smacks, and I am grateful to the Registrars and their colleagues there for putting up with my visits. To avoid peppering these pages with anything up to a hundred footnotes I have inserted these particulars, chiefly dates and dimensions, in the Index of Ships' Names.

For the role of the pilots and the salvagers' work with them I am grateful to Captain Robert Sanders, formerly Trinity House Superintendent Pilot at Harwich, who himself has in hand a history of the North Channel pilots which will undoubtedly make another major contribution to a belated understanding of bygone life on the East Coast and the Thames Estuary.

The Archivist of the Royal National Lifeboat Institution (Miss D C Rogers) has also helped me with illustrations and factual checking.

In view of these two acknowledgements I must add that if my old and imaginary friend has at any point done less than justice to either Trinity House of the RNLI I express my regret on his behalf. But it does seem to me that, despite its many activities in the interests of seafarers, Trinity House, along with the Board of Trade (which having neither a body to be kicked nor a soul to be saved merits no civilities), must be held responsible for procrastinations and prevarications which contributed horribly to the appalling toll of nineteenth-century shipwreck on 'the Burying Grounds'.

As to the RNLI, some will consider the controversy over self-righting lifeboats sterile and exhausted, and regard the idea of a steam cruising lifeboat as an irrelevant 'might-have-been'. In my view they are both part of a fascinating aspect of maritime history which has been too little considered.

My thanks must also go to that good friend of old Harwich, Mrs Winifred Cooper, and to Mr Roger Finch and Mr John Leather (himself the great grandson of Thomas Barnard), two authors whose books I have already mentioned and who have been generous with knowledge and advice.

Finally that most skilled exponent of English as she is typed, Mrs Sandra Hopwood, has cheerfully adapted herself to the illiteracies of my dear old friend in preparing his memories for the press.

Hervey Benham,
Feldy,
West Mersea
1980

BOOK ONE

THE SALVAGERS' CENTURY

'The Burying Grounds': Rescue and Pillage: Smuggling and Salvaging: Emergence of the Salvage Trade: A Week's Toll: Hazards of Navigation: Ships and Lives Expendable: The Salvaging Life: The First Lifeboats: A Campaigning Customs Officer: Working in the Dark: Limitations of the Lifeboats: Salvage and Pilotage: Bygone Glories of Harwich: Village Enterprise: A Brightlingsea Tradition: A Rich Man's Ruin: The Mayor Goes Salvaging: Pioneer Salvage Tugs: 'Of Ipswich': Other Harwich Celebrities: The Salvaging Smacks: Off the Beach: Suffolk Smacks.

THE SALVAGERS' CENTURY

The story of shipwreck in the North Sea in general, and among the sandbanks of the Thames Estuary in particular, stretches back to the furthest focus of history and beyond.

Yet only two centuries have passed since the first recorded evidence of real concern over the saving of life at sea.

And it was only in the nineteenth century that there emerged among the shoals and sandbanks of the Thames Estuary a body of men devoted both to the saving of life and the preservation of stricken ships which in previous ages would have been written off as wrecks.

This is the story of these men, the salvagers who ventured their craft. their skills and their lives in some of the most difficult and dangerous waters in the world. It was a strange calling, in which heroism and pillage were inevitably intermingled. The interplay of these motivations, along with some of the particular difficulties the salvagers encountered and the techniques they developed to overcome them, are the subject of the main section of this book, Memories of a Scroper's Son.

But first some background, historical, geographical and personal, is needed to appreciate the conditions under which the salvagers worked.

Within living memory man has, for the first time, not conquered the challenge of the North Sea – which will still find a few unpleasant tricks to play and surprises to spring to the end of time – but has at least developed the power of his ships and the capacity of his navigational aids to a point where he can accept the challenge on equal terms.

It was very different in the age of the salvagers, who began to establish themselves as a recognised profession in the early years of the nineteenth century, reached the zenith of their activities at the mid-century when they were joined but not superseded by lifeboats and steam paddle tugs, and saw their calling diminish and die out as the closing decades at last brought a decrease in the appalling toll of death and destruction which provided their livelihood.

'The Burying Grounds'

From the Tyne to the Thames the whole East Coast was a graveyard of ships throughout the age of sail. The Yorkshire and Lincolnshire beaches claimed in particular a toll from the great fleets of colliers staggering north in ballast, or struggling homeward or to foreign ports deep-laden. Craft embayed in the Wash, or making an ill-judged landfall from the Baltic, left their bones on the hump of Norfolk. But of all the death-traps for shipping, not only on the East Coast but anywhere round the British Isles, none was more terribly destructive than the sandbanks of the Thames Estuary.

Craft trying to enter the Estuary had to find their way between the Gunfleet, the Barrow and the Sunk Sands, reaching out like fingers to grasp their prey. To the south-east of these the Longsand and Kentish Knock stretched further still out into the North Sea, a hazard to every craft trying to find a passage from the North Sea to the English Channel, through the bottleneck between them and the Flemish banks. Here not only coasters but foreign-going merchantmen and passenger ships from Germany, Holland and the Baltic were at risk. Along with the Goodwins, the Longsand was thus the most awful place of all, earning its name, 'the Burying Grounds'.

All these sandbanks lie submerged and invisible at high water, and across them all the tides sweep treacherously, making navigation hazardous even for well-found ships with skilled and experienced masters. Big, well-manned passenger liners could not cope with them, so it is no wonder that clumsy collier brigs and leaky Norwegian timber barques fell easy victims.

Nowhere on the East Coast south of the Humber was there a harbour of refuge till Harwich was reached, other than the partial shelter of Hollesley Bay and Lowestoft and Yarmouth Roads, which gave little protection in a north-easterly gale. Many a skipper facing the fury of the North Sea prayed that he might be spared to see the shelter of that great natural haven, and many of their prayers went unanswered. For there were further traps across the approaches to Harwich, in particular the Shipwash and the Cork Sands, and if a vessel was fortunate enough to avoid them and reach Landguard Point she might be unable to brace up hard enough to make the harbour entrance. In that case she would drive down on to the West Rocks or the Pye, or would strike 'the Holidays', as the Halliday shoal was known.

Finally, as if the natural hazards were not deadly enough, they were complicated by human folly. The Beacon Cliff on the Essex side was so eroded during the first half of the nineteenth century, due to the removal of thousands of tons of cement stone, as to affect the tidal flow and cause Landguard Point on the Suffolk shore to extend out into the fairway marked by the leading lights, which thus became known as the misleading lights, and guided many innocent vessels to destruction.

It was possible, with local knowledge, to run up the Wallet channel, and, avoiding the Knoll and Eagle Sands, to round the bar and find refuge in the Colne or Blackwater, but this was an escape route unknown to foreigners and even to many Geordie collier skippers, who would sometimes brave the Longsand and the Goodwins in the hope of an anchorage in the Downs or, failing that, a lee under the South Foreland. No spider contriving a web across some of the busiest sea-lanes in the world could have drawn its threads with more cunning cruelty.

The area must have had an awful reputation throughout North Europe, Scandinavia and the Russian Baltic, wherever ships were owned and sailors met together. Many a little French, Dutch, German or Danish seaport must have received the news that yet another of its argosies had perished on that dreadful English coast. Those lucky enough to survive would be sent home by their Vice-Consul, who was in fact a local broker appointed with official recognition to look after foreign nationals' interests. Those less lucky were sometimes buried in Harwich churchyard (occasionally by the salvagers themselves) but more frequently in that cold and hungry graveyard, the North Sea.

Owners and merchants would hear news that their ships and cargoes, or what remained of them, were being sold by strangers to strangers in a strange land. In due course they would receive what was left after salvors, agents, auctioneers and lawyers had had their pickings.

Rescue and Pillage

Harwich and its neighbour Colneside thus became the centre of a strange trade – salvaging. It was a curious calling, for one day the salvagers were risking their lives in heroic exploits to rescue half-drowned seamen from sunken ships; the next they were back like a pack of hyenas to strip the wreck of every rope yarn and every scrap of movable cargo. Were they heroes or sharks? Sometimes they were in disrepute, but on the whole they were honoured. Even on the occasions when they faced charges of stealing or concealing wreckage, the magistrates, with a few notable exceptions, showed the respect with which they regarded them, often apologising for having to impose a minimum fine, and when they themselves took their claims before the courts they were usually treated sympathetically and even liberally.

Just how and when it all began is impossible to say. Rescue and salvage are always closely connected and must have developed according to the evolution of craft capable of facing the conditions involved. There is no evidence in this area of 'wrecking' such as is alleged to have been common in the West Country, that is to say the luring of ships to destruction by the display of false lights. It may have been done. There are stories of smacks lying in the Spitway showing bright lights to attract ships on to the Gunfleet Sand, but no real evidence, and it seems out of character with the well-documented records of what did go on.

Rights of 'wreck of the sea' were a medieval bone of contention. A mandate to the Sheriff of Essex from King Henry IV in 1419 laid down that such matters should be 'distrained, dealt with, tried and rectified by the Common Law' with the powers of the Lord Admiral confined to 'cognizance of the death of man, and mayhem done in great ships'. The office of Vice-Admiral became a decorative appendage to the title of the Lord Lieutenant, but the County Vice-Admiralty in some way passed into the nominal control of the Lord Warden of the Cinque Ports. The Lord of the Manor also had a finger in the pie, with rights over wrecks above the tidemark, so that if one had the misfortune to be 'wrecked on the manor' one might have to pay for the privilege of losing a ship.

In practice, from the seventeenth century onwards, the Board of Customs were really the controllers. This was the position in the early nineteenth century, with the emphasis on fighting the smuggling of salvage much as if it was contraband.

An Act of Parliament of George IV nominated Ramsgate, Deal, Dover, Harwich, Brightlingsea and Wivenhoe as places authorised for receipt of salvage, where it had to be delivered to 'the Deputy Serjeant of the Admiralty of the Cinque Ports'. This preservation of what was doubtless ancient tradition resulted in a curious anomaly – the existence of Cinque Port Admiralty depots as well as Deputy Serjeants at places having no connection with the Cinque Ports. Brightlingsea was an early member of this medieval confederation, and its only outpost on the East Coast, probably as a counter-poise to the influence of Yarmouth. It was also, by the times with which we are concerned, the only member save Dover to preserve any maritime activity. But the so-called Cinque Ports jurisdiction at Harwich, as late as 1842 when the Admiralty droits from the *Brunswick* were sold, is an example of the liberties legislators took with history.

With the mid-nineteenth century Wreck and Salvage Acts and the draconian Customs Consolidation Act of 1852 the Deputy Serjeants gave place to Receivers of Wreck, who were part of the Customs service, and to Lloyd's Agents. A mid-nineteenth century Act transferred the receipt of droits from the Agents to the Receivers, which provoked a row between these worthies at Wivenhoe in 1858. The interests of foreign shipping were the care of local brokers nominated as Vice-Consuls, and the losses of North Country colliers were sufficient to justify a local Agent for the Sunderland Policies.

It is thus evident that the salvaging of wreck was of importance for many centuries. The next question to be asked is, when did this occupation come to be of sufficient importance to constitute an occupation in its own right?

The certificates issued to smacks to protect their masters, mariners and apprentices against the press gangs begin to mention 'assisting vessels in distress' in 1811, but only as a third alternative to the usual 'fishing and coasting'. But since this occupation was within a few years being put forward by most Essex and Kent smacks it probably indicates the discovery of a useful new claim to exemption from impressment rather than a new trade, or even a big increase in an old one.

Such certificates were issued to the nine-man crews of the survivors of the great fleet of cod smacks which grew up at Harwich and its neighbour ports, Aldeburgh and Manningtree, in the eighteenth century. They undoubtedly took part in the saving of ships from disaster and the saving of life and property from ships which had met with it.

But offshore the Revenue cutters, powerful craft constantly on patrol, were the first to accept the responsibilities later adopted by the specialist salvaging smacks and the lifeboats. They continued to play a dominant part throughout the first half of the nineteenth century, working with and often supervising the growing fleet of salvaging smacks.

Smuggling and Salvaging

Indeed, the changing conditions in the North Sea are exemplified in the role of the Revenue cruisers. In the 1820s they were bringing smuggling craft into Harwich at the rate of almost one each week. The age of the armed smuggler prepared to fight it out with the cutters was drawing to a close, but there were still many specialist smuggling craft, often Kentish luggers, freighted with the traditional half-ankers of spirits, tea and tobacco, their crews prepared to take the risk of imprisonment or drafting to the Navy. These crews were often largely foreigners, who were exempt

from such penalties. The practice of leaving at least some of the contraband sunk at sea for later recovery was increasing, involving the Revenue
men in long hours 'creeping' with grapnels to discover it.

By the 1850s the specialist smugglers had largely been stamped out.
Fishing and salvaging smacks risked an occasional run (perhaps more often
than the records of detection reveal) but the smuggling cases before the
magistrates were increasingly concerned with trivial little ventures by
crews and passengers aboard the railway steamers. At the same time the
specialist salvagers were increasing in importance, and in conformity with
this trend the Revenue cutters' cruising patrols became less and less concerned with arrests and seizures and more and more with assistance to
vessels in distress. Their colleagues in the Customs service ashore likewise
became increasingly involved in the control and disposal of salvage rather
than contraband.

The redoubtable Captain Isaac Saxby of the Revenue cutters *Desmond*
and *Scout* was in the early years of his service busy seizing smugglers, but
when he died in 1872 at the age of eighty he was remembered as a life-
saver. 'Many are the castaway crews he and his gallant *Scout* have landed
at Harwich', ran the obituary in the *Free Press*. His best-remembered
rescue was from the schooner *Hero* in 1844, when his efforts led for the
second time to an outcry for a lifeboat, but many equally notable exploits
are recorded in the following pages. He must have earned good money
as well as a fair reputation from them, for he had powerful craft and big
crews provided at the Government's expense, and presumably the rewards
for their endeavours were personal perks for him and his men, as remains
the case to this day in the Royal Navy and the lifeboat service.[1]

Emergence of the Salvage Trade

The wreck of the Prussian ship *Curier* on the Shipwash in 1812 provides
an interesting picture of the closing years of the Napoleonic Wars, when
the East Coast was at last being freed from the scourge of the privateers,
and on the eve of the great expansion in maritime traffic made possible
by that freedom.

On this occasion the salvage was directed not by a Revenue cutter but
by the 150-ton privateer *Courier* which had been 'cruising after the *Curier*
upwards of three weeks', but only learned of the wreck when she came

1. For details of smuggling see *Once Upon a Tide* and Chatterton: *King's Cutters and Smugglers*.
It is possible that the financial arrangements made by the Customs for seizures of enemy ships and
contraband goods extended to salvage awards, but this has not been revealed in research for either of
these books.

into Harwich.[1] The smacks working with her were from Colchester, Harwich (then including Manningtree) and Orford, all to continue as centres of the trade. From Colchester came the *Indefatigable*, the first on the scene, *Providence*, *Welcome Messenger* and *Hebe*. From Orford came the *Virgo* and from Harwich and Manningtree the *Charlotte*, *Perseverance*, *Neptune's Increase*, *Nancy*, *Rover*, *Two Sisters*, *William and Mary* and *Mary Ann*. Of these, the *Nancy*, *Two Sisters* and *William and Mary* were Manningtree cod smacks destined to be lost two years later with all hands, including their captains, three sons of the owner, Samuel Howard, whose family fleet was to sail away from Manningtree thirty years afterwards to found the fortunes of Grimsby. These, then, were only occasional salvagers. So, according to their Protection Certificates, were the 39-ton *Providence*, the 31-ton *Hebe* and the 21-ton *Indefatigable*, all of which mention fishing and coasting as their first calling.

Five years after the wreck of the *Curier*, in 1820, smacksmen were warned off five wrecks on the Gunfleet and the Buxey, and another that had occurred on the Tongue in the same gales, but how many of these were specialist salvagers is impossible to determine. There is a suggestion in many of the accounts that the casuals behaved more rapaciously than the regulars. For example, when the brig *Lochiel* was wrecked on the Maplins in 1840 it was claimed she was looted by smacksmen 'except Captain Eagle of the *George and Eliza* of Wivenhoe and Captain Andrews of the *Fair Traveller* of Colchester'.

Reporting at this time was heavily influenced by local pride, and some of the salvagers clearly took trouble to present themselves in a favourable light, but my impression is that in the 1820s and 1830s, while every fishing vessel was on the look-out for the rich pickings available from wreck and rescue, a number of them began to find these interruptions so profitable that they could be treated as their main and then their full-time occupation, and that these men, while no angels, tended to act in a more professional and responsible manner.

Certainly, however it may have been shared between full-time salvagers and fishing craft that chanced to be in the right place at the right time, activity was at its height by the 1840s. The scale of operations is shown by the fact that after the *Ariel* got ashore in October 1846 on the highest part of the Gunfleet (which was then much higher than it is today, with great

1. The privateers represent another story waiting to be told. The *Courier*'s owner and master, Captain George Munnings of Thorpe-le-Soken, near Harwich, later became Commander of the Wivenhoe Revenue cutter *Repulse*. He died in 1837. For further details of the salvage of the *Curier* see *Once Upon a Tide*. For details of the Manningtree smacks and of salvage by the cod smacks in the nineteenth century see *The Codbangers*.

areas of sand a-dry at half ebb) no fewer than forty-five smacks joined with the Revenue cutter in a salvage claim, the result of which is unfortunately unknown. The crews of all these vessels totalled 226 men.

The *Ariel* was in the trade from Russia with tallow and hemp, which also involved two other wrecks with specially spectacular sequels – those of the *Fleece*, in 1849, when it was stated that 150 men were engaged in pillage and twenty-eight were charged, and of the *Regina* in 1861, when the depredations of thirty smacks led to the calling out of the marines at Sheerness and seven Brightlingsea men were fined £100 – the maximum penalty, rarely imposed, generally beyond any possible resources and so usually involving a spell in prison as the alternative.

The level of activity reached in the 1840s continued for another thirty years. It was then radically influenced and altered by the appearance of steam tugs and lifeboats, with the 1880s bringing a decline and the virtual end of traditional activities at Harwich, leaving the old trade to be carried on with many of the old craft out of Brightlingsea till the turn of the century.

Other places may have developed a sea-going, cruising salvage trade to a comparable extent, but if so I have not been able to learn of them. Kentish craft included 'assistance to vessels in distress' among their occupations in seeking protection certificates during the Napoleonic Wars – indeed, the first smack that I have noticed making this claim was the *Fox* of Margate in 1811 – but the trade does not seem to have been sustained and developed to the same extent as in Essex.

Ramsgate smacks participated in the rescue from the *Floridian* and the *Dyle* in 1849, and the pillaging of the *Deutschland* in 1875, but most of the rescues on the Longsand, which is about half-way between Harwich and Ramsgate, seem to have been carried out by Essex men. The chief Kentish salvaging ground was, of course, the Goodwin Sands. The terrible toll of wreck there and the continual demands of the fleets lying windbound in the Downs kept the Deal luggers busy, and may have provided enough occupation for the Ramsgate men also, with craft from Margate and the Medway sharing the Nore Sand with the Southend and Leigh men.

The fact that a diver named Rigden (possibly the former skipper of the Harwich *Cupid*) was working with a Faversham craft named *Invicta* in 1894 suggests the possibility that the salvaging trade was more important in Kent than has so far been revealed, but from existing records it certainly appears that most of the rescues on the Burying Grounds and other sandbanks in the Thames Estuary were made by Essex men.

A Week's Toll

At the height of the trade the salvagers certainly did not lack occupation. From the first gale in October till the end of March, hardly a week passed without their being offered a choice of opportunities.

To take one winter's gale at random, in the first week of January, 1863, the barque *August* of Stettin, run into while lying at anchor, was assisted into Harwich by the Colchester smack *Snowdrop*. The barque *Amy Louise* was assisted off the Sunk by the Harwich smack *Queen*, which lost her boat in the operation. The sloop *Prosperity* was assisted off the Longsand. The barque *Danzig* brought up near the Sunk and four of her crew boarded the lightship (presumably for refuge or perhaps for a pilot); they were unable to return and were replaced by men from the Harwich smack *Alfred*, who slipped her anchors and got her into Harwich. The *Johan Jacob* of Altona sailed from Harwich, and put back leaky to be unloaded and repaired. The French brigantine *Marie Amelia* was wrecked on the Longsand. Her captain was killed by a falling mast and her crew took to the rigging, where the cabin boy died and three men were saved by the *Scout* of Colchester.

All these incidents were compressed into one brief routine local news-paper paragraph under the weekly heading 'Shipping Intelligence'. The following week another such paragraph took up the story, with the saving by the *Alarm* of Colchester of the crew of the *Rosebud* of Arbroath, wrecked on the Barrow, and of four smacks assisting the brig *Henrietta* off the Gunfleet, while the noted Harwich salvager *Marco Polo* was in collision in the Swin with a Whitby brig with the loss of one of her crew who tried to jump aboard the brig.

With losses on such a scale two shipwrecks on one voyage were not uncommon. When the *Two Sisters* of Shields was wrecked in December, 1868, her crew took to the boats and were picked up by the *Triune* of London, which ran for Harwich. She also got ashore and both crews took to the boats to be picked up by the salvager *Volunteer*.

Some craft were specially unlucky, or particularly incompetently handled. The Norwegian barque *Oliver Cromwell*, salvaged after a week on the Shipwash in 1891, was again salvaged off the Whitaker or the Sunk (accounts vary) the following year. The schooner *Tino* was got off the Cork in 1851, and in 1853 was ashore on the Shipwash and sank in the Black Deep. The barque *George Robinson* was got off the Shipwash in 1858, hauled out and repaired in Harwich and sailed four months later, straight on to the Gunfleet where she was wrecked. The *Hugo* of Stettin, towed off the Kentish Knock by the Revenue cutter *Scout* in 1848, was also wrecked on the Gunfleet just a year later. Finally, there is the pathetic little tale of the schooner *Arrival*, which was in trouble in 1880 while still owing payment for a previous salvage. This was too much for the skipper, who hanged himself in his cabin.

As late as 1889, when the toll was decreasing, J H Vaux as agent at Harwich of the Shipwrecked Fishermen's and Mariners' Royal Benevolent Society received, lodged and sent home seventy-five shipwrecked sailors; fifty-three to London, five to Lowestoft, three to Goole and fourteen to Sunderland.

This service was for most of the nineteenth century one of the more humane aspects of a callous scene, even if it may have been originally prompted by an instinct to get potential paupers out of the parish. In the 1820s, however, destitute shipwrecked mariners still had to get home as best they could – if they could. When the Shield brigs *Ann* was wrecked in 1822, her crew were brought into Brightlingsea. Four of them made their way as far as Norfolk, and then got some Corton beachmen to take them off in a coble to hitch a lift home in a north-bound collier. A ship picked up their boat but towed it under and three of the men were drowned. The *Ann* herself was apparently almost as unlucky, for three months later the master of a Harwich packet reported he had seen her being assisted into Gothenburg, dismasted.

Hazards of Navigation

The concentration of shipwreck during the winter months is very marked. Partly this was due to the increased incidence of gales, and partly to the hazards of navigation at night, even though the lightships and lighthouses were more numerous during the second half of the nineteenth century than they are today.

Trinity House long resisted the idea of 'floating lights'. Lightships were provided at the Nore and the Dudgeon in the 1730s, and at the Newarp Sands, off the Norfolk coast, as a result of a disaster in 1789, when fifty ships and eighty fishing boats were cast ashore between Lowestoft and Cromer. When the Sunk lightship was established in 1802, along with the East Swin and Orford Ness lighthouse, it was considered that the 'North Channel' into the Thames Estuary was established, though the Mouse, Shipwash and Swin Middle light vessels did not appear till 1837 and the Kentish Knock and the Cork until 1844.

Yet an astonishingly large number of ships blundered into the Thames

Estuary when they thought they were entering the Channel, ending up on the Gunfleet when they supposed they were off the French coast, or even searching for the Humber under Orford Ness. There were lightships at both ends of the Longsand, but when the German emigrant ship *Burgundy* was lost in 1848 it was considered they could not be seen in thick weather.

Even when the basic navigation was correct some terribly difficult passages remained to be negotiated. Till the Gunfleet lighthouse was built in 1852, the Swin was a notable example. The main bottleneck on the North Channel, 'the King's Channel', as it was known, the Swin led between the Scylla of the Gunfleet and the Charybdis of the Barrow and Middle Sands. Once vessels had lost the flash of the Sunk light, which was a guide to the entrance, they had many miles of dead reckoning in the dark before picking up the next light at the Middle. This would have been difficult with the tide running fair through the channel, but setting hard across the top of the sands it carried many vessels to their destruction.

In December 1822 fourteen ships were ashore on the Gunfleet in one gale – surprisingly without loss of life, and with the loss of only two of the ships.

Three years before the Gunfleet lighthouse was at last built there were at the beginning of January 1848 at least three simultaneous wrecks on these sands, and later in the same year, in December, six vessels piled up there on one dark night, probably following each other. While the lighthouse was under construction a schooner and a brig drove ashore nearby on the same night, providing the contractors' tug with a nice little £100 bonus for salvaging the schooner. Though the Gunfleet continued to claim its toll for another half century (specially in foggy weather) it was never again on this scale.

Moreover, while the establishment of the lightships is recorded, there is less evidence as to when lighted buoys were introduced. The absence of these in the first half of the nineteenth century may well have contributed to the great increase in shipwreck during the hours of darkness.

Ships and Lives Expendable

The unremitting toll of ships and lives produced a fatalistic acceptance amounting often to apathetic complacency. Ships were expendable; they were expected to pay for themselves in a few years' trading and were often not even considered worth insuring. Lives were cheaper still and were squandered accordingly.

The numerous accounts of seventeenth- and eighteenth-century disasters on the East Coast seldom, if ever, include mention of rescues or attempts at rescue. For centuries shipwrecked sailors were doomed men unless they had the good fortune to get ashore in their own boats, or to be picked up by a passing vessel. And even passing vessels were often helpless. There seemed nothing surprising or shocking in the arrival in the Colne in 1844 of the Sunderland brig *Alpha*, reporting that she had been in close company with another brig which capsized, perhaps through not being properly ballasted, or perhaps through touching the ground, and sank in five minutes off the Sunk. She was near enough to see the crew of seven clinging to her side, and to read the word 'Scarborough' on her stern. Was it then impossible for her to heave-to or bring up and get a boat in the water? The idea must have been considered and rejected as too dangerous or downright impossible.

The tales of grim struggle to survive, as half-frozen men lashed themselves to the rigging of their sunken craft, tell their own story, but at the other extreme there is an extraordinary record of losses through such minor mishaps as falling overboard, or the capsize of a boat in harbour, or slipping off a quay. There was clearly a much smaller prospect of rescue than would be expected today, due no doubt to the fact that fewer seamen had learned to swim and that lifebelts and other life-saving equipment were conspicuous by their absence.

For example, thirteen men were thrown in the water on a fine summer's day in 1863, under the eyes of their mates 150 yards away, when a brig named *CSM*, lying ashore on the West Rocks, rolled over on to their boats. No fewer than ten of them were drowned. It is difficult to imagine such a toll today.

This helplessness extends sometimes to an impression of downright amateurism. What for example is one to make of the epic of John Cook, who was dredging cement stone off Harwich in his peter-boat in 1828 when his hat blew off? The consequences are solemnly narrated in an advertisement which he inserted in the following week's *Kent and Essex Mercury*, supplemented by the editor's explanation.

John pulled his foresail aback to make the peter-boat heave-to, and jumped into his punt to retrieve his hat. At which moment a breeze caught the boat and away she sailed, crewed only by his unfortunate dog. To make matters worse, she had no name on her stern, 'having recently been lengthened and the weather not having been suitable to put it on'.

So if any readers of the *Kent and Essex Mercury* had encountered a peter-boat, twenty-one feet by seven feet by three feet, jogging across the North

Sea under mainsail, foresail and jib, the foresail three-parts a-weather, with nothing on board bar a dog and about a ton of cement stone, John Cook would like to know. I hope she was picked up, if only for the sake of the wretched dog. (John Cook himself was born for trouble. Six months before this he was sick, and supported by the Seamen's Friendly Society. But he was seen painting the windows of his house, and payment was refused for 'working while on the box'. Cook took the Society before the Harwich magistrates who, however, 'deemed they were shut out'. Notice was given 'to move the King's Bench'.)

As early as 1821 a Society was proposed to supply salvagers with inflatable life-jackets, but there is no record of this being put into practice. A fruitless campaign half a century later to introduce life rafts is referred to subsequently. Even flares and rockets were seldom provided in small craft. It was cheaper to set light to a tar barrel – usually, though on one occasion this primitive distress signal left aboard a ship abandoned on the Gunfleet set fire to her and finished her off.

Whether the salvagers themselves troubled to put a bit of cork under the thwarts of their smacks' boats, which were so often sunk under them, I do not know. I doubt it. Seamen had small hopes of dying in their own beds, and that is one reason why so few did.

The salvaging skippers themselves certainly had nine lives and used up most of them. The few who paid the price of their hazardous calling included Joseph Thorpe of the *Prince Coburg* (1823), William Mudd of the *Samuel* (1833) (prompting speculation as to his connection with the William and Harrison Mudd who, eighteen years later, sailed from Manningtree to Grimsby and did more than anyone else to establish the fortunes of the world's greatest fishing port), Robert Wardley of the *Fair Traveller* (1839), Baldry of the *Fox* (1845) and George Wyatt of the *Alfred* (1869). Thomas Barnard of the *New Unity* saw one of his eight sons, Daniel, drowned under his eyes in 1877, and a number of other losses among the smacks' crews are recorded.[1] All things considered, however, the number remains small and the immunity of the salvage craft from major disasters remarkable.

The Salvaging Life

As has already been made clear, the salvagers had plenty to occupy them,

1. According to the *Illustrated London News* a Colchester vessel lost five hands at the wreck of the *Floridian* in 1849. But there is no confirmation of this in the long report in *Essex Standard*.

Salvage of the schooner Earl Grey *(180 tons) which sank in the* Whitaker Channel *on December 24, 1847, after being abandoned on a passage from Yarmouth to London with barley and malt. The* Illustrated London News *(June 17, 1848) states: 'This new method of raising sunken vessels is by flexible airtight cases and attached chains.' The tug is the* Fly, *which towed the wreck to Burnham, where the cargo was sold on April 10 after being three months under water. 'A good deal of it was afterwards retailed at 15s. a quarter.'*

at any rate during the winter months. What they did in the summer, when weeks often passed without the mention of a ship in trouble, is less clear.

Some laid up their smacks and exchanged their rough piratical calling for the charge of some nobleman's elegant yacht. Others returned to fishing, down Channel after scallops or across to the other side of the North Sea on the terribly dangerous Terschelling banks for deep-sea oysters. Others continued the tradition of mixing coastal freights with fishing voyages, using their speedy craft for fish carrying,[1] or sailing to the Channel Islands for a freight of potatoes.

There were also more surprising cargoes. The *Vanduara* took a freight of dynamite to Antwerp, and smacks often turned collier, with at least one meeting with disaster. This was Robert Tracey's *Robert*, which earned general acclaim and a letter of thanks from the master and crew for a fine rescue from the *John Hunter* in March 1837, and which a year later foundered off Scarborough with a load of coal from Shields for Brightlingsea, her young owner and skipper being picked up after five hours in his boat. Such employment for a smack that was only three years old prompts one to wonder what profit there can have been in the few tons she could carry, and what provision was made to secure the hatches, which must have been dreadfully vulnerable in such a trim.

But quite a number regarded themselves as specialists, and earned enough money to avoid the necessity for another occupation. After a well-deserved refit these would have resumed their cruising patrols in the hope that even in mid-summer a chance breeze of wind or a bit of carelessness on a skipper's part might put something their way. James Cook of the *Snowdrop* of Colchester, testified at a salvage hearing in 1861 that his only means of livelihood from January 1 to December 31 was assisting ships in distress, and on another occasion it was mentioned in defence of some rapacity that the men concerned had not earned sixpence between them during the previous eight weeks.

Smacks equipped with specialist salvaging gear were presumably among the full-time salvagers. At Harwich the *Aurora*'s *Increase*, *Cupid* and *Queen Victoria* were fully equipped as diving smacks, which must have involved big air pumps in their holds, for when they worked on the wreck of the passenger steamer *Bruiser*, sunk off Aldeburgh in 1866, the diver spoke of going down for some hours. It was perhaps with these pumps that salvage smacks inflated caissons under the sunken schooner *Earl Grey* to lift her in the Whitaker Channel in 1848.

1. See Chapter 20.

Diving gear was a speciality of the Lewis family (referred to later). They were employed to clear a sunken wreck from the fairway of the Spalding River in Lincolnshire in 1848, and after their success with the *Bruiser* they took the *Aurora's Increase* and *Queen Victoria* to the Scheldt to salvage a steamer sunk off Antwerp in 1868. Among the working divers were John Fulliger, skipper of the *Cupid*, Tom Rigden, and William Porrage, who called himself 'Don the Diver' and used Lewis's apparatus to walk under water across Harwich Harbour from Harwich to Shotley in one hour twenty minutes in 1848. Having taken up a good collection from the excited crowds he announced that he would walk on the bottom from Harwich to Landguard at a forthcoming regatta, but the report of that event includes no mention of the attempt.

Another specialist salvaging pump was Cottingham's Patent Fountain, the invention of Lewis Cottingham, a Harwich borough councillor and plumber by trade, who used it in an abortive attempt to provide the town with a water supply in 1844. (The service was not finally provided till 1875.) This device was worked by two men and with a 'double-action spindle and flywheel', and was claimed to deliver half a ton of water a minute. There was also a model worked by eight men, claimed to throw three tons a minute. It was credited with saving many craft, including the brig *Dervant* and the smack *Active*, both in February 1853.

When the brig *Shepherd* was got off the Gunfleet in 1862, and sank in the Wallet, she was got afloat and brought into Harwich by this means. For the *Dervant*, the *Aurora's Increase* sailed to Harwich to fetch this pump, suggesting that it was not then standard equipment carried aboard smacks, but there is a mention of John Glover of the *Increase* rigging 'his' patent pump to get the *Kronprincess Louise* off the Gunfleet at a later unrecorded date, by which time the equipment had perhaps been generally adopted.

Sometimes the smacks combined to work in groups. At Harwich William and John Lewis collaborated with their *Aurora's Increase* and *Tryal*, an arrangement which provided some mutual protection and 'back-up' in emergency, and sufficient manpower for heavy tasks such as jettisoning cargo, as well as allowing one smack to remain in possession of a prize while the other sailed to obtain further help. A wretched skipper in trouble would sometimes be confronted by a whole pack of smacksmen, but these had probably been gathered together by the attraction of his misfortune. There are, however, references in salvage claims in 1854 to the rights of craft jointly engaged, and a passing reference in 1849 to 'the lookout boat *Violet*' suggests that this Woodbridge smack was on that occasion acting as the eyes of a fleet or partnership.

The exact extent of the salvagers' legal rights remains obscure, even after studying many arguments in court. But while I have allowed my old narrator to express the common belief that a derelict, that is a deserted craft, was free for anyone to pillage, it is clear that this had no legal basis. Indeed, the chief purpose of bringing some prosecutions, such as those which followed the plundering of the *Fleece* in 1849, was to prove and to publicise this fallacy, which nevertheless remained the basis of working practice.

One aspect of these proceedings would be quite unacceptable by present-day standards. This was the right of the Customs to act both as prosecutors and as judges of the penalties. Over and over again the magistrates felt compelled to impose a fine which they urged the Customs to review and remit. Whether the Customs responded is unfortunately not revealed. The system may, in any case, well have been counter-productive, increasing the magistrates' reluctance to make convictions involving penalties which they felt unreasonable.

The First Lifeboats

Public conscience at last began to react to the incessant loss of life and property in the second half of the eighteenth century.

The first stirrings on the East Coast were in Suffolk and Norfolk, where shipwrecks even more numerous than those on the Essex sandbanks occurred on the shores and beaches. This meant they were right under the eyes of many horrified witnesses, and there was less difficulty in reaching them.

The Christmas gale of 1770 – still remembered a century later as the standard against which other gales were measured, with eighteen ships ashore off Lowestoft and, according to tradition, twenty lost on the Kentish Knock – prompted Edward Gillingwater, the historian of Lowestoft, to call for 'a vessel or machine upon such principles as should not be liable to overset, but should be capable of approaching any vessel in distress'. His hopes were fulfilled with the provision by the Suffolk Humane Society of the lifeboat *Frances Ann* at Lowestoft in 1801, followed soon after by another at Bawdsey.

Around the same time Captain George Manby, an artilleryman who was barrack-master at Yarmouth, was advocating the establishment of county lifesaving organisations, and taking part in the foundation of the National Institution for the Preservation of Life from Shipwreck, later to become the Royal National Lifeboat Institution. Combining vision with practical ability, Manby himself designed a lifeboat in 1825, and saw the need for a 'steam life ship' as early as 1839.

But his chief contribution was a mortar to throw a line from the shore to a wreck. This was prompted by another historic disaster, that of 1807, when the Norfolk shores were strewn with wreckage including the Revenue cutter *Hunter* and the gun brig *Snipe*, from which only twenty of her company of ninety-two were saved. Manby's mortars quickly proved effective wherever wrecks occurred within a few hundred yards' range of the shore, but neither they nor the early lifeboats provided any answer to the perils of the shoals off the Essex coast.

This was the situation when both Essex and Suffolk formed lifeboat associations in the 1820s.

The Essex Life Boat Association, prompted by the loss on the Cork of a schooner with nine hands, was formed at Colchester to provide lifeboats at Harwich and Brightlingsea. The Brightlingsea project had to be forgotten, since there was barely enough money for the Harwich boat, which was built on the lines of the Lowestoft *Frances Ann* by Graham, the first private lessee of the Navy Yard and predecessor of John Vaux, referred to later. She was named *Braybrooke*, after the Lord Lieutenant of the County, but funds did not run to a boarding boat, so in the winter she had to be kept ashore. In addition to the inglorious missions mentioned in the ensuing narrative, she did on one occasion assist HM cutter *Surly*, for which the Admiralty awarded £10, but she was no match for the salvaging smacks and did not justify her existence.

The Suffolk Lifeboat Association, originating in Ipswich, entrusted its project to Captain Richard Gower, a local designer with a notably inventive turn of mind. After going to sea as a midshipman in the East India Company he earned the title 'the young philosopher' at the age of twenty, and came ashore to concentrate on his inventions, which included two four-masted ships, *Transit* and *Royal Transit*, full of labour-saving devices such as came to be accepted in later years.

With characteristic originality he designed a double-ended whaleboat to be launched off the beach at Landguard. She was thirty feet long and only six feet beam, rigged with two spritsails, with buoyancy provided by cork and by copper air-tanks. She was intended to be light enough to transport from one part of the beach to another, but evidently her freakishly narrow beam was not a success, for after she had been damaged in a mishap she was rebuilt two foot six inches wider. She was used a few times but was in disgrace, along with the *Braybrooke*, when a brig, the *Elegant*, was lost on the Roughs with all hands bar the captain without the wreck even being reported.

The clumsiness of the collier brig and the tragic finality of shipwreck are epitomised in the wreck of the Lily *at Scarborough.*

The West Swin around the turn of the century, as seen by W L Wyllie. Today the Maplin lighthouse has gone and only an occasional craft passes through what was for centuries the greatest and busiest sea route to London.

She was sold for conversion into a yacht, and though the Admiralty replaced her with another lifeboat in 1845 there are no records of her service. It is not even clear whether she was ultimately stationed at Land-guard or at Harwich, or indeed at either. At a meeting to discuss this, Captain Washington accepted that she would be more useful at Harwich, and it was agreed to approach the Ordnance Board for the use of the old boathouse (perhaps one ultimately provided for the *Braybrooke*). But whether this came to anything is not clear. Since there are no references to her arrival, or the appointment of a cox'n, let alone any services per-formed, it seems doubtful.

The Suffolk Association for Saving the Lives of Shipwrecked Seamen, founded at Bury St Edmunds in 1824, also provided a little twenty-four-foot boat at Bawdsey in 1826, but lifeboats were not taken seriously in Essex till 1875, when, following the wreck of the German emigrant ship *Deutschland*, which provoked international repercussions, the RNLI estab-lished the *Springwell* at Harwich, paid for by Miss E Burmester, sister of the Rev George Burmester, rector of Little Oakley and for forty years a magistrate.

Other RNLI lifeboats followed; the *Albert Edward* at Clacton in 1878 (provided by the United Grand Lodge of Freemasons), the *Boys of England* at Southend in 1879 (provided through the *Boys of England* magazine), and the *Honourable Artillery Company* at Walton in 1884 (provided by the Dramatic Club of that regiment, which had recently been stationed at Walton). Volunteer lifeboats were established at Walton in 1894 and at Frinton around 1900, but while the Walton *True to the Core* was an estab-lished competitor with the *Honourable Artillery Company*, the Frinton *Sailors' Friend* may well have been primarily a visitors' pleasure boat, gaining kudos and financial support by taking the title of lifeboat.

Though I have allowed my imaginary old friend's still more imaginary father to grumble about the lifeboat, this is intended to indicate chiefly that he was a good old Harwich grouser. The lifeboats do not in fact seem to have been generally resented by the Essex salvagers. The RNLI itself gave rewards to salvagers as well as to its own crews and their volunteer competitors, and paid tribute to the way the Harwich 'hobbling' smacks performed their duty. (This, by the way, is the only occasion I have noticed salvagers given this ancient maritime description, more familiar in the title 'hovellers' for men with local knowledge who assisted sailing craft in tight corners.) The lifeboat cox'n was often a salvager, and so doubtless were many of their crews, attracted by the social distinction of an honoured service, by the payment of 10s for a day launch or £1 at night, and by the prospects of more substantial rewards in the form of special awards by the Institution or of salvage which the Institution allowed its crews to claim.

The Lowestoft *Frances Ann* was actually cut adrift from a wreck by beachmen who had taken possession of it in 1822, with the result that four lives were lost, but when a salvaging smack met the lifeboat going to a job it would often pick her up and give her a tow on the way, calculating perhaps that sharing the salvage award was a price worth paying to avoid the perilous use of the smack's own boat.

Difficulties did arise, however, when the Institution refused to allow lifeboats to be used for salvaging pure and simple (as distinct from rescues which might also lead to a salvage claim), and indignant crews even refused to launch in protest at Harwich in 1881 and at Yarmouth in 1864. But there was no such antagonism as existed between the crews of the Institution and the volunteer boats, who actually came to blows. Here again, the Institution men resented the volunteer crews' freedom to use their boat for salvaging as they chose without control by a committee.

A Campaigning Customs Officer

In view of the general acceptance of shipwreck as inevitable, it may seem that I have endowed my old friend with hindsight in crediting him with a rebellious impatience. But most of the words I have put into his mouth were those written by the editor of the *Harwich Free Press*. He was doubtless in touch with local opinion, which thus seems to have been more enlightened than official thinking in high places.

An equally interesting local witness and commentator was the Harwich Receiver of Wreck, to whom all salvage had to be reported, J W Wood, an intelligent, outspoken, independent-minded Customs officer. The waste of lives and of ships appalled him. He considered the first cause was the ignorance of mariners, and the second their wretched equipment. He urged that the first be tackled by the establishment of training schools or ships at the main ports, so that workhouse boys could be sent to sea with some knowledge of their trade instead of as helpless drudges.

His contribution to improving life-saving equipment was to design a raft which could be stowed aboard and launched more easily than the conventional ships' boats, which were so often smashed or swamped, often with loss of life. He read a paper to the Society of Arts in 1870, and he made a prototype with funds collected at a meeting called by the Mayor of Harwich. After demonstrating this at Harwich he tried to interest all the appropriate parties at his own expense, for he had renounced all commercial rights to the invention, and with results which show that faceless bureaucracy is a phenomenon by no means unique to our own age.

The Board of Trade considered the raft would be of great benefit but regretted they had no powers to compel its use. An international exhibition in Dublin sent him a medal. Lloyd's Salvage Association submitted it to a panel of four naval captains, each of whom promised to write an individual report in its favour. The Royal Humane Society 'highly approved'. And hundreds more crews died before the lifesaving float came to be universally adopted.

Another losing battle was fought by Wood when four Harwich smacks, *Volunteer*, *Paragon*, *John and William* and *Agenoria*, struggled for three days and nights towing in the bottom and one side of the 300-ton Norwegian barque *Justitia*, which they found adrift off Suffolk after she had been wrecked off Corton. The wreckage was sold for £108, and the smacks nearly lost any reward, for the Gorleston lifeboat which had rescued the crew claimed that the Act of Parliament gave life salvors the prior claim. This was rejected in court, but the maximum salvage that could be awarded was £79, which produced only 13s 6d for each of the twenty-one men aboard the four smacks. Wood wrote to Lloyd's, urging proper rewards for salvagers clearing up dangerous, drifting wreckage, but the committee turned down his plea.

He also frowned on deck cargoes of timber in winter, and quoted as one of his examples of dangerous ignorance an occasion when he visited a brig which had come into Harwich to replace a lost anchor and chain. He was horrified at the heap of rusty scrap iron on the foredeck and expostulated with the skipper, who assured him, 'Why, sir, that's far better than the chain I had before!'

Working in the Dark

Reverting to my old friend's bones of contention, Trinity House was over and over again guilty of parsimony and prevarication. It is difficult to believe that money was not available, for in 1841 the nett revenue from the Harwich light dues exceeded £13,000 a year.[1]

The scandal of the 'misleading lights' at Landguard, already mentioned, was the subject of an urgent report to the Admiralty in 1843 by Captain John Washington, RN.[2]

1. According to a Parliamentary report quoted in *Essex Standard*, December 13, 1844.
2. Later Rear Admiral and Hydrographer of the Navy, 1855–1863, a good friend to Harwich, which he knew from his surveying in HMS *Shearwater* and HMS *Blazer*. The report is quoted in full in Hughes: *History of Harwich Harbour*.

His warning was confirmed the following year by the wreck of the schooner *Hero*, as a result of which the Admiralty (doubtless at Captain Washington's prompting) soon provided Manby's rocket apparatus and promised the lifeboat already referred to. Yet Trinity House continued to issue ineffectual warnings for another seventeen years till a small light-house was finally erected in 1861, according to the *Essex Standard*. (The *Victoria History of Suffolk* says 1868.) Between 1845 and this date a light was left in a barrack room window, which may have salved consciences ashore but can have been of little use on a thick, dark night at sea.

During the same period, when the Sheers beacon on the Maplin sands was carried away, a lighthouse was erected nearby, but the old stump was left for nine years, projecting three feet out of the water at low tide, but invisible at high water. During this time, before it was removed in 1846, it was alleged that it caused the loss of eleven coasters. The Gunfleet light-house, built in 1852, was also clearly overdue by many years and scores of wrecks.

Most controversial of all was the failure to provide proper communica-tion with the lightships, which seems a century later quite indefensible. The wreck of the *Deutschland* proved beyond doubt the need for a tele-graph cable to the Sunk lightship, which was by then a practical proposi-tion, yet Trinity House spent eight years and countless lives convincing itself that carrier pigeons were no substitute.

The wreck of the sailing ship *Indian Chief*, which caused a comparable outcry six years later, in 1881, shamed the authorities into accepting an offer by the Telegraph and Maintenance Company to lay a line and main-tain it for a year free of charge. Then, after the trial year, the Board of Trade held an inquiry to decide if the result had justified the cost, decided it had not, and took the cable up again.

Twelve miles of submarine cable to a swinging lightship was not a simple task, and it may be observed that it was not till the same year (1885) that the Germans succeeded in connecting their Aussen Jade lightship with the shore. One of the problems was the risk of the wire twisting round the lightship cable as she swung to the tide. This was overcome by making a hollow swivel in the mooring with the wire led through it. An extra wire was also wound round the cable in a spiral as a reserve circuit in case the core broke as the lightship snubbed to the sea. Moreover, in a gale it was the custom to veer extra chain, so that the swivel would be left lying on the ground sixty yards from the lightship. But these problems were not insuperable, as the Telegraph Company's initiative proved.

Lacking telegraphic communication it seems beyond belief that no recognised code of rockets and flares was laid down. Any sort of signal was used indiscriminately, not only to indicate distress but to summon a pilot, or to attract the attention of a ship steering into possible danger, with the inevitable result that urgent calls for help were ignored or misunderstood, while lifeboats were sent on fool's errands of every kind.

Limitations of the Lifeboats

The continued ineffectiveness of the lifeboats is another surprising story. When Harwich received its inadequate little *Springwell* in 1875 the RNLI clearly stated that lifeboats were only expected to have a few miles' operating range. This provided no answer to the worst problem of all, the Longsand and Kentish Knock.

The Institution was at this time obsessed by self-righting boats. Unfortunately such craft were prone to capsize, and though they duly righted themselves they were liable to lose crewmen in the process, as occurred in the fatal upset of the Harwich and Clacton boats in 1881 and 1884. The Norfolk and Suffolk men, used to their sea-going beach yawls, would have nothing to do with the 'roly-polys', but insisted on beamier, stiffer craft, and their preference was followed by the Walton volunteer crew, whose *True to the Core* outsailed the RNLI's *Honourable Artillery Company* to such effect that the Institution later replaced her with the Norfolk and Suffolk style *James Stevens*.

The Institution's partiality for the self-righting type was explained in the *Lifeboat Journal* in 1881 (the year of the capsize of the *Springwell*) when it was stated that of 249 self-righters forty-three had upset with the loss of fifty-four lives, while of nineteen Norfolk type lifeboats five had capsized with the loss of no fewer than forty-eight lives. Despite this, by 1893, thirty out of the Institution's total fleet of 314 lifeboats were of the Norfolk and Suffolk type. The controversy continued into the 1930s, by which time less than half the fleet were self-righters.

Even the local RNLI secretary condemned the *Springwell* as 'like a bung on the water', and it seemed to be accepted that self-righters could not be made stiff enough to carry sail, or be given a good 'grip of the water'. Yet by 1870 the RNLI had produced in the much-admired *George Hounsfield* of Aldeburgh a self-righter that would go to sea. She was forty feet long, against the thirty-five feet of the *Springwell* and the thirty-four feet of the Clacton *Albert Edward*, so possibly these boats were just not big enough.

Certainly, whether due to her shape or her size, the *Springwell* was no great improvement on the failures which had preceded her. It was perhaps intended that she should serve as a surf boat, towed out to offshore wrecks, yet, though there were tugs in Harwich, no proper organisation for their employment was ever achieved, despite the existence of such an arrangement at Ramsgate.

It was an age of much enterprise and some goodwill, in which co-operation and concerted leadership were conspicuously lacking. First Harwich had had a lifeboat without a tug, then it had a tug without a lifeboat, then it had both a tug and a lifeboat which would not work together. Later it was to have, in the pioneer steam lifeboat *Duke of Northumberland*, the most modern lifeboat in the country (perhaps in the world) and no way of ensuring it was in the right place at the right time.

Salvage and Pilotage

From earliest times there was an association between salvage and pilotage.

Pilotage was not compulsory on the East Coast till the present century, but from its inception in the sixteenth century Trinity House was empowered to license pilots, who had prior claim over unlicensed fishermen. This system was confirmed and reinforced in many pilotage Acts from 1732 onwards.

The licensed pilots were obtained from twelve cruising cutters stationed at Aldeburgh, Southwold, Lowestoft and Yarmouth, with four or five pilots aboard each cutter, or from one of the longshore beach companies on the Suffolk and Norfolk coast. At Yarmouth there were seven companies of thirty or forty men each – over 2,000 men in all, while Lowestoft had its Old Company, Young Company and North Roads Company, with over 300 members between them, as well as seventy more in the Pakefield Beach Company.

The members took turns to man their towers, watching the procession of passing ships, on the lookout for a signal for a pilot.

Sometimes, however, the flag would be a distress signal, or a craft would, to the practised eye of the lookout, be clearly in distress without having to give notice of it, or maybe steering a course to take her on to a shoal, the existence of which she did not even know. Then the company would be called together for a different mission, perhaps loading a heavy brig's anchor aboard their frail yawl to haul off a ship ashore into deep water.

Unlicensed pilots, who could take a job if a licensed pilot did not claim it, were called 'brummagen pilots' or 'brums', a reference to Birmingham as the manufacturing centre of cheap substitutes. The Essex salvagers were not above picking up a 'brum' job when they could, but their opportunities were limited. Plenty of ships brought up or hove-to at the Sunk for a pilot (more than one drove ashore in doing so and required a salvager), but there were always Trinity House cutters on station there.

Attempts to pass off a 'brum' pilotage as salvage assistance usually failed when challenged by a prosecution. The *Volunteer* put a man aboard a steamer in 1869, and was challenged by the Trinity pilot, Robert Willson, lying off the Cork in his cutter. The *Volunteer*'s skipper claimed that the steamer was in distress, and the 'brum' pilot was let off with a fine of £1 and £1 costs – half his pilotage fee of £4.

The official pilot cutters and their tenders themselves took an occasional hand in salvage, and towards the end of the trade Trinity House hired some of the last of the salvaging smacks for pilot landing,[1] but in general on the East Coast the licensing system kept pilotage and salvaging separate.

Bygone Glories of Harwich

For reasons of geography already described Harwich was the principal centre of activity for the cruising salvagers.

The narrator of the yarns which follow was aware that he was living in the twilight decay of a place with a long, proud history. A thousand years before his time, in the year 885, King Alfred's ships had destroyed a fleet of sixteen Danish pirates at 'Stourmouth' – the first record of the harbour. And when our old narrator insisted that Shotley Spit is properly known as Bloody Point he may have been recalling that naval battle of long ago; it is at least an intriguing conjecture.

Yet despite the importance of the harbour, usually known in the Middle Ages as Orwell, the town of Harwich did not even rate a mention in the Domesday Survey, when it was still a hamlet of Dovercourt. Not till the mid-thirteenth century was it established as a town in its own right by Roger Bigod, Earl Marshal of England, Earl of Norfolk, and Lord of the Manor of Dovercourt-cum-Harwich, and not till 1600 did it achieve the dignity and authority of a charter – both events provoking a bitter rivalry with Ipswich, and an antagonism between the two towns which was also alive in our narrator's memory.

Many great naval expeditions have assembled in the harbour down the centuries. The departure of King Edward in 1340 may be cited as perhaps

1. See Chapter 20.

the greatest of all such occasions. 'On Thursday before midsummer 22nd June the King set sail with his great fleet assembled in the port of Orwell about the hour of prime (sunrise).' This fleet, perhaps the largest that ever sailed out of Harwich, numbered about 200 sail. It was joined off the coast of Flanders by another fifty ships and on the Saturday the Battle of Sluys was fought and won.

Two hundred years later, in 1588, Lord Howard of Effingham reported to Lord Burghley, 'My Lord, it is a place to make much of, for the haven hath not its fellow in all respects not in this Realm.' Around this time Thomas Cavendish of Trimley, on the Suffolk shore of the harbour, was the second Englishman to sail round the world in the *Desire* of Harwich, and many of his fellow townsmen were the professional masters of ships nominally commanded by gentleman captains from other parts of the country, including Drake's flagship *Revenge* and Lord Howard's *Ark Royal* at the defeat of the Armada, and Raleigh's flagship at Cadiz in 1599, of which the masters were John and Thomas Gray and Roger Hankin. Thomas Thompson, who commanded Sir John Hawkins' *Dainty*, was father-in-law of Christopher Jones, of Harwich, captain of the Pilgrim Fathers' *Mayflower*.

In the eighteenth century Harwich was the chief centre of the North Sea and Icelandic cod fishery, developed by Harwich enterprise in introducing well smacks and exploring the Dogger Bank grounds, till the town had nearly a hundred deep-sea smacks of its own, with as many more from other ports using the harbour. It was busy, too, with North Sea packet boats, whose captains were men of wealth and influence, and whose passengers, from the most famous personalities of the land to the humblest, filled scores of inns and boarding houses. The Revenue cutters, fighting an open war with the North Sea smugglers, were hardly less important, while the Navy Yard was busy building 'third rates', starting with the *Harwich*, which Pepys declared 'takes the palm from the whole fleet', and ending with the *Scarborough* of 1754 tons in 1812. With these three services in open rivalry Harwich has been described as 'a town of three navies'.

The Napoleonic Wars, however, proved a knockout blow from which the town never recovered. Naval building went to the Medway, the Post Office mail contract to Dover, the cod fishery first to Barking, Gravesend and Greenwich and then to Grimsby. These were some of the vanished glories of which our old narrator was half aware, with his sense of living in a town in decline.

Village Enterprise

The other chief centre of the cruising salvagers was the Colne Estuary and its three fishing centres, Brightlingsea, Wivenhoe and Rowhedge. All were part of the Port of Colchester, for which reason their smacks were described as 'of Colchester', though the town itself took no part in salvaging, or indeed in fishing.

Brightlingsea, as already mentioned, was of sufficient medieval importance to become a member of the Cinque Ports, and had King Henry VIII (who visited it and preferred it to Harwich) had his way it might have become a naval station. Wivenhoe and Rowhedge, further up the river, enjoyed a peaceful obscurity till they awakened in the nineteenth century to enjoy a period of much creative enterprise and prosperity. Both were concerned with salvaging, but the pioneering spirit came chiefly from Rowhedge.

Rowhedge, or to use its older name East Donyland (I have employed the former to avoid confusion), was a place with no history to recall and no natural advantages to explain its pre-eminence. Just why it should have produced an unequalled breed of adventurers, who in turn produced an unequalled fleet of smacks, is one of those enigmas which lend interest and colour to every study of human achievement and development. The connection with salvaging dates back at least as early as 1808, when Robert Prestney anchored his *John and Jane* of Rowhedge and went to work on a brig ashore near Foulness. The smack broke adrift and carried two lads (one of them Prestney's son) to destruction on Sheerness.

The affairs of Rowhedge were of necessity closely entangled with those of its neighbour on the other side of the Colne, Wivenhoe, and by the mid-nineteenth century Wivenhoe begins to figure more prominently in the story. Though the two places were linked by a ferry, a bend and bottleneck in the river's course meant that derelict shipping could reach Wivenhoe but not Rowhedge, for which reason the former was, as already mentioned, recognised as a port for the receipt of salvage, and the description 'of Wivenhoe' came to be used sometimes for smacks from both places.

The energy and enterprise of these two places may well have been stimulated by the arrival at Wivenhoe of a remarkably colourful and creative shipbuilder, Philip Sainty, who sold the shipyard at Brightlingsea and made the move in the first years of the nineteenth century. By 1820 his reputation was such that the Marquis of Anglesey, home from the French Wars after losing a leg at Waterloo, sought him out to build his yacht *Pearl*, one of the champions of her time.[1] This started a tradition of yacht building and introduced Colneside men to the glamorous and rewarding trade of professional yachting, where they quickly distinguished themselves. These men turned to fishing and salvaging in the winter and demanded smacks no less stylish than the yachts to which they had become accustomed.

These splendid craft, the salvagers of the second half of the nineteenth century, were produced not only by Sainty but by his successors and neighbours on the Colne, Harvey of Wivenhoe, Harris of Rowhedge and Aldous of Brightlingsea, which, being more conveniently situated at the mouth of the estuary, became predominant in the salvaging trade by the end of the nineteenth century and continued it after it had died out at Harwich.

The Colneside salvaging smacks were thus more numerous than those of any other place, though it is possible that the smaller Harwich fleet included a higher proportion of specialist salvagers. Certainly there is no record of diving smacks on Colneside. However that may be, there are accounts of thirty Colchester smacks on one salvage job in the 1830s. In 1875 there were eight Colne smacks engaged in pillaging the wrecked *Deutschland*, against three from Harwich and half a dozen Kentish-men.

A Brightlingsea Tradition

Throughout the second half of the nineteenth century Brightlingsea was as much a salvaging centre as Harwich or Rowhedge.

'The Knock John Ship' became part of local folklore, though in the process the identity of the wreck seems to have been lost. The legend fastened chiefly on the treachery of a woman who revealed the whereabouts of hidden salvage. A 'Knock John Fair' came to be observed, at which the woman rode through the town on an ass and was then burned in effigy.

According to a lengthy doggerel poem:[2]

The salvors, thinking no one had more right,
To a share of these goods, for they risked their life,
So they went to work to remove the things home
That they might remember the wreck of Knock John.

---

1. See *Last Stronghold of Sail*.
2. Unpublished MS in papers of Dr E P Dickin at Essex Record Office.

At this state of affairs it was whispered about
An informer there was who began to spout
And she being angry with her neighbour for one
Declared the things buried from the wreck of Knock John.

So neighbours and friends, now pray don't you think
The name of informer a long time will stink
In the nostrils of those who the sand went upon
To try for to save the goods from Knock John.

This may throw some light on the strange encounter in 1849 between
a Customs officer and a Brightlingsea mob including a woman riding a
donkey, referred to in Chapter Five. Did they run into the Knock John
Fair?

A Rich Man's Ruin

Most, if not all, Colneside salvagers were skipper-owners, but at Harwich
two of the leading citizens took an interest in the trade – John Watts and
John Vaux.

John Watts was primarily concerned in the Harwich stone trade, the
story of which is told for the first time in Chapter One. He also owned
sailing barges, including the *John Watts*, named after himself, and the
famous *Alice Watts*, named after his daughter. He had a finger in most
Harwich pies, and started the first Harwich–Felixstowe steam ferry with
the launch *Felixstowe*. He also owned the salvager *Albatross* and a half-
share in the *Volunteer* with Thomas Adams, who also owned the *Marco
Polo*.

In the 1870s he introduced the first Harwich steam paddle tugs, *Liverpool*[1] and *Promise*. The latter only features in this story once, when she and
the *Volunteer* salvaged the Londonderry brigantine *Roma*. The *Liverpool*,
under the command of another salvager, John Carrington, former master
of the *Agenoria*, made the belated rescue of the survivors from the
Deutschland and a month later saved the crew of the Norwegian barque
Hunter.

Shortly before this time, however, John Watts had retired, successful
and respected and, according to gossip, worth £30,000. Within three
years his whole enterprise was brought to ruin by his son, Walter Watts.
It makes a sad little story, all too representative of the continued failure of

1. Clinker-built on the Tyne in 1870, 116 tons. Licensed to carry ninety passengers.

Harwich enterprises to put down roots and produce growth, from one cause or another.

John Watts trusted all his affairs and assets to his son without any formal agreement, and settled in his farm at Dovercourt, making daily visits to his office, where he was bewildered by such extravagances and foolish speculations that in 1877 he himself had to sign a petition to make the family business bankrupt. He had already borrowed heavily from his own bank, for the barges, smacks and tugs were mortgaged to the hilt. The bankruptcy revealed debts of £11,000 and assets of only £2,700, including claims (which sound speculative) of £1,000 against the owners of the *Deutschland* for services rendered and of £600 for salvage of her cargo. It is perhaps an example of Walter Watts's judgment that his claim for £275 after the salvage of the *Roma* by the *Promise* was dismissed as 'monstrous'. He was awarded £50, threatened to appeal, and was tersely told he had no power to do so.

At the bankruptcy inquiry he complained that the preceding winter had been bad for salvaging, despite the fact that in April, 1876, the *Albatross* and *Liverpool* were awarded £1,046 for salvage from the barque *Orto*, soon after receiving £800 for towing the *Atlantic* into Ramsgate. He also claimed he did not receive what he expected from the *Deutschland*, which is borne out by the fact that crates of wine and spirits, laboriously salvaged by divers, were charged with duty and so only realised 5s a dozen bottles. Despite this, Walter Watts admitted that he went to the sales of *Deutschland* wreckage at Brightlingsea and Woodbridge and bought himself a plated tea service. One other scrap of salvaging information emerged at the hearing, when Watts mentioned that he allowed five per cent on salvage to the *Liverpool* and seven per cent to the *Promise*. I presume this was bonus to crews retained on a basic wage.

Poor John Watts first offered 2s 6d in the pound. Then at the resumed hearing he said he had been thinking of a physician's warning that if he wished to spare his son's life he must keep him quiet, and offered to pay another 2s 6d after three months. Despite the Registrar's doubt whether he had any right to make such an offer (meaning, perhaps, any obligation) this was accepted. So ended one of the principal Harwich enterprises. John Watts himself, ruined by his own principles, died in 1896 'in far from affluent circumstances', according to the *Harwich Free Press*.

The Mayor Goes Salvaging

After the departure of the *Liverpool* and *Promise*, sold away, no doubt, after the debacle, the next tug-owner was John H Vaux, whose failure with his *Harwich* to reach the wreck of the *Indian Chief* involved him in a controversy even more bitter than that over the *Liverpool* and the *Deutschland*.

Vaux (who died in 1894) succeeded his father in 1874 as proprietor of the Harwich Navy Yard, which in his day was kept busy not only with new building but with salvaged ships hauled up on its two slipways for repairs. Yarmouth and Lowestoft could not be used for half-sunk derelicts drawing as much as twenty feet, which thus had to be towed to Harwich from far afield, adding to the repair jobs at the Navy Yard.

Both father and son were men of substance and of affairs, busy in the public life of the town. Between them they owned, at various times, the *Cognac Packet* (a snow built in 1792 at Bursledon, trading in her youth to the West Indies, reputedly with four guns, but in Vaux's day a collier and finally a coal hulk); the *Victoria* (lost in 1854); the barque *Antipodes* (trading Swansea to China in 1870); the barquentine *Princess of Wales* (built by Vaux in 1866); the schooners *Terresita* (feared lost in 1870 but found safe in Bridlington Bay), *Alma* (lost in 1878), *Vecta* (assisted into Yarmouth in 1882), and *Inverness* (built in Newfoundland in 1839, she ended her days sunk off the Navy Yard, one of several vessels used as breakwaters); the schooner barges *Stour* (built by Vaux in 1857) and *Lymington* (built by Vaux in 1880, wrecked in 1889); the ketch barge *Doric* (part-owner, built by Vaux in 1892, lost in 1894); the three-masted schooner *Clacton* (built by Vaux out of the wreck of the Swedish *Jacob Landstrom*) and the barque *Walton* (built by Vaux in 1875, she was imprudently launched with top-masts and yards aloft, nearly capsizing, and drowning one of three spectators who were thrown in the water. On her second voyage she left New York on January 20, 1876, with bagged wheat for London, John Shields master, and was never heard of again.). These are merely some of the craft that passed through Vaux's hands; there were doubtless others that have not come to my notice through some newsworthy misfortune.[1]

Yet, with all his possessions, responsibilities and dignities, J H Vaux chose, in 1880, when he was Mayor of the town, to take personal command of his precious and uninsured tug *Harwich* in an abortive attempt to tow the Harwich lifeboat out to the *Indian Chief*, and by his failure to accomplish his mission earned unprecedented and vitriolic obloquy. It is

1. Basil Greenhill in *The Merchant Schooners* (Vol. II) says 'The smaller vessel his name is usually associated with is the *Frances and Jane*, a three-masted schooner built by Vaux for Mann of Mistley in 1863, and later rigged as a barquentine, afloat in 1939 in Chichester Harbour and the last square-rigged merchant vessel ever registered at a port in the British Isles.' Despite the interest of this vessel, she is not linked with Vaux's name in Harwich memories.

a fascinating story of human motives and behaviour on which I have allowed my old narrator to make his own comments.

Pioneer Salvage Tugs

Though they did not last long at Harwich these primitive paddlers were of course precursors of the huge salvage tugs, mostly Dutch and German, which today range the oceans of the world and continue the tradition of the trade on a scale which would doubtless astonish the old-timers whose exploits furnish these pages.

The *Harwich* herself was a wooden paddler of 123 tons, 100 feet long and drawing ten feet. She had a 50 hp engine and two boilers with two funnels side by side. After Vaux's death she was sold to the Tyne where she was re-boilered and reduced to one funnel. It is also said that some of the oak so lavishly built into her by Vaux was removed to make her less heavy. Later she made another move to Blyth, where she finished her days, working according to one report till after the Second World War.

It was for long a tradition in the Vaux family that their fortunes had been founded on the sideline, salvage, rather than on the main business, shipbuilding and owning. Since Vaux did not include salvaging smacks among his interests, this would be a memory of the days of the tugs *Harwich* and *Robert Owen*. Certainly in their brief heyday these craft must have been gold mines to their owners, specially as they could fill in the summer with passenger trips and look for a third income from commercial towage all the year round.

Though salvaging was in decline when J H Vaux died in 1894 and the *Harwich* was sold away, there were still lucrative pickings, which fell chiefly to R & W Paul, the Ipswich merchants, and their characterful captain, Ernest Delhi Tovee, as owners and master of the tugs *Merrimac* and *Spray*, and the steam barges *Swift* and *Speedwell I* and *II*. The *Speedwell II* was built on the lines of a trawler rather than a barge, suggesting the possibility that she was chosen with salvaging in mind.

'Of Ipswich'

Several smacks, including *Celerity*, *Marco Polo* and *Paragon*, are referred to both as salvagers and stone-dredging smacks. Many of the early salvagers were 'of Ipswich', including *Agenoria*, *Princess Royal* and *Spy*, which in 1832 was credited with saving twenty-three lives in the past eighteen months and went on to save another crew before the year was out. Two years before this her owner, Jennings, saved a crew with the *Pearl* of Ipswich. Another salvager, the *Seagull*, was stone-dredging when in 1846 one of her crew was killed by the flying buoy of a dredge which came fast.

All this suggests a major participation by the Pin Mill stone fleet, particularly in the early days, with the emphasis moving to Harwich as the stone trade died out and the full-time specialist salvagers developed. It also shows that the stone boats were by no means all rough old 'tore-outs', as has often been assumed, but included many craft of quality. Assuming that these smacks carried on the two trades at the same time it is not clear how they mixed them; salvaging in the winter and stone work in the slack summer season would seem a logical probability.

Other Harwich Celebrities

The many Harwich and Colneside families who made their living and sometimes gave their lives in the trade of wreck and rescue must make their own appearance as this tale unfolds. Two Harwich families, the Lewises and the Tyes, however, deserve some introduction.

The exploits of the Lewises date back to 1826, when Edward Lewis was involved in a curious little tragedy with the *Aurora*. He left two of his crew in the smack's boat, lying to a ship's anchor, perhaps while he sailed into Harwich for help to recover it. A Rowhedge smack, the *Hope*, came up and, claiming the job was hers, anchored so close that her cable overrode the painter of the *Aurora*'s boat, which was pulled under. Both men – who were from Brightlingsea, serving a Harwich skipper – were drowned, and the Rowhedge skipper was sent for trial on a charge of manslaughter, with what result I have not discovered.

The following year Edward bought the *Aurora* from a Willam Lewis, who thus may have been his father, but the family is not easy to sort out, for there were two Edward Lewises, senior and junior.[1] One of them was active in the 1830s with the *Endeavour*, which he sold in 1842, three years after the building of the *Aurora's Increase*, which perhaps took her name from being a development of her predecessor.

She was jointly owned by the two Edwards and by another William Lewis, who was probably Edward senior's son. His other son, John, was in partnership with his father and brother in the *Tryal*. After Edward senior's death about 1850 the brothers continued in partnership, receiving

1. Two brothers Lewes (*sic*) were lost in the Harwich smack *Four Brothers* in 1823, but there is no indication of the connection, if any.

many medals and awards for meritorious services. As well as the *Tryal* and *Aurora's Increase* they owned the *Queen Victoria* and *Cupid*.

Their partnership ended sadly after William was injured working on a wreck, and suffered bad headaches. One night in 1871 John heard his brother go outside and found him hanged by the linen line in the yard. John carried on, acquiring the *Albatross* after Watts's bankruptcy, and his son, William Lewis, with the *Volunteer*, saw salvaging through to its last days.

Another member of the family, Robert Lewis, preferred sailing barges. After being the first skipper of the *Dunkerque* he went on to own a number of craft, as did a member of another branch of the family, Jimmy Lewis at Woodbridge.

Of the Tyes less is known. William Tye was one of the crew of Lewis's *Tryal* to earn a silver medal for the rescue from the *Etoile de la Mer* in 1852. John Tye (perhaps his son, but there is no evidence of the connection) was apprenticed to Groom's Harwich cod smacks. He twice absconded, and on his second conviction in 1848 was sentenced to three months' hard labour along with another apprentice, Thomas Randall. Three years later he was in trouble again when, as a member of the crew of a Colchester smack *Good Agreement*, he was caught with a bottle of Dutch gin intended for his Christmas treat. Later he was skipper of Lewis's *Queen* and *Tryal*, and when Harwich had its first RNLI lifeboat in 1875 he was appointed cox'n. When he retired he kept the Three Cups inn and was prominent in model yacht racing. (This reconstruction is of course dependent on the assumption that there was only one John Tye, to whom all these references apply.)

The Salvaging Smacks

The Rowhedge–Harwich connection was two-fold, apart from the fact that the Colne smacks naturally made much use of Harwich harbour as the geographical centre of operations.

At least one Rowhedger, John Glover with the *Increase*, found it worth moving to Harwich, and there were probably others who did the same thing.

In addition, the Harwichmen also increasingly came to use Colne-built smacks. The eighteenth-century Harwich cod smacks were very thick and tubby, with up to seventeen feet beam on an average length of fifty-two feet. In the early years of the nineteenth century Colneside smacks were a little less extreme, but still big heavyweights which must have sacrificed speed and handiness for seaworthiness. Examples include *Adventure*, built at Rowhedge in 1814 (52 ft × 15 ft × 8 ft), *Indefatigable* (Wivenhoe, 1808,

41 ft × 14 ft × 6 ft), *Ino* (Rowhedge, 1806, 45 ft × 15 ft × 6 ft) and *Prince Coburg* (Brightlingsea, 1816, 42 ft × 15 ft × 7 ft). The style was continued as late as 1840 in the Ipswich-built *Agenoria* (56 ft × 14 ft × 6 ft, square stern), but in general the end of the Napoleonic wars saw a demand for smaller craft, from thirty to forty feet, with an intense activity in their building on Colneside in the 1830s. These craft were leaner and lower in the water, with an increasing preference for counter sterns, due to the influence of yachting already referred to.

Many of the early salvagers were thus under forty feet long. *Good Agreement* was only thirty-three feet, *Running Rein* thirty-four feet, *Fair Traveller* (which was among a fleet seized oyster dredging off the French coast in 1833, the year she was built) thirty-five feet, and *Phoenix, Blue-Eyed Maid, Prince of Orange* and *Adamant*, thirty-six feet.

The need for a return to larger craft was evidently felt, for these little vessels cannot really have been man enough for knocking about the Longsand in all weathers. Partly this was met by building bigger. Size increased decade by decade through the nineteenth century, the length often corresponding by quaint coincidence with the date, from the thirty-footers of the 1830s up to the sixty-footers of the 1860s.

Among the North Sea fishing craft the traditional cutter rig was generally abandoned at this point in favour of ketch or dandy, but the salvagers seldom saw this transition. There were a few ketches among them, including *First* and *New Unity*, but generally the trade began to die out by the time the cutter had reached its zenith in such craft as *Aquiline* (65 ft × 15 ft × 8 ft 6 in) and the fifty-four-foot *Volunteer*. Both these had counter sterns and looked more like yachts than fishing smacks. Surprisingly however, Glover in 1857 preferred a square stern for his *Increase* (59 ft × 14 ft × 6 ft), possibly because the long counter, the secret of the smack's great speed, was also vulnerable to damage, though the smacks with their deep draught seldom risked going alongside wrecks. Indeed, their inability to get to close quarters, and the consequent reliance on boatwork, was their great problem, the chief cause of loss of life and the main advantage of the shoal draught lifeboats.

Some owners, however, could not wait to replace their small smacks with larger ones, but adopted the alternative practice of re-building them with extra length. Among craft lengthened in this way were *Cupid* (from forty-one feet to fifty-three feet), *Pheasant* (from thirty-one feet to thirty-eight feet in 1837) and *Rumley* (from thirty-nine feet to forty-three feet in 1843). *Aurora's Increase* was lengthened twice, from thirty-four feet to forty-seven feet in 1844, and to fifty-three feet in 1853, according to her registration (though it should be mentioned that there are often curious variations in the different registrations of the same vessel).

Some of the early salvagers were clinker or clench built, including Edward Lewis's thirty-six-foot *Endeavour*, built at Broadstairs in 1814, and the thirty-five-foot *Atalanta* (Gravesend, 1826), but among Essex builders carvel was almost invariable. The oddest craft among the regular salvagers was 'the lugger *Aid* of Colchester', as she was always referred to. She was clinker-built at Deal in 1809, 31 ft × 9 ft × 4 ft, and came to Wivenhoe as a three-masted half-decked eight-ton lugger in 1826. The same year she was reduced to a two-masted lugger and within a few years had one mast and a sliding bowsprit, suggesting she was finally rigged as a cutter smack. She was sunk by a steamer off Greenwich in 1891.

Off the Beach

In addition to the decked, cutter-rigged smacks of Harwich and the Colne, open boats working off the beaches joined in the trade.

The Suffolk and Norfolk beach yawls, manned by the beach companies already mentioned, have received their due recognition as perhaps the finest open boats ever produced. In particular the sixty-nine-foot *Reindeer* of Southwold is remembered for challenging the schooner *America* to a race for £200 – an encounter which, alas, never took place, since the yachtsmen demanded a prohibitive stake of £1,000.

Though there were some shoals and sandbanks off the Suffolk and Norfolk shore, most of the wrecks were vessels driven on to the beach, and thus better dealt with by these open boats which could make the short passage to them and get alongside.

Elsewhere the beach boats have been less considered than they deserve. Those in Essex never rivalled the splendour of the Suffolk yawls, but some were quite formidable craft. At Clacton, for example, the *White Swan* was licensed for ninety-six passengers and the *Skylark* for ninety-seven. The latter was classed as a thirty-two-tonner and is said to have been able to take 130 passengers.

The Leigh and Southend boatmen also reaped a rich harvest off the Maplins and the Nore, and had their established customs and traditions; for example, when a number combined in a partnership this was broken if one boat dropped out for a tide. After the collier *Peggy* got ashore on Leigh Middle in 1852, no fewer than twenty 'yawls' manned by sixty men claimed salvage. As the award was £80 few of them can have ended up much the richer.

At Frinton, beach boats were owned around the turn of the century by former Lowestoft beachmen, including David Cook, three of whose sons were in the crew of the Walton volunteer lifeboat, *True to the Core*. One of them, also David, had a thirty-two-foot surf boat called *Godsend*, rigged with a single dipping lug, which he renamed *Sailors' Friend*, using her for salvaging in the winter as well as for a pleasure boat in the summer. After a while she was replaced by a real forty-foot Norfolk and Suffolk lifeboat, also called *Sailors' Friend*, specially built by Cann of Harwich, and maintained by a Society with Ted Cook as cox'n, another Cook as second cox'n and two more members of the family in the crew. Her adventures include a service to a Russian schooner on the Blacktail when one of her crew, Cecil Bambridge, was knocked overboard and lost as they were lowering the mainsail to hail the Swin Middle light vessel for directions.

Some years before the launch of the Cann-built lifeboat, the Cooks launched their boat to a ship ashore on the Gunfleet, and John Hezekiah Cook was drowned when she capsized, though his brother David Edward Cook was saved. The family were strict teetotallers, forbidding liquor aboard and even christening the lifeboat by breaking a bottle of sea water on her bow.

These Clacton and Frinton boats had a good start over their competitors in a race to the Gunfleet, but just how much salvaging they did is not clear. Investigation is not helped by the boatmen's habit of referring to their 'lifeboats', to give them prestige and perhaps to collect money. When Cook's *Will o' the Wisp* took part in a salvaging exploit she was unequivocally called a lifeboat, probably at her owner's instigation. The grandly named *Dogger Bank* joined the tugs and lifeboats in salvaging ss *Brighton* on the Gunfleet in 1892. Was she so styled in an effort to get away from the 'Skylark' image?

Most of the larger Clacton boats worked off the pier, along with a number of small deep-keel cutters kept on moorings there. These were similar to Colne-built smacks, but half-decked. Two of them, *Gracie* and a smaller ten-ton *Skylark*, were later decked for use as oyster dredgers and survive to this day as smack yachts. But while their owners doubtless took part in the hilarious proceedings which attended the institution of boatmen's licences, the little craft would hardly have been man enough for knocking about among the sandbanks in salvagers' weather.

Suffolk Smacks

While Suffolk was primarily beach yawl country there were also a few salvaging smacks in the rivers Deben and Alde.

At Felixstowe Ferry, or Bawdsey, at the mouth of the Deben, the *Wonder* and *Violet* were perhaps used as an alternative to the beach yawls according to weather conditions, for Ablet Passiful features in these tales sometimes as owner of the yawl *Pride of the Deben* and sometimes as master of one of these smacks, or on one occasion (in 1858) in charge of the *Jessey* of Woodbridge.

He was a Felixstowe Ferry pilot, and brother of Edward Passiful, captain of the noted Woodbridge schooner *Bernard Barton*. He also acted as skipper of Edward Fitzgerald's yacht *Scandal*, deputising for another salvaging skipper, Tom 'Bassy' Newson, whose connection with the Harwich Newsons I do not know, but whose smack, according to a letter from Fitzgerald, 'had a Good Thing on the Shipwash lately'.

Fitzgerald himself took a lively interest in all aspects of longshore life, and on one occasion mischievously provoked an argument between Newson and his better-known skipper, 'Posh' Fletcher, over the merits of Lowestoft and Felixstowe salvagers. Newson maintained that while the beachmen at Lowestoft were more numerous those at Felixstowe were better organised, accepting the leadership of pilots such as himself. Next day Fitzgerald returned in the role of peacemaker. 'Posh, you had your Frill out last night?' 'No, no – only I didn't like to hear the Lowestoft chaps weren't so good, specially before the Stranger Men from Harwich.'

In the Alde, *Jemima* was owned by Samuel Whyard of Orford, who shared with John Carrington of the tug *Liverpool* the credit and the rewards for the rescue from the barque *Hunter*. He is remembered as a broad-shouldered, powerful old man with side whiskers, who always wore a top hat to morning service in Orford church. He also owned the Woodbridge schooner *Ariel*, employing a skipper till, in difficult times, he had to take her himself. He came out of Seaham with a load of coal for Orford and disappeared with the *Ariel* in the gale of November 1893.

And now, having set the scene and introduced some of the characters, let our old friend the narrator take the stage, and tell us how these strange and stirring times might have appeared to one who lived through them.

BOOK TWO

Memories of a SCROPER'S SON

CHAPTER ONE

Bathside Boy

I was born and bred a Bathside Boy. That's the arse end of Harwich, round the corner and up above the Gasworks Creek. They had old public baths there once, and later on they tried to make a new town, but the baths died out and the new town never come to nothing, so that was like a lot of other plans and notions in Harwich.

There's nothing to see now but a great old concrete sea wall, but that was all marshes and saltings in my young days, before they built the wall to stop the flooding which come pretty regular. The road down to the shore divided. One part runned down to Jiggy Baker's piece of land where the Anchor stands now. He dried washing for the women. He set up lines and pegs and he took the washing in at night. He had an oven too where they could do their baking. He charged a penny for this and a penny for that and got a living that way. You could carry on like that, that time of day.

The other road led to the Noah's Ark. That was an old man-of-war high and dry by the cant of the saltings. That had doors and windows in the side and a roof built over the deck to make four cottages, with brick chimneys sticking up through the roof. At one time there was planks up to the doors, but later they made an earth ramp. They didn't have no lavatories – just a pole on the seaward side. You sat on that and done your business over the side. The tide washed it away. There was a tarred rope for you to hold on to. That was so old and hard you could hardly tell it was rope. That was alright from the shore side because no one could see nothing, but that wasn't so pretty if you was messing about in a boat anywhere nearby.

There was a windmill down by the beach and another up the top of Mill Lane, used for grinding up stone to make cement, and an old battery on the shore with a gun in it. That's where us Bathside boys used to play.

Old Ben Norman built bawley boats and barges in a bit of a creek there. One of them was a great old ketch called the *John Wesley*.[1] He had five

1. 128 tons, built 1873, at which date she was the biggest barge built in Harwich.

sons, all shipwrights, but only two worked with him, Isaac and Richard. They came to look at a boat one day and just stood and stared at her. They never measure nothing. Then Ike says, 'I've got her in my eye, Rich', and off they go to make a start on the job. Some people used to say they were rough builders compared to George Cann and John Vaux at the Navy Yard, and that's true they built a stone boat called the *Matilda* that wasn't the same shape both sides, so she was always cranky on one tack, but they built some winners too. When the Bathside was walled in they had to move up the Gas Creek and shared a yard with Cann.

When we couldn't think of nothing else to do down by the Bathside we'd go off into the town. We'd sing our song as we marched:

We are the Bathside Boys
We are the Bathside Boys
We know our manners, we spend our tanners
We are respected wherever we go.
When we go marching through the Bathside
Doors and windows open wide
We can dance and we can sing,
We can do the Highland Fling
We are the Bathside Boys.

We'd climb about on the ships building in the Navy Yard, and when the foreman turned his back we'd slip in and nick a handful of copper nails. Then we'd go and sell them to old Burgess, the rag and bone dealer that lived in one of the Noah's Ark cottages. Next day when the old girl his wife wasn't looking we'd steal them nails back again.

If there was a cod smack a-coming in we'd go up to the Post Office and take any letters aboard. The skipper would give you tuppence for that. Or there might be a boat to mind at the steps time the old captain was ashore. That was nice because you could have a scull round in the Pound.

There was a lot of regular licensed boatmen round the piers and of course you wanted to keep clear of them. They got a living all sorts of ways, taking out visitors, sailing gangs off to the grain ships, carrying a message to a ship or bringing the captain ashore, and all such. Tom Bell had a little old spritsail-rigged thing called the *Good Intent*, and took the doctor off to the ships. Edward Cattermole had a boat called 'The Darker the Night the Better the Deed'. I suppose that had another name but that's what she was called and that give you an idea what he got up to. He'd take people out and then say he wouldn't put them ashore again, not without they paid him another couple of shillings. They kept having him up and fining him for being drunk with people in his boat and he did that once too often. They sent him to prison for a week to cool off.

Elijah Barnard, some visitors at the Great Eastern Hotel told him they'd like to go off and see the railway boat sail, so he takes them out into the middle of the harbour, no light or nothing, and the ss *Cambridge* goes right over the top of them. That's a funny thing, but only just before that the *Cambridge* had run down a pleasure boat in the Scheldt and drowned four members of good Antwerp families. Swarms of Dutchmen lived by plunder on that river. Every time they stripped a body they just weighted it and put it back in the water.

Or we might go round by Groom's timber yard and pinch a bit of firewood, but I'll tell you how that was stopped. The old boy on the saw, he wondered where his offcuts was going, so he took three billets and drilled a hole in each of them with a one-inch auger. He filled them holes up with black powder from his punt gun and put in a plug. A week or so later a house not far from ours had the fire blown out right across the room, and then a shrimping bawley out in the Wallet had the copper blown right over the side. The old saw-man said, 'That's all I wanted to know. I wish now I hadn't done the other bit.' No one never heard nothing of that one, which was funny, but my father say, 'You go down the shore and fetch home driftwood from now on.'

On the way home we'd go round by 'Pussy' Clarke the butcher's and shout 'Miaow, miaow, any cats wanted?' till he came out after us and then we'd run like hell.

I'm only telling you these things to give you an idea what we used to get up to in my young time and what sort of a place Harwich was. Being as it was my home I thought Harwich was the head town in England and the Bathside was the head part of Harwich. I couldn't make out why my father was always shaking his head over the place, though I found out later, as I'll be telling you.

Of course I knew it had seen better times. My grandfather would tell me about the times when the inns were full of travellers waiting to sail to Holland or Hamburg in the Post Office packets. He said he didn't know which were the prouder men, the captains of the packets or the Revenue cutters. You can still see the bow-front houses they lived in on St Helen's Green. That was just after the war with Bonaparte, and he said even then they were forever remembering the good old days before them wars, when the royal yachts used to come in and princes and princesses would be brought ashore in state.

That was the head town for fishing in the North Sea then, and some bit of that still went on when I was a boy. We used to run down to the pier before breakfast to see them kill the codfish for the market. They would pull them out of the fish chests all alive, and how they'd jump and thump before they cracked them on the head and loaded them into the rail vans! But my grandfather, he say, 'That's nothing to what it used to be. What smacks we do see now is all Greenwichmen bar half a dozen or so. Why, before the French wars we had nigh on a hundred of our own here, with God knows how many shipwrights and sailmakers all owning shares in them.'

He told me, 'Things is a bit better since we had the railway, and not before time. But you mark my words, there won't be nothing left here for you when you're my age.' I couldn't see then what he meant, but he wasn't far out.

The first of the old trades to go was the stoning. There was two hundred stone boats when I was a nipper – a lot in Harwich itself but more still at Pin Mill, with some at Shotley and Trimley. Some of them were poor old things, but there was some smart craft among them. They weren't bawley boats, they had booms and hang-over sterns, and they would sail. The *Paragon*, that belonged to Pot Miller the baker, would hustle along with the scroper *Volunteer*, which was the fastest thing on salt water, but my father reckoned the *Tripping* and the *Red Jacket* were the fastest. They belonged to John Watts, and so did the *Jessie* and *Flirt*. He bought the *Tripping* from Pin Mill. They had their own race in the regatta every year, separate from the bawley boats. The *Hero* of Pin Mill was another that won it one year, though another race she broke her mast. The Butt and Oyster at Pin Mill was a real stone men's pub then.

Dullick Smith had the *Celerity* that he got from Brightlingsea, and there was the *Reliance* at Pin Mill and the *Victor* that belonged to Raisin, and the *Portly*, *Marco Polo*, *Koh-i-Noor* and *Oyster* – any God's amount of them. There was one called the *Who'd-a-Thought-It* – not William Good's bawley that came later, but another one. Her skipper went into Middleton's, the ship's chandlers in Harwich, for some gear. The clerk said 'What name?' so as to write it down and charge it to the owner. The skipper said, 'Who'd a Thought It' and the clerk said 'I don't want none of your sauce.' They used to say, 'Who'd a Thought It, the stone men bought it.'

There was a bit of stone up the Stour, right in the channel, but mostly they raced out every morning to the West Rocks to get the best ground, out where the Stone Banks buoy is now. Low water time they'd anchor fore-and-aft in a pool over some big old lumps. Sometimes they'd use four anchors. They were mostly two- or three-handed, but some carried four hands. You wanted three for croming, which was the principal way of stone fishing.

The crome had metal claws on the end of a thirty-foot staff, with a long strop fixed to the ironwork and leading up the staff, so the eye was by the rail with the crome on the bottom. The croman wriggled the claws under the lump and sang out 'Tackle!' Then his mates hooked a mast-head tackle into the strop and heaved the lump up. The tackle went to a winch on the mast, one man winding and the other guiding. The croman had to see the stone didn't drop off or drive the crome through the smack's side. He had to be strong and artful, but several of the best cromen were little wiry chaps. Or you could grip a lump in tongs and put a tackle on that. Nippers we called them.

If the lump was too big to lift it was broken by a tool called a studyer, something between a spear and a chisel, so you could have the chisel end on the stone and welt the other end with a maul, standing on deck. Small bits you got in a dredge, which was like a big oyster dredge, all made of iron rings. That was high water work. The big lumps made the best price, and if you got just sandy rubbish you had to move off. Of course dredging you were under way, and not at anchor.

End of the day they all raced in again to get first turn with the stone guesser. He came aboard and judged the amount. He didn't do no weighing, he just knew. Then they tipped it all out again on the stone heaps. From there it was picked up by barges that took it all round the coast, or by Dutch and German schooners going to Hamburg and such foreign parts. There was sometimes thirty foreign ships in the harbour waiting to load. There was a stone heap between the Gas Creek and where the train ferry pier is now, and another across on Shotley Spit, or Bloody Point as it should be called. Some cargoes were delivered at Brightlingsea and Mistley, and at other places in the Stour and Orwell.

Several times they had to go out on strike to get the price up, and that meant hardship those days. They were out for weeks in my father's time, with no stone worked and ships lying idle in the harbour awaiting for it. Then at last things got so bad some of the Brightlingsea boats went back to work and a few Harwich men with them, but the Pin Mill boats and some of the other Harwich men, they sailed after them with double crews aboard and flags a-flying and they rammed them and took them in tow till the whole fleet came back in with a lot of broken spars and broken heads.

There was a Brightlingsea smack dredged off the West Rocks when one of ours sailed into his boat towing astern and smashed it up to teach him better. Then the Brightlingsea man does the Harwich man's boat the same way and after that they got at each other till in the end the Brightlingsea man takes the fid out of his bowsprit and sails full tilt into the Harwicher. The bowsprit runs in and he hits our boat abaft the channels with his iron stem band. She was damaged so much she only just got round the break-water and sank on the Beach End.

But after the strike, when they'd got a better price, it wasn't a bad trade. You might get, say, two tons a day, sixty or eighty tons a month or up to seven hundred tons in a year's work, worth about 6s 6d a ton. Before you could make cement out of it, the stone had to be broken up and burned and then ground into powder in mills. Pattrick had a big cement works at Dovercourt and there were three factories in Harwich, one owned by John Watts, where the gasworks is now, and the others where they built the coastguard station and the Salvation Army Citadel. There were factories at Colchester and Ipswich and Brightlingsea and Leigh and other places too.

In the old days before the wars with Bonaparte the stone was dug out of the Beacon Cliff till that done so much damage with the tide flowing everywhere that they had to stop it and build the breakwater to make the tide run fair and scour the harbour.

They used it just for building material then, till they found out how to make it into cement. When they pulled down the old church to build the one we've got now they found it was built with Beacon Cliff stone. They got hundreds of pounds selling that rubble to the cement factories. This cement notion was invented in Kent originally. I suppose that's why some of our chaps came here from Gillingham. They brought their boats with them and they kept their Kent registration numbers to the end.

I can only just remember the stone, time they was a-croming of it. That all came to an end when they invented making Portland cement out of mud and chalk and didn't want our sort no more. Pattrick's factory went over to the new stuff and might have made a fortune supplying the building of Parkeston, only he spent so much on fancy machinery for the works and a fancy house for himself, the Towers, or Pattrick's Folly we called it, that he went bust instead.

The Harwich factories all shut up shop. John Watts made a fortune out of the stone-dredging, him and his partner, William Colchester, the Ipswich barge-builder. Watts was mayor a time or two and owned several trading craft and a steam tug besides his stone boats. He was worth £30,000 when he retired. Then his son busted the whole concern up in a matter of months. He ruined himself playing off the debts and died in poverty, that's what poor old Watts done.

There was a bit of an oyster fishery too when I was a lad. The grounds being right in the harbour you might dredge up all manner of things besides oysters. One old boy gave as his day's catch:

A wash of great and a bushel of small
A silver buckle and a two-headed maul.

But we couldn't keep the Brightlingsea men off it though we tried to, and I reckon they ruined it. Anyway that died out too, though shrimping picked up soon as the railway opened. That was one trade did increase in my time.

For a while the old stone men and oyster dredgers could generally get a bit of work unloading timber ships for Groom's, who had a good timber business at Harwich, as well as owning a lot of barges and a few cod smacks. Then Paul's, the Ipswich merchants, they would employ anything up to seventy men unloading grain into lighters out of the big sailing ships from Canada. They sailed the men off in boats with dipping lugs. But while I was growing up the new Ipswich docks were being made, and soon more and more trade began to go right through our harbour and up the Ipswich river.

There was still some work with Groom's, and the old Navy Yard kept a hundred hands going on shipbuilding and repairing. The owner in my time was John Vaux. We called him the Vice-Chancellor of Harwich. I'll have some more to tell you about him before we're through with this lot. But beyond that there was only the Trinity House and the railway, and the worst thing of all was when Harwich fell out with the old Great Eastern. That was expected they would extend the quay, but they couldn't come to terms. Some said the town was too greedy over dues, and some said the railway was too close-fisted and tried to make the town pay for everything. Anyway, the upshot of it was they humbugged off up the Mistley river and built their own port at Parkeston.

Yes, all the time there was some old trades dying out or moving away and next to nothing coming to replace them. But there's one side of things I haven't come to.

There may have been fewer ships coming into Harwich because they had business there, but there was still a hell of a lot coming in that hadn't no intention of doing so when they sailed, and a hell of a lot more that tried to get in and never made it.

The one thing they couldn't take away from Harwich was that it was the only harbour of refuge on the East Coast. It was the one place a sailing ship could find refuge between the Humber and the Thames in an easterly gale. When I was a boy I once saw 200 ships lying windbound here and in my father's time there was sometimes twice that number.

When that came fine that was a sight to see them muster. Yes, for a week on end you'd see them rolling and pitching at their anchors all over the harbour, and more coming in day after day and looking for a clear berth to let go, and then the wind would veer into the north-west and the sun would come out and it was all like a huge regatta with sails as far as you could see whichever way you looked, only a few of them was sure to get foul of each other in such a scrummage and have to come back in for a new stick or two. Like everything else, that got less as I was growing up, with fewer ships on the coast and more of them steamers, but all the time I'm thinking of, which is up to the time I went in the railway boats, there was always some vessels come in for shelter every time we had a breeze of wind easterly.

They were the lucky ones. Harwich was a good harbour once you got in, but if the devil himself had had the job of creating the earth instead of leaving it to God almighty, who come to think of it didn't a lot better, he couldn't have schemed up a worse lot of traps at the approaches to it. There was sandbanks everywhere, all just out of sight at high water, with the tides setting everywhere over the top of them. They'd knock the bottom out of a ship in a couple of tides and sand her in level with the deck in a week.

The Sunk and the Cork and the Shipwash and the Gunfleet was all laid out to catch you whichever way you come from, and if you was running down from the Tyne in a northerly gale, you might get right to Landguard and then maybe you couldn't brace up sharp enough to weather the breakwater. In that case you'd pile up on the Pye or the Holidays or drive down on to the West Rocks. A lot of the old Geordie collier skippers never even knew they could have runned up the Wallet past Clacton and fetched into Colne. If they been taught that a lot would never have been lost.

The worst place of all was the Longsand and the Kentish Knock, further off the land. All the foreign-going ships from Germany and the Baltic, as well as English vessels from the north, had to find their way round that place to get out of the North Sea and down Channel. That's where most of the biggest wrecks happened, and it was a terrible bad place to get at, being midway between Harwich and Ramsgate, and too far from either for comfort. We called it the Burying Grounds.

There was only one good thing about our sandbanks. If a ship didn't knock herself to pieces or fall over or sand in, you'd got a chance to get her off – not like some of them West Country shores that was all rocks. A craft wouldn't last a tide on rocks, on account of they'd poke up through her bottom. The West Rocks was the only place on our coast played that sort of trick on you.

The chaps that made a living out of such places as these were called salvagers. Some of them old Suffolk boys called them salt-wagers and spoke of going salt-wagering. At Southwold that was saul-wagering done by sauls. But they were very broad-spoken in Suffolk, and you don't want to take much account of them. In Harwich we called it scropering and our salvaging smacks was scropers. Yes, I reckon that was the proper name for it.

CHAPTER TWO

When Revenue Cutters Ruled

My father was a scroper, same as his father was before him. Scropers weren't like fishermen. They got their living saving ships, or if they couldn't save the ships saving what they could out of them.

Of course that meant saving the chaps aboard, and they done that too. There weren't no one else to do it in the old days. There weren't much money in saving life, not beyond a bit of life salvage and maybe a few pounds one of the societies might send you, or maybe a silver cup or a telescope presented by the Board of Trade or one of them foreign governments.

But once you'd got the crew out of her a vessel was yours. That was like this. So long as the old skipper stayed aboard you had to try and get a ship off or help her into shelter and you mustn't touch nothing. But once she was abandoned you could help yourself, though you were supposed to declare what you got to the Customs ashore.

You'll hear tales of salvagers doing away with shipwrecked sailors so as to claim a wreck, but that's silly. No, you don't want to believe half what you hear, like tales of smugglers making underground tunnels or leaving boats full of Revenue men with their throats cut. That's shore folks' talk. I've heard people say we showed false lights to get a ship ashore. We couldn't have done that if we'd wanted, most of our wrecking grounds being miles off the shore, and anyway there weren't no need.

There was one job in my father's time when the skippers of two of our smacks, the *Marco Polo* and the *Alfred*, are supposed to have put a brig on the Longsand on purpose. She was a Liverpool craft called the *Alciope*, bound from Shields to the Black Sea with coals. They got her off and into Harwich, and Oliver Williams, the Lloyd's agent, paid them £225. Then word got about it was a put-up job with the skipper of the brig, and Williams stopped the cheque. They had them up in court and argued it for five hours. The captain stuck to this story, but he'd had the sack and the magistrates said they weren't prepared to convict on his evidence.

Rowhedgers

Above: Jack Spitty, noted as a salvager with his Bluebell. In later life he fished from Bradwell.

Left: Thomas Barnard (1816–1896). He and his eight sons were concerned in many notable salvages, particularly with his New Unity.

Below: Smacksmen in old age. A group at Rowhedge about 1890.

Aldeburgh beachmen, from a painting in the Moot Hall Museum. Most were members of the North and South Beach Companies, manning the yawls which worked off the beach. The names, as also recorded in the museum, are:

Behind: James Ward ('Dony'). *Second row from back:* William Ward ('Drooks'), his brother, Jim Fisher; Jack Catmore; Sam Filby (who always wore a blue jersey).
Third row from back: Robert Easter ('No-Thank-You'); Sam Ward (sexton and gardener); Charlie King (brickmaker and 'Professor' on all festive occasions).
Fourth row from back: Charlie Nicholls ('Sanko'); George Cable ('My Lord'); William Cable ('Dick McCarthey'), his brother; John Scarlett.
Fifth row from back: Robert Thorpe (a man with a red hat who belonged to a trading coaster); Jack Brame ('Twee'), with a Dutch-style cap; Ned Burwood.
Sixth row from back: Charles Burwood, his cousin; Christopher Fisher ('Kit'); Robert Wilson, who was employed on the Lloyd's Signal Station.

The elegance of the Colne smacks
ed in the rough trade of salvaging
shown by this photo of Sunbeam,
eva and Xanthe, all of Row-
dge, racing in the local regatta.

CK73

The 18-ton Globe of Brightlingsea,
re seen entering Newhaven about
joo, was built at Wivenhoe as
rly as 1805. She gives an im-
ession of a powerful cutter smack
fore the ultimate refinement of
e yacht-like Rowhedge racers.

Tripper boat working off the beach at Lowestoft. Fine craft like this, with much of the style of a Norfolk and Suffolk lifeboat, made a summer living from holiday visitors from Yarmouth to Southend, and were quite capable of taking part in the salvagers' sterner trade.

A beach yawl, her shingle ballast bags ready on the staging at Yarmouth, with a fleet of collier brigs in the Roads waiting a fair wind or tide.

But we didn't need to try such tricks as that. We got wrecks enough without contriving them.

Before I get round to some of the things I can remember I'll tell you a few more tales I had from my father about what went on in his day, and maybe some he'd heard from my grandfather.

Grandad could go right back to the time there was a big fleet of cod smacks at Manningtree, before they all cleared out to Grimsby. Several of them that got lost off Heligoland soon afterwards were in the salvage of a Prussian ship called *Curier* that was lost on the Shipwash in the last years of the wars with Bonaparte. There was a privateer took charge of that job. Such craft as that were before even my father's time, but in his day that was often the Revenue cutters that done the rescues and controlled the smacks as well.

There was two of them at Harwich, the *Desmond* and the *Scout*, as well as a tender called the *Flying Fish*. Isaac Saxby had first the *Desmond* and then the *Scout*, and whichever he had was always in the thick of things. When we get to the lifeboats I'll tell you about how he tried to save the crew of the *Hero*, which is what he was chiefly remembered by, but he done any God's amount of better jobs than that. Yes, in my father's time he was saving more lives than any man, being always cruising on the lookout with a fine craft that could stand any weather.

He'd take control of a salvage too when there was smacks working on it, and saved a lot of pillaging that way. Them old boys in my father's time, they were proper terrors and didn't have no respect for God, man nor devil, but they dursn't defy the Revenue cutter, not so long as she was there to keep an eye on them and had her pennant flying. Mark you, Saxby was in the salvage job along with the rest and put his claim in same as they done, so he must have earned a lot of money, what with all his expenses being found by the Government.

Some of the most wicked wrecks was the old emigrant ships, time they were shipping thousands of Germans out to the colonies. They crammed them aboard of ships that hadn't got no idea how to find their way out of the North Sea.

One of them, called the *Johann Frederik*, got on the Gunfleet when he thought he was off the French Coast. The smacksmen pulled 150 of them Germans, mostly women, through the surf and got them ashore before she broke up. A few years before that the *Cumberland*, with another 150 aboard, she was fetching along between the Longsand and the Sunk and

c

thought she was in the English Channel. They had a hell of a job to make that captain see sense before they took him into Harwich. The *Scout* got another, an American ship called the *Forrester*, off the Longsand, but others that got ashore there weren't so lucky – if you can call that luck to be hauled ashore with no home and no hope and what few things you had all gone.

I'll tell you presently about the *Deutschland*, which was in my time, but now we're talking about my father's days. The time the *Deutschland* was lost he was all on about a couple of other jobs happened a long time before – the *Floridian* and the *Burgundy*.

The *Floridian* was another Yankee ship chartered to some people in Antwerp. She sailed from Flushing for New York on a Tuesday evening with a fair wind for the Channel, along with an East Indiaman called *Dyle*, bound from Antwerp to Havannah. That night the wind veered into the south-west, and the captain, sighting what he took to be the South Foreland light, put about and stood off the land for two hours in snow. By noon on the Wednesday he had to heave-to in a gale, heading to the north-west. In the afternoon she touched the ground so gently that wasn't hardly noticed, and they tried to put her about. But she struck again, and no mistake this time.

There was 160 passengers with thirty women and twenty children and the whole lot in a panic. The crew of fourteen couldn't do nothing. Two seamen jumped in a boat to bale it out but them passengers tried to pull it alongside. The men thought to save the boat. They cut the painter and just disappeared. Captain Whitmore, he got into the ship's lifeboat to make it ready for his wife and other women, but the passengers thought he was abandoning them. They stormed in, swamped that boat and drowned the captain and chief mate. They tried to cut away the rigging but couldn't find no axes. They tried to call up the *Dyle*, three miles away, but blessed if she didn't get ashore and broke up. The passengers were being washed off the *Floridian*'s decks. Some of them clung to floating cargo that was forced up through the broken hatches. The house on the poop was washed away with scores of people in it or on it. That came ashore on the German shore weeks later still carrying two battered bodies.

Then that *Floridian* broke in two. The stern sank, but a handful of survivors clung to the bow all through the Thursday night. Then on the Friday evening the only surviving passenger and three of the crew were taken off by the Revenue cutter *Petrel*. Our cutter *Scout* saved all hands bar one from the *Dyle*.

That's a funny thing, but the *Floridian* got forgotten in Harwich, though there was twice as many Germans drowned as there was from the *Deutschland* that caused such a set-to. That was partly because such things were taken for granted that time of day, and partly because our craft didn't have much to do with it. There was some cargo and a lot of corpses got in, but that was done by the Kentish men from Ramsgate and Margate.

The *Burgundy* was lost the year before. She was a big ship of 800 tons out of Bremen for New Orleans with about three hundred Germans aboard. The first we knew of her was signal guns from the Longsand. The Revenue cutter *Desmond* and some of our smacks went to her, but she was right up on the top, done for. John Lewis, that was about the head salvager as ever was, and a man I'll have a lot more to tell of, was there with the *Tryal*. He smashed his boat up trying to get to her, and was lucky not to lose the chaps in it. The carpenter aboard the *Desmond* patched the boat up, and Lewis and his crew pushed it through the surf to the wreck. They came back with ten passengers. Then back they go again. Seven times they done that, getting ten each time, till they'd saved sixty-eight. The *Desmond* got some and a French schooner took the best part of a hundred into Ramsgate.

In all there was ninety-nine brought ashore at Harwich. They sent the *River Queen* steamboat to take them up to Ipswich, and they gave a cheer for Harwich when they left. At Ipswich they gave them whole cartloads of clothing and sent them to London by train. At the end of it, most of them were as well set up when they embarked in another ship as when they first left their homes, though some of the better-off passengers lost their fortunes.

That will show you something about them German emigrant ships when I tell you another of them called the *Atlantic* was lost on the Goodwins the very next day. The captain, two passengers and a boy got swept overboard, but the Deal luggers and the Ramsgate smacks looked after the rest of them.

My father reckoned the worst smash-up in all his time was when the Sunk lightship got driven off her station in a gale. Along comes a fleet of colliers looking to steer by that mark, which was all they had to guide them. But knowing he was in the wrong place the Sunk dursn't show no light at all and eight of them pile up ashore, one after the other. Most of the crews was lost. The captain of one managed to swim to another ship, but they reckoned there was around twenty-five drowned.

A fleet of colliers running up from the north with a fair wind was always

terrible wild. They'd carry on regardless, half out of control and God help
you if you was anywhere in their way. But that lot you could not blame,
poor devils. No one can allow for a light vessel not being where it ought
to be.

The survey ship HMS *Fairy* sailed out of Harwich into that self-same
breeze and just disappeared. Months and months they were looking for a
trace of her and never found nothing. That was a blow to Harwich, for
her commander, Captain Hewett, lived here. The Hewett Channel at
Yarmouth is named after him. Only a few months before, her bosun's
mate had made himself a proper hero in the town. He climbed up the top
of the church tower and fetched down the weather vane that was damaged
by lightning, and when that was repaired he climbed up and put it back.
They reckoned the *Fairy* had too many boats on deck for her survey work,
and that made her top-heavy.

Yes, my father often spoke of that gale. There was fifteen ships ashore
at once off Harwich, and all the inns in the town full of shipwrecked sailors.

When there was a craft towed in he'd say, that's nothing. He'd be all on
about an Aldeburgh smack called *Mary Ann* that picked up a Prussian
schooner off Cromer. She was called *Iris*, and she'd been ashore on the
Lemon. The *Mary Ann* towed her for three days and got her into Harwich.
She got £500 for that, and my father reckoned she earned it, specially as
she was run into and damaged off Orford Ness by one of them colliers.

According to my old chap there was never such a sale of salvage as came
out of the *Eugenee*. She was a nearly new American barque, and when they
broke her up there was enough timber to build half-a-dozen craft and
enough gear to rig them, as well as a beautiful great carved stern frame,
fit to go over a Duke's mantelpiece. I wonder what happened to that?

He'd make out that was all great wrecks then, like the *Horatio* that had
a cargo worth £30,000 from India, or the *Marquis of Huntley* that had
forty-five men aboard. They pitched 4,000 muskets overboard to lighten
her and at the end of it that took a year to make the Government pay up.

Then there was the *Robert* that had a freight of mahogany, and an East
Indiaman called the *Marquis of Wellington* that got on the Mouse. There was
advertisements in the papers week after week threatening penalties of
£200 and transportation for concealing stuff out of them, with rewards
of £20 for information, but for all that the wagons still kept on taking
that mahogany inland. They had some sales of cotton and rice at Wivenhoe out of the Indiaman but her anchors and cables and a lot of her gear
the salvagers sold straight out of her to north-bound ships as they were

passing. She lay handy for that on the Mouse. Then some of the sugar that was in the Admiralty warehouse, they broke in and stole that back again.

Yes, they had some good pickings in the old days by all accounts, but from what I can make of it the work was mostly collier brigs on the Gunfleet before they put the light there, and there was a hell of a lot more work than profit chucking black diamonds overboard.

CHAPTER THREE

A Night in the Rigging

Some of the salvaging was done by craft that just fell in by chance with vessels in trouble. That might be a cod smack working on his long lines down the shore or round the back of the Sunk, or maybe bound home from the Dogger. Or that might be the stone boats working off the West Rocks. From there they had a good view of the Gunfleet and a head start to get there, so if they saw a vessel strike they'd have the dredges on deck and be after her.

Even amateurs might chance on a job. There was a little yacht come out of the Crouch on a day's wildfowling, and he sees a barge called *Pride of the Colne* on the Whitaker. The crew had been taken off by another barge, so the skipper says, 'Right. This is better than a few black geese and a pair of widgeon.' He goes aboard and along comes three smacks, the *Daisy*, *Laura* and *Mason*, which he engages, and they get her off into Colne.

But that was just a fluke. With our regular scropers that might be like this.

After a blow we'd be out at first light and have a look along the Gunfleet and down to the Sunk, and then if there wasn't nothing there we'd have a cruise to the Burying Grounds. As like as not we'd see a vessel up on one of these sands, or maybe we'd see a craft making a course that was going to take her there. Then we'd say 'Oho! Do she don't wend or wear in a minute she's ours.' Perhaps one of the lightships would be watching her and he'd fire a gun to warn her, but as like as not she wouldn't take no notice because half the time these foreigners didn't know where they were.

One time one of our pilots, Robert Willson, went to a Russian schooner brought up just inside of Orford Ness, and he thought he was in the Humber! Another time a Norwegian barque called the *Cromwell*, bound from the Baltic to Barcelona, was on the Shipwash, but he bumped over. The crew of the *Gipsy* boarded him but he wouldn't take them. Then blowed if he didn't run her on the Cork in broad daylight. That one thought he was off the coast of France. There came a gale that night and the tug *Harwich* couldn't shift him, though they threw his timber overboard, but they got him off a week later.

That same craft[1] was in trouble again a few years later when she was on the Whitaker. The *Welcome* took off the captain and then got on the Buxey herself. That was a Monday and she never got home till the Wednesday.

Albert Jefferies, the Lloyd's agent at Brightlingsea, sent Fred Salmon in the *Dauntless* and also Bowles's smack *First*. The *Dauntless* took the captain off the *Welcome* and the Clacton lifeboat picked up the rest of the crew, and then between them they got the old *Cromwell* off and into Brightlingsea.

She lay there a long time, and every tide she just picked up then sank again, so that people could watch and see a ship founder every day. Then they pumped her out with windmills and she was bought to make the head of a jetty in the Colne. But nothing came of that scheme and in the end a Thames Conservancy steamer pumped her out properly and dumped her on the East Mersea shore, which is where they broke up a lot of craft.

Over and over again a vessel come running into the Thames Estuary believing she was going down Channel.

There was a three-masted schooner, the *Ornan*, got on the Gunfleet, bound for Portsmouth with firewood. He said he took Orford Ness and Harwich lights for the North and South Foreland, and the Gunfleet for the Varne, so then he made out Clacton must be Dover. The *Volunteer*, the *Varuna* and the Clacton lifeboat went and got the crew off, and next day the smacks came back with Fred Salmon's *Emily* and got her off into Colne.

Another three-masted schooner, the *Ocean Pride* of Guernsey, made the self-same mistake, taking the Gunfleet for the Varne, and got on the Sunk. They never got her off, but the Clacton lifeboat took the crew, and five of them Colne smacks – the *Queen Victoria*, *Emily*, *Emblem*, *Ella* and *Thought* – stripped her. They even got the masts out of her and brought them in.

You could understand them foreigners getting confused, but you'll find it hard to believe when I tell you we had a full-rigged ship, the *Hawksdale* of Liverpool, with a pilot on board, get on the Gunfleet when she was

1. On the first occasion she is referred to as the *Cromwell* and on the second as the *Oliver Cromwell*. There may have been two Norwegian barques so similarly named, but I assume they were one and the same.

bound from Hamburg to Melbourne. They reckon that pilot mistook the lights of Kent for the coast of France, but they couldn't ask him because the poor beggar was drowned with two of the crew, trying to get a boat away. The Clacton and Margate lifeboats saved the other twenty-five, and then Salmon and the *Emily* had a go at her too. He brought in chairs and lamps and furniture of all kinds including several pianos. She was supposed to have five hundred pianos aboard. They had a special auction sale at Brightlingsea for her salvage and sold the pianos in that.

Most of the craft we went to were ashore, but sometimes we'd find one disabled at sea. That might be a craft that had been on one of the banks and knocked over on her own. Perhaps she'd be making a lot of water and want hands to pump her into Harwich and up on to the mud. Or a lot that got ashore knocked their rudders off; that generally meant getting a line aboard to tow or help her steering.

Towing an old ship half full of water, with her rudder busted, was a funny job, but the old boys managed it. That was usual to have a smack or two pulling ahead and another towing astern to steer. You could sheer the smack back and forth so as to pull the ship's stern round. That's how they fetched the *Hugo* of Stettin in off the Kentish Knock, with the Revenue cutter *Scout* towing and the *Agenoria* steering astern with a rope to each quarter. Right over the top of the Longsand they towed her, and got £200 for the job, though there was twenty-six men in the two crews had to share it. The funny thing is that *Hugo* was wrecked on the Gunfleet within a few months of repairing her and giving her a new rudder.

If you were on your own, sometimes you could set a bit of canvas on a ship so as she'd drive ahead, and trim it so she tried to luff head to wind. Then you'd hitch your smack on her weather quarter so as to check her back and keep her sails full. You couldn't jockey a vessel into a berth like that, but you could keep her going where you wanted, same as into Harwich or Colne, specially if you had a good old tide under you doing most of the work.

One time old Lewis had the *Aurora's Increase* all rigged up under the stern of a Spanish ship called the *Independiente* ready to try this. They'd got her off West Rocks and anchored her in deep water. Lewis gets aboard to help weigh the anchor, which was a job with the windlass pawls busted as usual. The Spaniards was pointing at Walton Naze, saying it was the South Foreland, and they must be on the Goodwins. Then one of them cuts the stopper lashings holding the cable, and the ship makes a stern board right down on to the smack. Lewis had to hop back aboard sharpish and sheer her clear, else that ship would have gone over her and smashed her up, and she was only three years old then.

The wind was too northerly for Harwich, so away they go up the Wallet for Colne, with the *Aurora's Increase* still astern steering. Then Saxby comes up in the *Desmond* to give a hand. He reckons they mustn't try getting her into Colne like that, with the wind a bit shy and a lot of craft lying in the fairway. So they decide they'll get the *Brocklebank* from Colchester if she'll do the job for £15. She was an old Colchester-to-London steam packet, one of the first they had there.

So next day Lewis goes into Brightlingsea and gets a lift into Colchester. He finds the *Brocklebank* laid up, but he rouses her chaps out in the Seahorse pub. They want £25 for the job on account of they have got to buy fresh coal, but in the end they settle for £20, to come out of the salvage, not dealing with them Spaniards, and £5 to come back if they get the job to tow her back to Harwich as well. So they get her up to Wivenhoe, and after all that lot the beaks only award £450 between three smacks and the steamboat. They were going to appeal, but the Spanish vice-consul had the sense to add another £100 to stop them.

There was a lot of ways ships could be disabled without being stranded. Some had lost sails and spars in a squall, or had their jib boom carried away in a collision. A lot had lost their anchors or smashed up the windlass. They'd bring up in the Roads off Yarmouth or Lowestoft, and then maybe there came a lot of wind and sea and they couldn't get their anchor again and had to slip, or maybe they'd pitch so much the strain would either bust the chain or smash up the windlass pawls or pull the bitts out.

Yes, the windlass at one end of the ship and the rudder at the other end were two of a craft's weaknesses. Then there was nothing for it but to slip, and either way they'd as like as not be glad of a hand into harbour, though when you got them in they might turn on you and say they could have done alright on their own.

Suppose you had a ship ashore, you'd get the old smack as close as possible, beating up under the lee of the sand if you could, so as to get a bit of shelter. Mostly you couldn't get very close, for our old scropers drew five or six feet of water, so there was no banging alongside like the lifeboats could do later on. No, you had to anchor if it was fit, or heave-to if it wasn't, and then the skipper would take a couple of hands and try to get across in the boat. You'd wait till the tide had ebbed off the sand so you could get a bit of lee.

That boat work was generally the worst part of the job. A Brightlingsea smack called the *Fair Traveller* once found a Dutch schuyt on the Gunfleet, and that took the master and an apprentice two hours to row seventy fathoms to her. After that they were upset and drowned, and so were the three Dutchmen.

There was a lot of smacks' boats upset too when a steamer called the *Battalion* finished up on the Longsand. Three of our Harwich men were drowned in one of them. The crew were brought in by a Ramsgate lugger and the *Qui Vive* of Rowhedge,[1] but they never got that ship off. The master blamed it on the Longsand Light having been moved, but that didn't stop them suspending his ticket.

The worst loss of that sort I heard tell of, though, was on a fine day with calm water.

There was a London collier brig called *CSM* got on the West Rocks by Goldmer's Gat. A Colchester smack called the *Pheasant* brought her crew in, and then a week later our *Koh-i-Noor* and the *Lord Howe* of Colchester and two Pin Mill boats, the *Cyrene* and *Ranger*, they thought they'd go and have a look at her. She was listed over to the eastward, and thirteen men in their skiffs were boarding her on the other side when the tide pushed her up and rolled her over on to their boats. The whole lot was in the water looking like a lot of buoys, all around the wreck. The smacks were lying-to about 150 yards away. They took too long to get there. At last the *Cyrene* closed in and picked up three, but the other ten was all drowned.

I never heard before that of a craft rolled right over from one billage on to the other, but that was common for ships to fall over. They'd kind of hang up as the tide left them, and then over they'd go all of a sudden – not only sharp-built things, but round-bottom ones as well. If you wasn't lucky enough to catch hold of something you'd get thrown overboard when that happened.

If the sea was too bad to use the boat you'd have to dodge about, lying hove-to on one tack and then jogging back hove-to on the other, perhaps all day and all night, and you might see the chaps washed out of the rigging and nothing you could do for them. But that didn't do to leave a wreck. That made a lot of difference to them aboard to see you. That would give them a bit of hope and make them keep hanging on to some-

1. In *Once Upon a Tide* I recounted a tradition that Tom Barnard twice ran the *New Unity* alongside the wreck of the *Battalion* and took off the crew. This account was included in Barnard's obituary, but the above is the contemporary account in the *Essex Standard*. A possible explanation may be that Barnard was at the time skippering the *Qui Vive*.

thing, specially if their vessel had sunk under them and they had had to take to the rigging.

That weren't a very luxurious place to spend a night, not perched up in the rigging of a ship sunk under you, wondering the whole time if the mast was going to stand, specially winter time when you was wet through and three-parts gone with cold, without no proper clothing around you nor yet grub inside you. There was some stuck it out, say two nights and a day and were still alive when our chaps got to them, but not many. Mostly they couldn't hang on that long. They just dropped off, or else we'd find them stiff and cold, still held by such bits of lashing as they'd got round themselves when they first had to go aloft.

That often happened that chaps would have the strength and courage to endure a night, and in the morning they'd see our scropers dodging and they would think they were saved. Then at the end of it before our chaps could get to them the damned mast would go and take them with it.

That sort of thing was something several of our chaps had a taste of for themselves.

There was a Faversham schooner called the *General Cathcart* got on the Shipwash, and the crews of our *Tryal* and *Aurora's Increase*, and the Woodbridge *Wonder*, got aboard of her, eighteen men in all. Then that came on so bad they couldn't get away from her. They lost two of the smacks' boats trying, and finally a third one got back to a smack. Next thing is this schooner beats over the top of the sand and sinks in deep water, leaving her crew and our chaps in the rigging. Luckily as the tide ebbed that smoothed the water a little under the lee of the sand and the third smack got them off. The Board of Trade sent £6 reward to the *Wonder* over that and £5 to the *Aurora's Increase*, and the Society[1] sent Ablet Passiful of the *Wonder* 25s for the loss of his clothes.

A week or two after that a Sunderland brig called *Darius* was on the Longsand. Her crew capsized their boat trying to get it away, and three or four of them was lost. The rest had a night in the rigging and in the morning the *Volunteer* tries to get to them. There was too much wind and sea for boat work, so she sails as close by to windward as she dares and casts her boat off, hoping it will reach them, but it drives past, so she sails round and picks it up and lays by. By this time the tide is making and they see two more chaps drop out of the rigging into the water, so they reckon they've got to do something. They take the *Volunteer* into ten feet of water, so with that sea it was touch and go if she'd strike, and

1. The Shipwrecked Fishermen's and Mariners' Society.

they manage to sheer their boat into the rigging and get the survivors.

The ship being all gone they'd no claim beyond life salvage, but the Board of Trade sent £5 and a telescope to Thomas Adams, who was skipper and half-owner of the *Volunteer* at that time, with £3 each to five men who had manned the smack's boat and £2 each to the four others in her crew. That was mentioned at the presentation that about three years before Adams had done much the same sort of rescue with the *Marco Polo*.

Before my time there was a brig called *Palemon* sunk on the Andrews. Some of our chaps got aboard and smashed their boat up doing it. No one else could get to her for two days, and all that time the skipper that had a broken leg was being hoisted up to the tops each flood and lowered down when the ebb left her. He was in a bad way when they got that crew in the end.

The worst thing of all was when women got mixed up in that sort of business. The way some skippers took their wives with them, that makes you think they didn't understand themselves the half of what might happen to them on our bit of coast, specially winter time.

There was a Goole schooner called the *Thrifty*, bound from Grangemouth to Rouen with pig iron, got on the Longsand. The *Paragon* had two goes to reach her with her boat, but that was hopeless, so she tried to sail round to windward of the sand, but she shipped such seas she had to put back into Harwich. That was no use messing about there in the dark. She come in about ten at night and the crew got some grub and dry clothes.

They sailed again at one o'clock in the morning and got back to the *Thrifty*, all sunk by then, with the crew in the rigging. They found both the skipper and his son, the mate, had their wives aboard, and they was both done for. They took the four men into Harwich and the next day they came back and found the body of the mate's young wife, but the skipper's wife was gone altogether. The Institution gave Tom King of the *Paragon* their Silver Medal for that, with £3 each for his crew of six, and the Board of Trade sent him a telescope with another £3 and £20 for his crew.

An Aldeburgh smack called *Laurel*, she fell in with a boatload of Danes in the Swin. They were the ship's company of a vessel lost on the Goodwins. They'd been adrift fifteen hours with next to nothing by way of covering, and when the *Laurel* got them into Harwich the skipper's wife and twelve-year-old daughter, they wouldn't come ashore, not till they was decent. You'd think they would have had enough, but no, they stayed aboard that smack till they sent ashore and got some clothes for them.

There was a poor devil of a barge skipper at anchor off Sheerness. He'd got his sister and five children from thirteen to three years old along with him. His wife had been drowned only a few months before and this sister had come along to look after the kids. This barge, the *Rochford*, was pitching bows under and making a lot of water. When that was deep enough in the cabin to put the fire out, he bundles the whole lot in the boat. The *Emblem* found them and dragged the man and woman out, but the children they never got. The skipper said he thought three of them was drowned in the boat already.

Yes, some of them jobs don't bear thinking about. It's a wonder really more of our old skippers wasn't lost, but most of them must have had nine lives.

One that was unlucky was George Wyatt, that had the *Alfred*. He took her to a Danish schooner called the *Alvilda* on the Longsand, with the *Agenoria* and the *Paragon*. They see this schooner at dawn, February time, all on her beam ends so she was dipping her topsail yard in the water and tide still flowing. She'd lost both her own boats, but the *Paragon* and *Alfred* got their boats to her. Two of them Danes were just a-going to jump into the *Alfred*'s boat when all of a sudden this schooner gives a lurch and flops her square foresail, that was still set, right down all over the boat and upsets it. Most of the hands jumped aboard the wreck, but one was left in the boat, and poor old George Wyatt was overboard.

There was nothing they could do for him, but they still had to get them Danes, and they could see it wasn't safe trying to work her lee side. So they got round to windward and anchored the *Agenoria*'s boat. They dursn't risk trusting to the boat's anchor, so her chaps stood to the oars and slacked in a boat from the *Celerity* that had turned up, and then the *Paragon*'s boat. They got close enough so they could haul the Danes through the surf. Then the *Celerity* sailed after the *Alfred*'s boat and picked that up.

They thought Albert Tillet of Brightlingsea, that had the *Honour*, had gone the same way, but the funny thing is he hadn't, not by no means.

He got aboard a German schooner ashore on the Mouse. The *Honour* was laying off waiting for a tug, and all of a sudden they see this schooner go over on her side. They reckoned that was all up with anyone aboard of her, and they bore up for home and reported the skipper lost. That caused a to-do in Brightlingsea, the more so as Tillet's son-in-law had been lost just a twelve-month before. Then, while they were all a-grieving, in he comes by train about seven in the evening.

What had happened was the German skipper was lost when she fell over but Tillet got back aboard. On the flood the schooner came afloat and drove past the Mouse lightship, which dipped her flag and fired a gun so as a P & O steamer picked him up. I'd like to know what he said to his mates, and what they found to say to him.

CHAPTER FOUR

Pulling Off and Bumping Over

When you found a ship ashore, most often that started with an argument.

The old scroper he'd say, 'You ain't in a very nice place, Captain.' And the captain would say, all easy like, 'She'll be off and on her way before high water. But since you're here you can lay out an anchor if you like.' And the old scroper would say, 'That'll take more than an anchor to get her off. We'd best set about lightening her.' That meant chucking the cargo overboard.

There was generally some big old water casks on deck and the first thing after getting the boats overboard was often to knock the heads out of them. That made the old skipper understand you was aboard and something had to be done. Most times he'd got to come into Harwich or Colne if you got him off, or maybe you'd run him up to Sheerness if the wind was northerly, but once his water was gone that stopped any argument as well as taking a bit of weight off his deck. Cargo and stores of any value you tried to get aboard your smack, but coal and such just went overboard.

Scropers often worked in pairs, because a salvage job might need two smacks' crews, and besides if one got in trouble the other could help him. Or in my time, when there was a tug to help, one old skipper might say, 'While we're doing that my mate can go into Harwich and fetch some steam.' The other crew would stay aboard so as not to lose the job. But in the old days they had to manage as best they could on their own, and a lot of ships never got off that would have done with a tug to help. Some smacks carried a brig's anchor so they could lay that off well clear to windward and veer in with the cable, which was easier than trying to get the ship's anchor off to windward, lashed on a boat's stern.

Well, after a while the captain might say, 'Alright. Which way do you want to work?' That meant, shall we make an agreement now or take it to court later. 'You can have the job for £50,' he might say. And the old scroper, he'd look round and he'd say 'Good God! From what I can see it's going to be worth every bit of £200.' So they'd argue about a few pounds, with the old ship hammering her guts out under their feet and her sails flacking into ribbons over their heads, and as like as not they'd come to terms. If they didn't it would be settled in court later.

Some of them Rowhedgers, they set about the old skippers and didn't give them no peace. They'd hunt maybe in a pack of six smacks, and that might mean twenty smacksmen all haranguing some poor devil that was tired out and wet through, not knowing where he was or what the hell to do next. There was plenty of jobs they got by bullying and browbeating shipwrecked crews, that I'm bound to say.

Once you was engaged you was in charge, same as a pilot. You told the skipper what to do, what sail to set and all such. If you done it wrong you were to blame. That's what happened when the *Atalanta* got a Prussian barque called *Neptune* off the Longsand. He took her off on the wrong tack and got her ashore again, so he had his salvage claim dismissed.

First thing you'd got to decide was whether she'd come off the same way she went on, which you couldn't always do without a tug, not unless the weather eased. But sometimes you could manage it if you had the time and the hands to lighten her.

John Glover with the *Increase* was down by the Sunk when he saw a brig called the *Consort* go ashore on the weather side of the Longsand, to windward of him. That was soon after high water and the tides were taking off. He'd got eleven hands aboard so he sent four in the boat across the top of the sand and sailed the *Increase* round the end of it. By the time he got to the other side the crew of another smack, the *Elizabeth*, was aboard too, and they'd helped the brig's crew heave 2,000 sleepers overboard. There was too much sea to get the brig's anchor off to windward, so he took in two of his own anchors, with eighty fathom warps on each, and they pulled her off just before the next high water. The two smacks got £250 for that.

If you couldn't shift her to windward the way she'd gone on, and that was still a-blowing when you got aboard, the only chance was to set every bit of sail you could and make her bump and drag over the top of the sand on the high water. That didn't do her bottom no good, but it was better than letting her batter herself to bits where she struck, or sand herself in.

First thing most old skippers did when they got ashore was let to an anchor. If the ship didn't drive on to it and hole herself on the fluke, it just held her on the sand. So we'd often wait till a craft was nearly afloat and slip the cable. Then we'd clap on canvas and hope to reach the deep water the other side.

Of course when you got her into deep water she might sink on you, which was vexing, but it's wonderful what a hammering some of those old wooden ships would put up with. Plenty of them have been abandoned as total wrecks and then, when the tides have made, by which I mean come round to spring tides, they've floated off and been picked up derelict. Sharp-bottomed vessels was horrible to get ashore in because of the way they'd go over when the tide ebbed and as like as not never lift again, but sometimes you could press them so hard with sail they would heel over and draw less water, and like that you could make them squilt across.

Sometimes you had to work the weather side on account of that being too far to get across the sand to a wreck from the leeward. That wasn't very nice, because you hadn't got no shelter and if you made a misfetch you'd soon be up alongside the wreck yourself.

One old boy came out over Bawdsey Bar towing his boat astern. The old smack wouldn't hardly fetch and there wasn't a chance she'd wend, nor yet room enough to wear her round. So they chucked the boat adrift to help her and she just squeezed out.

There was a Russian timber brig on the Shipwash flaring away, and now they hadn't got no boat to get aboard, so what they done is this. They kept sailing back and forth close to windward of her, hollering out to them to chuck a rope. First they couldn't make themselves understood, and then them Russians couldn't chuck nothing to windward far enough to reach them. The fourth time they pass her the end of a line from the Rusky comes across the smack's rail and one of them chaps manages to slip it round hisself, catch a couple of turns and hold them with both hands. He hadn't no time for a bowline or such. So over the side he goes and them Russians soon hauled him aboard.

That ain't where you might choose to be, not aboard a wreck on your own with a lot of foreigners and no way of getting off again, but he was lucky. He told them what to do and they was soon off and into Harwich. They got £200, so that time it paid to act crazy.

Another time there was ten smacks' crews got aboard a Spanish brig called *Torre del Ovo* that was on the Kentish Knock. There was four from Harwich, five out of Colne and a Ramsgate lugger. They was working aboard thinking to get her afloat, with the smacks and their boats lying off, and then they begin to see she was a goner, with the sea breaching over her. They thought she might fall over and they cut the main mast away to keep her upright.

With the ship's crew there was fifty-three men crowded together on her stern and only the brig's boat to get help with. She hadn't so much as an oar about her, but eight smacksmen jumped in and cast her off. One of the smacks picked the boat up and give the word to the others and between them they got everybody out of her, all except a little old boy that was killed by a spar falling.

Mind you, that wasn't always bad weather, though you might think so, hearing all these tales. When that was fine and quiet you could get a smack alongside at high water and shift some cargo without wasting it overboard, or even risk lying alongside a wreck on the ebb when the sand was a-dry. And you could get a vessel's big anchor right off to windward. That was hellish hard work, but the old boys done it.

I'll tell you how that was done to save the *William and Anne*. Yes, that will be the best way of explaining how you could work when you had the weather on your side.

You could anchor your smack to windward and maybe pull a ship right off with a rope to your capstan. Of course you wanted a good anchor, which they had, same as for the stowboating[1] – great heavy things with big sharp iron palms fixed to the flukes. And you'd got to flop that anchor down just the right place. Too close and all you done was pull your smack hard up to the wreck. Too far off and you couldn't reach. About a hundred fathoms was the most you could stretch.

Even with the anchors them smacks had you'd got to watch it when you got the full strain on your capstan. If you broke your own anchor out there would be two of you ashore. Such work as this you could only do tide-time, with water enough to get close, or else on the edge of a steep bank. That was no good trying to drag a vessel across flat ground, even if you could get near her.

Well, this *William and Anne* was a Newcastle collier got on the Burrows on a fine winter's night. A Colne man named Levett found her with the *Gipsy*, around three in the morning. He gets aboard, chucks her boats off the deck and puts a light in her rigging to call up three more smacks, the *Eagle, Elizabeth* and *Adamant*. They're aboard by six o'clock, and with that lot of hands they'd thrown a lot of coal out by ten.

Then they decide they'll get her big bower anchor off into deep water.

1. A method of sprat fishing, using a huge net under the smack rigged to the anchor cable. See *The Stowboaters*.

That weighed twelve hundredweight, so the only thing was to sling it under the *Gipsy*'s bow. She's off at anchor in the deep water, so they slack her away from her anchor on a long rope and haul her in alongside. Once she's got this anchor she starts to heave off again. That's when they needed a damned good anchor. Even so, they can't drag the ship's great old chain as well, so every fifteen fathoms they rig a boat to take its weight. In the end of it they had five boats, which is all they'd got between them, strung out at fifteen-fathom spaces. Like that they laid ninety-three fathoms of chain. With the anchor the whole lot weighed two and a half tons. They smashed the collier's jolly boat up doing it.

Then they give her all they can on her windlass and on the high water she shifts, which was as well seeing the tides was taking off and next tide might not have lifted her. They had a line on to the *Gipsy* and were heaving on that as well, so when they picked up this collier's anchor there she was laying astern of the smack. Soon as they could cant her head the right way they give her some sail and away she goes. She lay that night under the Sheers, and the four smacks with her, and next day's tide she's off on her way up to London.

That did some bit of damage to the *Gipsy*, both her stern with the strain of the hauling and her bow with slinging that anchor, but they picked up £240 between them for that job so it all got paid for.

That was some of the regular problems the scropers had to expect, but there was all sorts of queer things might happen to them.

There was a steamboat called the *City of London* got on the Gunfleet. The Revenue cutter *Scout* and the *Fox* went to her. She was thrashing with her paddles, trying to get off, and the skipper of the *Fox* and one hand were in their boat. They got too near and this paddle draws the boat to it. They get sucked right under it and it kills the two of them.

That was years ago, in my father's time. They didn't know much about steam then, but all my time we was used to it, and that altered things – particularly having tugboats. Unless you could see that would be right easy to get a vessel off you'd go and rouse up the paddle tug, and if the wreck was to windward as like as not you'd leave your smack in the harbour and come back aboard of her. She'd pull a craft off to windward as clean as drawing a tooth, or she'd tow a lifeboat to windward of the wreck, and the lifeboat could let go her anchor and drop in right alongside.

Then of course once a vessel was afloat the tug didn't have no trouble getting her into Harwich and dumping her up on the mud if she was too leaky to lay afloat. But wind anywhere easterly those old scropers would generally tow a craft in. People seem to think you've got to have steam to do a bit of towing. Don't you believe it. Give them a fair slant of wind and a couple of old smacks would soon fetch a brig or a schooner in, same as I've told you already. The *Perseverance* had a go at towing a disabled screw steamer, only nothing came of that, on account of she busted her boom and the steamship sank on her. When we first had lifeboats they often gave them a pull too. But of course you can't expect a sailing craft to tow to windward.

Mind you, the old skipper might not even let you aboard. He might tell you all bloody scropulators was worse than sharks and where to go and what to do. Then you'd try to put the wind up him, telling him he's in a hell of a horrible place and all such, and if you could see he was soon going to change his tune and start hollering for you then you'd keep dodging. If the old boy was right and likely to come off the way he went on time the tide flowed a bit then you'd humbug off and look about for something else.

There was a Spanish steamboat got on the Eagle off Clacton. The *Topaz*, a Dover smack that belonged in Brightlingsea at that time of day, heard him blowing his whistle in thick fog and went to him, but all he done was he covered the ship's name and tried to shake the skipper of the *Topaz* off his ladder, with the Spaniards threatening the crew with knives and pistols. They got his name, which was *Ciscar*, but they never found what he thought he was doing there, nor yet what become of him.

That still went on when they had the lifeboats. Them Walton chaps will tell you how they went to a Russian steamer on the Gunfleet and the skipper says, 'Gents, I dursn't ask you to set foot aboard but if you like to lay alongside I'll give you some coffee,' which he done. That was better than another time they was chucking grapnels in a ship's rigging to get hold of her and the ship's crew with axes cutting their grapple ropes.

Yes, sometimes it was a job to get aboard a vessel and sometimes it was a hell of a job to get the skipper to leave her. You might have to throw the poor old fellow into the boat.

There was a French brig called the *Anne Marie* on the Sunk that smashed both her boats trying to get them in the water. They'd made a raft by the time the *Marco Polo* turned up next morning. The water was too shallow to get his boat to the brig, so he slacked it in as far as it would go and threw them a line from it. With that he pulled them Froggies through the surf to the boat. But they couldn't make that captain come. They had to leave him. He was picked up off that raft later by another craft, and the raft came ashore at Clacton.

Yes, them old skippers varied. One day my dad went to a schooner on the Gunfleet. The skipper had his old woman with him and they'd got such gear as they could all packed and ready to go. 'Thank you, boys,' he says. 'This ain't the first time for me and I'd rather lose a dozen more craft than have anything happen to my dear wife.'

Yet another time there was a schooner called the *Arrival* on the Cutler. The *Dawn* of Woodbridge got her off and into the Haven not too much damaged, and when they came back blowed if the skipper hadn't hanged himself in the cabin. That was the second time he'd been salvaged that month, and he hadn't paid for the previous job, so that all seemed a bit too much for him, poor old boy.

CHAPTER FIVE

Settled in Court

If you hadn't made no agreement at the time of a salvage, then you had to go to court to settle what you was to get.

Any kind of wreckage that came ashore had to be declared to the Receiver of Wreck at the Custom House, or to the coastguards who acted for him. If it just washed ashore you had to report it and you might get some reward for finding it, but if you brought it ashore you got around a third of the value.

You could try for more if you'd done a lot of work or taken a lot of risk or suffered a bit of damage and weren't getting nothing to show for it. After the wreck of the *Deutschland*, what I'll have to tell you a lot about all in good time, the divers got up a lot of crates of wines and spirits, but what with having duty to be paid on them the wine only sold for five shillings a dozen, so John Glover and Watts, that owned the tug *Liverpool*, they put in for half value instead of a third. Otherwise, they said, they wouldn't trouble to go salvaging no more. The Receiver at Harwich done what he could but they huffed and puffed at the Board of Trade and they never give nothing.

When you brought a crew ashore you could claim life salvage, but there weren't a lot of money in that.

The *Aurora's Increase* and the *Ranger*, they saved twenty-three men out of a barque called the *City of Carlisle* on the Kentish Knock. Oliver Williams, the Harwich Lloyd's agent, only offered them £28. They refused that and took it to court and got £50 between them. That didn't make a big shareout, not after you'd as like as not had a boat or two smashed up on a job of that kind.

Yes, that was often terrible unfair. John Lawrence with the *Martha*, he's going to a brig called *Severn* ashore on the Gunfleet. He falls in with the skipper and his wife and crew leaving her in their boat, and he picks them up. He's taking them ashore when he sees five other smacks going to the wreck. So he brings up and tries to row back, which is too far, so he comes back and gets the *Martha* under way, but by the time he's back to the wreck these other chaps won't even take him on. She was theirs by then, you see. All he can do is collect the crew's belongings and humbug off again.

These other craft get the *Severn* off and he has to see her sold for £800, and two-fifths of that awarded to them. That's beyond bearing so he applies to the magistrates for compensation. The beaks had to decide whether anything for him should come from what the other scropers had had or be paid by the owners, which seemed only just. But the owner's lawyer wouldn't have it. 'Lawrence saved nothing but the clothes of the crew,' he says. 'Then they count their lives as nothing?' says his lawyer. But the answer to that was that the skipper and crew forfeited their claim on the owners by forsaking the vessel – which of course they shouldn't have done, but this skipper was another that saw fit to have his old woman aboard and I daresay that made a difference. Anyway, the beaks said Lawrence was to have £40, but the owner's man just said he'd appeal, so whether that was ever paid I don't know.

They used to lead some of them Receivers a dance chance times. The Margate chaps off the *Eclipse* handed in some gear and three *empty* seamen's chests. I reckon that was a taunt.

But our Receiver, John Wood, he was respected. He had some sensible ideas. He was all on for training schools or ships at different ports so boys could go to sea with some knowledge instead of being sent straight out of the workhouse into ships as drudges, and he thought up the idea of lifesaving rafts that could be stowed away aboard ships. He was preaching that years before the idea caught on.

Yes, he tried to see things done fair and square. Sometimes they'd make a life salvage claim just for bringing in a shipwrecked crew that had rowed up to them in their own boat. John Barnard tried that one when he brought in the crew of the *Aspendus*, and so did Ablet Passiful when he picked up a boat from the *Grace Millie*, time he had the *Violet*, but Wood say, 'Humbug off. You ain't done nothing what anyone else wouldn't have done.' He wouldn't give them no life salvage reward though he told them they knew which form to use for a claim on the boat. But he would always fight for a salvager who had a fair claim, though his high-ups wouldn't always give him his way.

He had a lot of other jobs, like arresting ships that weren't seaworthy. He wouldn't let them sail till they'd been properly done up, and sometimes he'd have to look after hands aboard who were stuck in Harwich without wages. The owners didn't fancy paying out money to men who had refused to sail in a ship and had put them to the expense of doing her up. The beaks would not help them but Wood found them a few pounds to get them home.

Then he had his regular auctions to arrange, with his superiors demanding receipts for this and vouchers for that all the time. That might be a ship put up for sale that somebody had brought in, or just a collection of old anchors and chains that they sold when the price was good. At one time marked anchors and chains had to be tested before they were sold, but there weren't no test house near Harwich so they had to break them up. That was so troublesome and expensive that in the end Wood got permission to sell them as they were without guarantee or warranty. Yes, he had a fiddling sort of job.

One time there was a spar come ashore at Felixstowe, worth a couple of quid, and he fixes up a salvage claim for the coastguard, and then up comes Colonel Tomline saying that as Lord of the Manor he's entitled to five per cent groundage. That kept the lawyers busy till they decided there was an ancient right of that sort and they had to pay Tomline 1s 6d. The Colonel owned all the land from Landguard to Bawdsey, in fact they said he could ride home from Woodbridge to Felixstowe without once going off his own property, but he meant to have his eighteen pence, though that can't have covered his expenses.

Another time, when the *Jeune Ludovic* was wrecked, the whole shore from the Naze Tower to Harwich was covered with timber. The carts cut the land up so much getting down to the beach that Eagle, the landowner at Walton Hall, wanted compensation and Wood got him £10.

There was everlasting of cases claiming salvage when there hadn't been no agreement made at sea. The smaller claims were heard by the local beaks, but the bigger ones went to the Admiralty Court with a special assessor. They'd hear from the salvagers what a hell of a time they'd had and what a lot of risk they'd taken, and then the owner's lawyer he'd describe how that was a nice quiet day and the smacks was as much a hindrance as help.

They didn't have much trouble in seeing the rights of it. They'd say that's worth, perhaps, £50 for a little everyday job up to several hundred pounds for a valuable ship and cargo that had been in a real bad place. With the scropers claiming as much as they dared and the owners offering as little as they thought they could get away with, that was often just a matter of splitting the difference. In the end what you got depended on the value of the vessel and the cargo as much as on what you did and what risks you run. Now and again you'd get a mean lot of beaks that tried to cheat you, but then you could appeal to the Admiralty Court.

Yes, you had to make the best of the value of a ship and her cargo on account of the other side would make the worst of it. Turner Barnard, in the *New Unity*, he fell in with a Goole ketch called *Brilliant*[1] on the Barrow. She was bound up to London and got caught in a squall. The skipper had his wife and three kids for passengers and only his mate and a boy for crew. Barnard goes aboard with three hands and gets her off with an anchor and a spring to cant her head round the right way. Then he jills about till there's water in the Spitway, takes her through and gets a line aboard the *New Unity* which tows her into Colne.

All he gets offered is £40, so he takes it to court and asks £125. He couldn't claim much on the cargo, which was shoddy, worth about £3 a ton, but he makes out the ketch is worth £300. 'Do you know she's thirty-seven years old?' says the lawyer. 'Maybe so,' says Barnard, 'but look how old you are, and you think you're better than me.' That made them laugh in court and upset the lawyer, who meant to have the best of it. 'I see she was built in '41,' he says. 'That's right,' says Barnard. 'She's the same age as I am.'

He didn't get asked no more after that and they gave him £100. That was right enough when you think the *New Unity* was worth £500 and he'd put her at some risk, leaving just two hands aboard while the other four crew dealt to this *Brilliant*, which, by the way, was still knocking about years afterwards when she was over fifty years old.

There was some huge awards in my father's time.

Them tallow ships from Russia were always worth something. One of them called the *Brothers* got on the Gunfleet with a cargo worth £10,000. There was fourteen smacks working a fortnight on her and at the end of it the beaks decided to give £28 each to the sixty-four men aboard of them so that was the best part of £2,000. The owners appealed to the Admiralty Court but that award was upheld.

Another time a brig called *Clarissa* got on the Girdler and broke up, bound from Marseilles to London. She was worth over £6,000 with her cargo, and they gave £1,286 in awards – £460 to the *Liberty* of Colchester that saved the crew, £320 to eleven other Colchester boats, another £320 to the Whitstable boats, £30 to the *Mary* of Margate, £100 to the other Margate boats and £50 to the Milton boats. Them Kent chaps didn't fancy so much going to Essex, and they went to appeal.

1. 53 tons, built in 1841 at Leeds – an unusual building place.

The old judge said he reckoned the Margate boats did more harm than good and he didn't think much of it at all, he didn't. He said he wouldn't alter the total but he'd share it out different. He said £320 must go to the smacks that got there the first day, which was John Barnard's *Prince of Orange*, the *New Unity* and seven Whitstablers, and the other £320 must be divided between the remaining Colchester and Whistable men. That give you an idea what a lot of craft got around a big wreck that time of day, specially when that was handy for the Kentishmen as well as our salvagers to get at it.

There was a Whitby brig called *Regina* on the Swin Middle with tallow from Cronstadt, and within a day or two there was thirty boats having a go at her. The Lloyd's agent at Whistable, he sent a telegram to the Wreck and Salvage Association in London and then he called out the Marines from Sheerness. They took some of the smacks into the Medway under armed guard and the rest soon cleared out. They had seven Brightlingsea men up at Sittingbourne and fined them £100 each.

That caused a stir, that did. *The Times* said they were only doing what

Wreck of the schooner Renown *on the Nore. The Southend boatmen shown were branded as 'wreckers', and the Receiver of Wrecks was ordered to return salvaged stores to the owners without payment, 'leaving the pretended salvors to seek their own remedy for any claim they may consider themselves entitled to'. The illustrations and quotation are from an undated cutting from the* Illustrated London News.

the Seamen's Act empowered them to do, seeing as they were going to report to the collector of salvage and claim their share. 'There have happily been no such persons as wreckers known upon the Essex coast for many years', that's what that paper said. The magistrates thought different, and said it was a gross outrage. The Brightlingsea men took it to appeal but that didn't do them no good.

Another brig on the self-same voyage, tallow and hemp from Russia, she got on the Gunfleet and there was a hell of a great law case over that. She was called the *Fleece*. The *Agenoria* bumped her over, but that didn't do her no good and they couldn't get her into Harwich. No, they had to put her on Walton flats in three fathoms of water. That was before they had them patent pumps that would pump half the North Sea through a craft to keep her afloat.

The stone men thought she was fair game and they set to work picking her bones. They arrested nine of them on the spot. The captain engaged the Revenue cutter *Scout* and the *Agenoria*, *Aurora's Increase*, *Tryal* and *Success*. That gave him thirty-five men to salvage what they could. He tried to hire barges in Harwich but he couldn't get any. When he came back there was 150 men aboard. They'd even cut the rigging out of her so he couldn't use the masts to sling the cargo out.

The upshot was they charged twenty-eight men from Harwich, Brightlingsea and Pin Mill. They hired the biggest room they could find to try the case, but of course that wouldn't hold half the crowd tried to get in. These chaps said the *Scout* was only in charge so long as she was flying her pennant and her ensign and when she hauled them down at night it gave them a right. A few got off because they weren't properly identified but in the end they fined four of them £4 or two months in prison and the rest £2 or one month.

I've told you already how some of our Harwich men were accused of making a put-up job of a wreck. They had some of them Rowhedgers up for a conspiracy too.

They got hold of a Welsh brig called the *Trixie Wee* that was on the Longsand. The skipper refused them and she came off, but he didn't know where he was so next thing he put her on the Sunk. This same lot of Rowhedgers get aboard again, but the old man still won't have them, and he goes and gets his head down for a few hours. When he comes back on deck they are still on at him. The mate tells the hands to man the windlass, but one man refuses till they've got rid of the smacksmen. At last the skipper says, 'I suppose I shall have to employ you.'

They told him they'd give him £80 if he'd make an agreement to take the brig to Dover for £300. The mate said he didn't know what to put in the log, so one of them writes the words on the log slate for him to copy. After that they beat up to the Sheers and anchor for the night. They'd been telling the poor old skipper he was 200 miles from Harwich, but next morning when that was a fair wind for Harwich and a head wind for Dover they change their tune and alter the agreement too before they run into Harwich.

The tale got out and they had them up in court. They'd washed the chalk off the log slate, but if that was warmed the wording still showed up, so that's what they done in court, and they could read it. They told the mate to read what he'd writ in the log and he said, 'If you was to give me a thousand pounds I could not read it.' That was all a lot of lies, he said.

They sent Thomas Barnard and four others to the assizes, but they wouldn't hear the case on account of some legal snarl-up, so they got off. Some years later this *Trixie Wee* went ashore near Aldeburgh and broke up.

There was a tale too that when a Colchester sloop called *Susannah* got in trouble the smacksmen offered to give the skipper a receipt for £400 if he'd pay them £200. That he wouldn't do and they say they tried to knock a hole in the vessel's bottom.

Some of the old skippers wasn't above playing a trick or two on the salvagers if it come to that.

My father told me one of them French luggers got on the Shipwash – a Chase-Mary[1] he called her. Edward Lewis gets aboard from the *Aurora's Increase* and tells the skipper to pick his anchor up, which he does. Then this Froggie starts saying 'How much?' and Lewis suggests to leave it to the gentlemen ashore. That's how he put it. The Frog won't have that, so Lewis suggests £50. He gets offered £15 and just after he's refused that up comes the *Agenoria* and a Woodbridge smack called the *Jessey*. The skippers, John Carrington and Ablet Passiful, come aboard and they agree to humbug off and leave the Frogs to cool down a bit. The mate tries to keep them. He says the skipper has had a drop to drink and he ups with a bottle of brandy, so they all have one, but then away they go just the same.

After half an hour that's breezing up nicely, so back they come and tell

---

1. The chasse-marée, that strange combination of heavy, almost billyboy hull with a rakish lugger's rig, was quite common on the East Coast at this time, particularly in the coal trade.

the skipper he'll have to leave the deal to his Consul. Then, while they're at work, the Frenchman calls Lewis down to his cabin. He says after the job he'll need to know his name, so will he write it down. He gives him a pen and ink and three sheets of blank paper and he gets Lewis to write his name in the middle of one sheet and again at the bottom of the next. By this time this Chase-Mary is coming afloat and Lewis gets hold of the helm and sails her into Harwich. I recall her name was the *Reine des Anges*.

Next day in Oliver Williams' office Lewis gets shown an agreement for £5 with his signature to it. That was argued two days in court, with Lewis giving it as I've told you, and the other skippers saying he wasn't below in the cabin above a few minutes, not long enough to make an agreement even if he'd been daft enough to want to. But the French skipper and mate, they swore every word was written down while Lewis was in the cabin.

I reckon they ought to have been had up for falsehood and lying, but the beaks must have had some doubts, because they took a long time to discuss it and then they only gave £5 to each smack and each side to pay its own costs.

The Rowhedge and Southend boats, they sometimes worked partnerships. They'd agree to be as one, but that didn't always work out.

The *Blue Eyed Maid*, *Gipsy* and *Prince of Orange* were working that way. The *Blue Eyed Maid* was to keep down Swin, while the other two had a look higher up. They found a Dutchman ashore, but when the *Blue Eyed Maid* took them to court for her share it was ruled there couldn't be no partnership if one partner wasn't there at the time.

At Southend they had a different custom. A partnership was on so long as they all kept at sea, but if one boat went in for a tide then she didn't have no more claim.

The Harwich custom was one share for each smack and a half-share for a boat, and that seemed to work alright. But some of the bawleymen fell out after a Maldon brig called the *Berthold* got on the West Rocks. She refused the lifeboat, but employed the bawleymen to throw her cargo overboard. They got paid £70, but Denney that owned the *Irex* had to go to court to get her share.

But they were only bawleymen and didn't know no better. No more did the stone men when they got mixed up in it.

Some of them found an anchor with eighty fathoms of hawser on it, time they were a-dredging. Blowed if one of them didn't go up to a coastguard when they got ashore and tell him, 'We're a-going to run an anchor and cable tonight.' Tried to persuade him to look some other way.

Of course there was a reception committee waiting for them, and they fined a couple of them £5 each.

That was just a bit of nonsense. But that caused a real stir when the Customs summonsed leading salvagers for concealing stuff they'd brought ashore. Of course there was always a bit of that done and I reckon they thought they had to bring a case every now and again to keep it within reason. The court was always crowded with smacksmen and they didn't keep quiet either.

Sometimes if you was caught red-handed there wasn't nothing you could do. James Cook that had the *Concord* came into Colne one day, and he hands in a few bits of wire and rope to the guardship. He signs a declaration that he hasn't got nothing else, and when the coastguard asks him if he is sure of that, which might have put him on his guard, he says yes and he wants to hustle up to Rowhedge that tide.

The coastguard says he'll have to rummage, and he shines his bull's eye into the scuttle butt beside the mast. That's full of bottles of Geneva, nearly up to the top of the water. There's more bottles in another water cask and glasses and decanters and God knows what stowed about her. 'That's a bad job,' says Cook. 'I shall have to get clear of it as best I can.' He'd got that stuff out of a vessel called the *Francesco Ferrara*, that had got on the Longsand bound from Rotterdam to Buenos Aires.

When it come to court Cook and his crew couldn't do nothing but plead guilty. They had to make him pay double duty, which was £26 15s, but they kept the fine down to a £5 note and the Collector said if he'd done him under some new Act of Parliament he and his crew might have gone to gaol, with the smack and any salvage claim forfeited and a £100 fine on top of that. Soon after they did do George Orman of Brightlingsea under that Act, and fined him the full £100, though they recommended the Customs to reduce it to £25.

Jim Cook hadn't got a leg to stand on, but mostly when the old salvagers were had up they weren't apologising for nothing. No, not by no means. They'd tell the old magistrates 'If you carry on persecuting us like this we shan't think so much about saving a few lives at sea.' And you could see the magistrates were often on their side. They reckoned just bringing them to court was enough of a warning.

They had Bill Wheeler, skipper of the Brightlingsea *Excellent*, that was another famous scroper, up in Colchester Town Hall, saying he hadn't declared everything he'd brought ashore out of a vessel called the *Explorer* that had been run down by a steamer near the Mouse Lightship. Wheeler hands them up a copy of the *Brightlingsea Parish Magazine*, which was as good as the *Shipping Gazette* for seafaring news, time old Canon Pertwee was the rector there. That had the tale of a rescue Wheeler had done a year before when he got a bravery award from the Netherlands Vice-Consul for rescuing the crew of a craft called the *Anna* that was water-logged in the North Sea. The magistrates said they were liable for a fine up to £100 as well as forfeiting their salvage claim and paying double the value of the salvage. Then they just said to pay a fine of a shilling each and the double value of the salvage, which they put at £4 10s.

Them old Brightlingsea boys, they played the Customs up worse than we dared do in Harwich. One time after the wreck of a ship on the Knock John the Customs seized some stuff from a house and were taking it to the Custom House when they were met by thirty or forty men, all with muskets and bludgeons and fowling pieces. There was a woman riding a donkey among them, though what she was doing I can't fathom, nor yet the beaks couldn't either.

The chief boatman was man enough to walk right through them, but one of his chaps behind him hadn't the sense. He tried to take a pistol off one of the Brightlingsea men, saying it was off the wreck, and that started a set-to. Two men were had up in court. They claimed the Customs had a right to search but not to seize and they got the cases dismissed. I dare say they thought that having them up and giving them a scare was enough. What the hell was the use of sending them to prison?

About the only thing you were allowed to pick up was coal. When a collier got ashore at Felixstowe and broke up, the beach would be smothered with coal all the way from Landguard to Bawdsey, and that you might have. But they seemed to think if you so much as picked up a bit of driftwood the whole country would be ruined.

They had a whole lot of cases over that when I was a lad. When they done George Death of Brightlingsea, that was one of the best respected skippers there, and several other chaps for having a few shillings' worth of wood aboard their boats, that was mentioned there had been several cases lately and the bench would be surprised at the amount of timber found in hedges and ditches as a result of bringing them.

Around that time there was two timber ships, called the *Charles* and the *Herbert*, got wrecked and covered the shore by Clacton with boards and staves. The Receiver of Wreck at Harwich summoned about a dozen people, including Mrs Giles that had a big farm, with a governess and servants and all, that had been picking up this wood and laying it out in one of her fields. The magistrates had to fine them all, but they didn't like it. They asked the Board of Trade to remit costs and their lawyer said he would do what he could.

When the Bench next sat, the chairman, old Yellolly Watson, that wrote a history book[1] of those parts, said 'Have you heard anything from the Board of Trade?' The clerk said he hadn't. 'Well, I have,' said Watson. He knew that lawyer wouldn't do nothing so he'd writ off right away. He read out in court what he'd said: 'One poor labouring man earning 13s a week having a large family to support has to pay £5 in six weeks, or go to prison, in either case bringing ruin and beggary upon his family.'

Of course the Board of Trade just sent him back a bit of flannel. They said his letter would have careful consideration, but as to the man he spoke of, 'the Board would not be justified in recommending any mitigation, the case being regarded as a very bad one.' Watson said to extend the six weeks he'd allowed for payment by another month to see what their careful consideration was worth.

Smuggling wasn't nothing much in my time. In the old days Saxby and the *Scout*, they was all the time bringing in luggers full of gin and tobacco, and a lot of crews did six months inside, or got sent to the Navy if they was fit for that, but in my time it was mostly just railway boat chaps getting fined a few shillings week after week in the police court. The beaks didn't seem to worry much, they just took ten bob off them for bringing in a bit of tobacco, so as it must have been worth keeping on doing it.

Now and again they had to make an example. The Dutch fishermen used to sell tobacco to the lightships and one time they had seven of the crew of the Trinity yacht *Satellite* for bringing it ashore. They said every basket in the focs'l seemed to have half-pounds of Rising Sun brand in it.

I daresay there was more done by our smacks than ever come to light. The *Two Brothers* got caught badly. She had 600 lbs of leaf and 300 lbs of cut tobacco as well as 32 lbs of cigars, all worth £323. They fined three chaps £100 each, which they couldn't pay so they got sent to prison during Her Majesty's pleasure. After that the *Two Brothers* was sold away to Grimsby.

I only remember the King's Pipe at Parkeston being lit once. That's what they called the furnace for destroying contraband. They burned two huge crates of cigars that had been in bond for five years, and some bottles of spirits with some strong German beer which some of the labourers tried to drink, but that was up. But the chief point of that was to burn

1. *The Tendring Hundred in the Olden Time.*

Wreck of the emigrant ship Floridian on the Longsand, February 1849. This Illustrated London News impression depicts the Revenue cutter Petrel rescuing survivors from the bow, which alone remained above water after the Floridian broke in half. Only one of the 160 passengers survived, with three of the crew of fourteen.

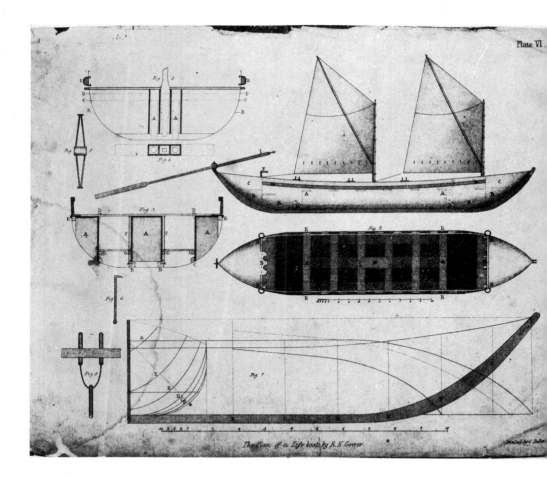

Plate VI

The Plan of a Life boat by R.H. Gower.

When Captain Richard Gower of Ipswich was asked to design a lifeboat for Landguard in the 1820s, he favoured a little thirty-foot surf boat with only six foot beam, light enough to be moved from one part of the beach to another, and rigged with two spritsails.

Design by John Smeaton for a beacon to be placed on 'the Hook of the Gunfleet' in 1784. It is mounted in a hull about thirty-five feet long with nearly twenty-five feet beam, ballasted with eight blocks of stone, each weighing four-and-a-half tons. It was to be towed out and sunk on the sand after the removal of the deck.

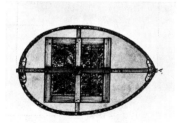

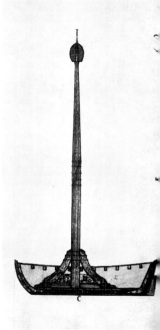

The Right Hon. Sir Francis Thornhill Baring Bart. M.P. First Lord of the Admiralty.

One of the two slipways at Vaux's Navy Yard, Harwich. *The capstan on left had twenty bars and could be manned by sixty men. When the salvaged* Friesland *(between 700 and 800 tons) was hauled out in 1859, she was the largest ship to be so handled, and four purchases were rigged to re-inforce the capstan. The small building on right houses the ancient treadmill crane which is still preserved – the only surviving relic of the shipyard.*

Harwich from the sea. An aquatint after W J Huggins, published in 1841, showing the low and high lighthouses, the church and the cement factories' chimneys smoking. The vessel shown at anchor probably suggests the style of the Agenoria, Aurora's Increase *and* Tryal. *The high and low lights were kept in line as a guide to Harwich till Landguard extended into the fairway which they marked, and they became known as the 'misleading lights'.*

J H Vaux (right, as Mayor of Harwich) and his tug Harwich, *which failed to reach the wreck of the* Indian Chief. *The photo above, with the Pier Hotel and Great Eastern Hotel in the background, shows what a handsome craft she was, though the later photo (below) is less flattering. The guardship, HMS* Hotspur, *dates it between 1893 and 1897, after the tug had been sold to Pauls of Ipswich and before they sold her to the Tyne.*

some hundreds of pounds' worth of mats. Braintree had a mat factory then and the boss had been to a Belgian penal colony and seen them made there. They'd just passed a law against foreign prison-made goods, so he got them on that.

Of course when they salvaged a cargo of liquor that was liable to lead to trouble. There was a brig went to pieces on the Longsand with every man aboard lost, right under the eyes of several of our smacks that couldn't get near her. She was supposed to be from Bremen. When they did get to her she was full of spirits in demi-johns, a hundred of them. Ben Dale, he tried carrying one home, wrapped up in a bit of tarpaulin, but they had him. He tried to make out in court he didn't know what it was! They can't have thought much of that for a tale, but they let him off with a fine of 14s 7d, which was supposed to be the value.

Then one of the crew of the Revenue cutter *Scout* went mad drinking it and died of apoplexy. There was a few questions at the inquest how the stuff came to be aboard. Finally they rummaged the *Agenoria*, time Hezekiah Baker had her, and found a couple of these demi-johns. That cost him £100.

D

CHAPTER SIX

The Smacksmen

There was two sorts of salvagers, the smacksmen and the longshore boatmen. Us Harwichers and the Colne men from Rowhedge, Wivenhoe and Brightlingsea done the smack work, cruising all about everywhere same as I've told you, with two or three out of Bawdsey and Orford taking a hand as well.

We worked easy with the Colne men on salvaging, though we'd fall out with them other times. They come and cleaned out the oysters which used to be a nice little trade in the harbour – but then they done that all round the shores of England and Wales and Scotland. Hundreds of oyster grounds they must have ruined, the way they come and cleaned them out. I've told you the set-to there was when they tried to break the stone men's strike. Another time the Brightlingsea stone dredgers had a go at the oysters in the Ipswich river and some of them got sent to prison for stealing them. They was like pirates when oysters was concerned.

But salvaging we got on together very well. You couldn't waste time arguing on that game. My father said the Rowhedge men were some of the head salvagers. Several of them moved to Harwich, because Colne was a long way to leeward to work from, wind north-easterly.

John Glover, that was respected as much as any of the Harwich scropers in my time, he came from Rowhedge. He had the *Increase* built a-purpose for him. He got a telescope from the Kaiser after he went to a Prussian barque called *Karl Agrell* on the Longsand round Christmastime and got thirteen men out of her. He had the crew of the *Reindeer* as well as his own crew aboard the *Increase* that time.

He was a man liked to stand by a job. That way he could do something the later lifeboats couldn't. There was an Italian barque called the *Raffaele Ligure* on the Longsand. The crew would not leave her, so off the lifeboat goes, and though she comes back next day the Italians are still obstinate. The day after that the barque begins breaking up and they wish they'd taken their chance, but Glover he's in his element dodging about there two days and two nights in his *Increase*, and he brings all eleven of them in.

Another time he and two other Colchester smacks, the *New Gipsy* and *Atalanta*, found a brig called the *Traveller* on the Gunfleet with the crew in the rigging. That was a February gale and nothing they could do but hoist a colour and lay-to all day Sunday and through the night. Then at last, though that wasn't no better on the Monday, they got a boat away from each of the smacks and picked up the ten hands. They were so swollen and stiff after thirty hours in the rigging they had to cut their clothes off.

Another craft he went to was a Scotchman called the *Dane of Argyle* on the Sunk. He got two hands out of her and they told him the third man was too far gone to be worth taking. But Glover said, 'Never mind. Dead or alive we'll get him,' and that's what he did.

Besides him there was no end of Cooks. I recall Harry Cook with the *Aquiline* and James Cook with the *Concord* that David Martin also had at one time, and others of them had the *Snowdrop*, *Beulah* and *Blue Eyed Maid*. Long before my time two of them were drowned in the job I told you about on the *Marquis of Huntley*.

Tom Barnard and his eight sons had the *New Unity* and *Prince of Orange*, James Mills had the *Pheasant* and Jack Spitty that moved away later to Bradwell, he had the *Bluebell* and when he lost her went copering with an old Dutch smack he called *Umperell*. James Mason had the *Liberty* and Charles Crosby the *New Blossom*, and at Brightlingsea there was Bill Wheeler with the *Excellent*.

But there, I shan't never recall the half of them, nor yet the things they got up to. Some I've mentioned already and others will come to me as we go along with this yarn.

Two that kept at it to the end were William Cheek of Rowhedge with the *Faith*, and Fred Salmon at Brightlingsea with the *Emily*. Just before my time old John Salmon got a telescope for saving five hands out of a craft on the Barrow with the *Emily*, but in my time it was Fred Salmon had her – him that got the pianos out of the *Hawksdale*, same as I've told you.

He used to get into everything. He goes out of Colne one Saturday afternoon and finds a brig called *Winifred*. He stands by her all night and in the morning tows her into Colne. Off he goes again and there's a Norwegian on the Gunfleet. He and the Clacton lifeboat get her off and run her up to Sheerness.

Then he starts off for home and finds a ship called the *Fiery Cross* on the Red Sand. She was a famous tea-clipper, and being as sharp-bottomed as a yacht she was lying on her side with the crew taken out of her. He and some Leighmen got her up somehow and he leaves his mate aboard in charge of her. The *Emily* gets home Tuesday night. That weren't a bad weekend's work, was it?

Among the Harwich scropers there was Hezekiah Baker that had the *Agenoria* and owned the *John and William* along with John Carrington. Thomas Adams had the *Marco Polo* and the *Volunteer*, Crane had the *Queen* and the Wyatts had several craft, among them the *Alfred* that drowned one of them. Before that William Newson had the *Alfred*.

But the most famous of all was the Lewises. There was two brothers, John and William. William had the *Queen Victoria* and the *Tryal*. He had the Institution's second service clasp for a rescue he done with the *Tryal* from a Goole sloop called the *Maria* on the Longsand. He'd already got the silver medal but I can't tell you how he come by that.

John had the silver medal too, for getting the survivors out of a brig called *Stanton* on the Gunfleet. He had several craft. One was a bawley called *Dauntless*. His *Queen* was called the tobacco box because she was caught smuggling and condemned to be cut in half, which is how they used to treat such craft to discourage the others. John Lewis could see she could do with lengthening, so he buys her cheap, puts the saw through her careful and builds a few extra feet into her.

Both the *Dauntless* and the *Queen* were fishing boats, going shimpering and doing a bit of long-lining for cod round the Sunk, but John Lewis also took on the *Aurora's Increase*, that was mixed up in as many salvages as any before she was run down lying off the Sunk where she'd been working on a wreck. A Norwegian barque blundered into her and she went down in a few minutes. She saw a lot of lives lost and saved in her time. Once she was laying in the Spitway when a schooner drove ashore and fell over with everyone aboard lost, and all at the same time the sea swept a young chap overboard off the smack.

Another time she went to a Sunderland brig called the *Loyalty* on the Whiting and got her off. John Lewis saw her go ashore and put his brother aboard. Then he smashed up one of his boats, and some of the brig's crew made off in their longboat, which left them with only one boat. That took six hours to get her off and bring her up with four-and-a-half feet of water in her.

Next day, the *Aurora's Increase* went back and got the sails, and blessed if they didn't have them up in the Town Hall for failing to report them. They got fined fifteen guineas, which was double the value of the sails and gear, but the Shipwrecked Fishermen's and Mariners' Royal Benevolent Society answered that by sending them £20 reward for the job.

The following year the *Aurora's Increase* and the *Tryal* worked together on the wreck of a French brig called *Etoile de la Mer*. She was another got on the Longsand, and when the crew cut her mainmast away they were unlucky, for that fell right across their longboat and smashed it in two. They see two smacks come near and bear away, and then they see the *Aurora's Increase*. Lewis and four of his hands got her boat under the bowsprit and six of the Frenchmen dropped into it. That took an hour to get them to the smack, but then back they come, the same chaps, and got the rest. There was silver medals for all that took part in that including Thomas Tye. That was another famous Harwich family. John Tye that was skipper of the *Tryal* was the first lifeboat cox'n. When he retired he kept the Three Cups and took a lot of interest in model yacht racing.

I was only a nipper when the *Aurora's Increase* was lost and about the same time old William Lewis done himself in. He hadn't been right since he and his brother took a hammering against a wreck they were working on. After that they sold the *Queen* to Ramsgate and the *Queen Victoria* back to Brightlingsea, where she went on a-salvaging. So I don't recall them nor yet the *Tryal*, which old William sold to Bawdsey before his death.

But my father told me the *Aurora's Increase* and the *Queen Victoria* were both regular diving boats, pumps and all. Our scropers didn't go away out of home waters much, but they did once or twice.

There was a passenger steamer called the *Bruiser* lost off Aldeburgh. Run into by a steam collier called the *Haswell*, she was, and sunk with twelve passengers and three of her crew. Oliver Williams gave the Lewises the job of getting what they could out of her. They had to cut her yards and rigging away under water to get at her, but they done so well that when another steamboat, the *Sultana*, was sunk in the Scheldt Williams gave them that job too.

She was going into Antwerp, and our railways steamer *Harwich* that was coming out very nigh cut her in half. She had a lot of valuable horses aboard and a cargo of cotton bales and pig iron. So the *Aurora's Increase* and *Queen Victoria* went off to Holland. They got the cotton out but couldn't do nothing with the pig iron. God knows what happened to the poor old horses.

Later on, in times I can remember better, John's son, Bill Lewis, that went on to the *Sultana* job as a lad, had the *Cupid*. She was a diver too. Her skipper, John Fulliger, was a dab hand at going down in one of them great suits and helmets. So was Tom Rigden, that owned a schooner barge called the *Laura*. After the trade died out in Harwich there was a diver at

Faversham named Rigden done a lot of work with a boat called the *Invicta*, but whether that was the same chap I don't know. The *Albatross* was one Walter Watts bought a few years before he busted his father's business, and Lewis had her after that happened.

But the *Volunteer* was the favourite. Walter Watts's father, John Watts, once had a half share in her with Tom Adams, her skipper. She was fifty-four feet long and went twenty-six tons. She was bigger than the *Cupid* but no so big as the *Aurora's Increase*, which was a better seaboat, but I reckon the *Volunteer* was the fastest thing on salt water.

She was Brightlingsea-built like a lot of the smartest things in Harwich. They knew how to build racers there. In the summertime a lot of the Colne salvagers were skippers of the finest yachts in England and in the wintertime they brought them home to lay up. What with sailing of them in the summer, and looking at them all winter, they could get a good idea what shape a boat ought to be. Anyway that *Volunteer* would go. They got Aldous to build the cod smack *Olive* after her model, and she was a goer too, though she couldn't touch the *Volunteer*.

John Vaux at our old Navy Yard built a bit heavy, I reckon, though some of our chaps thought they built a bit light on Colne. One old cod-man done most of his life in one of them Brightlingsea smacks and when he'd retired he took a look at her being broken up. 'Good God,' he say, 'if I'd a-known she was only inch-and-a-quarter I'd never have set foot in her.'

That *Volunteer*, she was for everlasting racing with the Revenue cutter *Scout*. Those two couldn't see each other without having a go, only of course they didn't have to pay for their own gear with the *Scout*, same as Lewis did with the *Volunteer*.

One day Lewis see his *Volunteer* cracking along like it was regatta day, and he say, 'We shall have to clip her wings.' So next time she was up for a re-fit he cut a few feet off her boom and stuck a little dandy's mizzen on her stern.

At the end she went back to Brightlingsea where she come from. John Cross bought her to replace the *Conquest* that was lost in the skilling fishery.[1] He bought her big old cutter's sail as well, and she used that when she went down Channel dredging for scallops, but when she was a-stow-boating she was a dandy. When Cross come to buy her he was shaking his head and pleading poverty to get the price down. But when they done

---

1. The deep-sea oyster fishery off Terschelling, one of the most punishing parts of the North Sea. The *Recruit*, *Conquest*, *Pride* and *Mascotte* were lost, in each case with a crew of six, in 1883 – the worst of many disasters in this trade. See also Chapter 20.

the deal he smiled and say, 'The name alone is worth the money, Mr Lewis.'

Besides Glover and the Lewises, Forster the sailmaker, that owned the ketch barges *Gem of the Ocean* and *Emma*, had another old square-stern cutter called the *Reindeer* that got wrecked later on the Gunfleet.

Then there was John Carrington that first had a little thing called the *Argo*, that did more scropering than fishing, and afterwards a big old box called the *Agenoria*. She was square-sterned, too, and a real old-timer.[1] Before Carrington's time, Hezekiah Baker had her, and after him Pinner took her to a Whitby brig called the *Julia* that got on the Longsand. The skipper had his wife and a four-year-old child with him, and the mate, that was part-owner, he'd got his wife and a child in arms, same as they used to take them on a voyage summertime.

First they knew of the Longsand was when they saw a schooner strike. They hauled up as smart as they could, but that was no go and they're on too. They had two boats but smashed them both trying to get them away. Then the *Agenoria* sees them and has three tries to get to them, but she can't manage and has to give up. In the morning she goes to her again and finds her all broken up. All she can save is two out of the crew of seven on a raft made of wreckage. They reckoned the schooner must have gone too with all her crew.

As I've told you, that was generally a matter of pride not to leave a wreck, but I daresay Pinner couldn't do nothing else. Anyway, the Institution sent him £12 to show they thought there was nothing to be ashamed of.

I used to hear my father speak of the *Aurora's Increase* and the *Agenoria*, and as he rolled them great names off his tongue I used to think they must have been huge craft. They were a bit bigger than the later smacks I knew, but the chief difference is they were heavier and deeper. The later ones Aldous built at Brightlingsea were more like yachts, with long counter sterns. They'd go to windward like greyhounds after a hare even though that made them a bit wet. But you can't have all the advantages, not in any sort of craft.

---

1. Built Ipswich, 1840, 56.3 × 14.1 × 6.4, 27 tons.

CHAPTER SEVEN

The Suffolk Shore

On either side of us the salvaging was by longshore boats. That was different work to what our chaps and the Colne men did, cruising in their smacks.

The Suffolk and Norfolk men used clinker-built open yawls off the beach all the way from Woodbridge Haven right down to Haisborough. (Folk ashore say 'up to Haisboro', but that's only because they're used to looking at maps and don't understand the tide ebbs down to the nor'ard and floods up to the south'ard.)

There was everlasting of ships off that Suffolk coast when I was a boy – a regular procession. In the springtime the ice melted in the Baltic and out came all the Finns and Norwegians and Russians – Scowegians we called them. Some was emigrant ships bound for America or the Colonies, or coming to London to unload human cargoes into steamers for Canada. Some was ice barques bringing lumps of ice for the London cold stores before they learned how to make their own with electricity.

A lot more were timber ships, and half of them as leaky as sieves. Timber ain't like grain, you see. You've got to have a tight ship for grain or the cargo will spoil, but wood don't mind getting wet, and in fact it will keep a ship afloat. I recall a Norwegian timber ship laid for weeks in Harwich. She looked quite smart, only just a bit low in the water, and it weren't till you got aboard you could see she'd had most of her bottom knocked out of her. They used to have windmill pumps on deck. You could hear them pumps grunting and groaning half a mile away. We called them ships 'onkers' from the noise the pumps made.

Now you'll understand nothing couldn't move in the Baltic when that was all solid ice. Some ships would be held up there weeks, so they hadn't got no grub left by the time they got to sea. Craft would go out to meet them with sides of beef in the rigging to sell to them. When a man's down and out and hasn't got two ha'pennies to rub together you'll still hear people say, 'Poor fellow seem straight off the ice.'

When the ice cleared in the spring there was hundreds of these ships. There used to be sixty pilots stationed at Aldeburgh, Southwold, Lowestoft and Yarmouth, cruising in twelve cutters, with four or five pilots aboard each. Some years these pilots didn't wait for them to come. During the winter, while they were a bit hungry for work, they'd have a meeting and decide whether to humbug off to Holland and pick up a bit of duty-free stuff or whether to go off to the Baltic. In that case they'd make for Elsinore and find something to do till the fleet could sail. They bought themselves Elsinore hats, made of dogs' skin with flaps to keep your face warm.

So one way and another most of these foreigners had got pilots by the time the Suffolk beach companies picked them up, but sometimes there was still a job going. When the lookout saw a ship showing a colour his company would launch a sailing yawl or a rowing gig and off they'd go. If they'd showed a colour they had to take a pilot. If they refused you when you got off you could take them to court.

Pilotage wasn't compulsory on our coast, not till just before the war, but there was a rule that an unlicensed pilot mustn't take a ship if a Trinity pilot was available. The unlicensed men were called brummagen pilots. That means Birmingham where they made cheap imitations. Of course the brums tried to get round it. Sometimes they would make out they were doing salvage, but the Trinity had them up in court. Our smacksmen would take a brum job when they could but we was too much under the nose of the Trinity. They always had cutters cruising around the Sunk.

Bad weather them Suffolk beach-men were looking for trouble, same as our scropers, but they didn't usually have so far to go after it. Once you get below Harwich the coast changes altogether and you can sail away all down round Orford Ness in deep water so close to the beach you can toss a biscuit ashore. Of course they worked the Shipwash, that was the chief knocking ground for their yawls same as the Gunfleet and the Burying Grounds was to us, and the Whiting and the Cutler which are no distance to get to, not so far as the Gunfleet was for us. But apart from them a lot of the Suffolk jobs was right up on their own beaches.

And my word, they had some craft piled up there! I've told you there might be 300 craft sheltering in Harwich harbour in a gale. Well, at the same time there might be 3,000 making the best of it in Yarmouth and Lowestoft Roads. That was nothing to have a dozen vessels all ashore together between them two places. I dare say trying to tell you the things that went on around our sandbanks I'm only remembering the half of it, but I couldn't have made a start on it down there, and no more couldn't no man. No, there was too much for remembering. That's no wonder there was thousands of men in them beach companies and scores of yawls always ready on the beaches.

Them yawls was proper salvagers. The *Pride of the Deben*, that belonged to Ablet Passiful, had got a five-hundredweight anchor aboard when she went off to a Newcastle brig called the *Ismyr* on the Cutler. She used it to cant the brig's head round to get her off. The skipper offered £5 and then £10 but Passiful wouldn't make no agreement. He took it to court and got £50.

They needed anything up to a dozen hands to sail them, them big yawls did, and they didn't have no trouble manning them, seeing they belonged to Beach Companies with hundreds of members. There was a Maldon brig called the *Victoria* parted from her anchor off Harwich and went driving down that coast. Off Aldeburgh she lets go another anchor and parts from that one too. She gets foul of a schooner and that's enough for the crew. They scramble ashore in the boat and leave the old skipper aboard on his own. He burns his tar barrel and the next thing is he's got twenty-three beach-men aboard. They soon hustled him into Lowestoft. I reckon that was alright till it came to the share-out. Fifty quid wouldn't go far, not with that lot wanting a bit each.

There was a smack or two as well in them Suffolk rivers, same as the *Wonder* and the *Violet* at Bawdsey and Sam Whyard's *Jemima* at Orford. She made a name for herself when another of them Norwegian barques, called the *Hunter*, went on the Shipwash one January night. The *Jemima* was dodging under the lee of the sand and she spotted the barque at day-break. She tried to get near but she couldn't so she runs into Harwich where they'd got a tug called the *Liverpool*.

Having raised the tug, the *Jemima* beat back to the Shipwash, and all that day the chaps aboard the *Hunter* could see her still a-dodging. When they looked out the next morning she was still there and then just as the barque was breaking up along comes the *Liverpool* and four of her men succeed in putting off with a boat and getting the nine men out of the Norwegian. The Institution sent £10 to Sam Whyard and his crew of six. John Carrington, master of the *Liverpool*, got a silver medal and £5. The four men who took the boat off got £9 and the other ten men aboard the tug got £10. With fourteen men aboard I reckon Carrington had shipped a scroper's crew, which was often done.

You may be wondering why that tug left it a day before she mustered. Well, she didn't. She'd been out the day before but couldn't find the wreck. On the way home she fell in with a French schooner half sunk, and put four hands aboard of her, losing her own boat in doing it. Carrington towed the Frenchman into Harwich, got another boat, came straight out again and saw the *Hunter*, but as it was coming on dark he couldn't do nothing till morning.

My father used to meet the yawl men on the Shipwash, but our smacks didn't go down below that a great deal and they didn't come a lot on our patch. Once we got the steam tugs that was all different. My father never got used to the tugs, and was always swearing about them, but I never remember the place without them. They worked all down to Aldeburgh, seeing as the next place with tugs was Lowestoft.

After the *Liverpool* we had the *Harwich* and the *Robert Owen*. They got a steamer called the *Bedder* off the Shipwash with the help of two yawls, the *Jane* of Orford Haven and the *Deben* of Woodbridge Haven. The court gave £900 to the tugs and £1,000 to the yawls.

A month or two later there was another steamer on the same place, a three-masted screw ship called *Enrique de Calvet*. The *Wentworth* yawl from Aldeburgh, Langmaid's yawl from Orford and Percival's yawl from Woodbridge were on her and the *Harwich* turned out as well. There was an agreement over that one for one-third of the value. She was supposed to have been insured for £12,000 so somebody must have bought his wife a new bonnet out of those two jobs, I reckon.

But I'll tell you some more about them tugs when we get back in home waters.

CHAPTER EIGHT

The Essex Boatmen

The other side of Harwich, to the south'ard, there was longshore boats at Walton and Clacton, and then again when you get to Southend and Leigh.

I don't count them in the same class as the Norfolk and Suffolk men. They were really holiday visitors' tripper boats. A few of them had the gear and knowledge to do a bit of salvaging, and in the nature of things they must have saved a good few crews that were wrecked nice and handy. But they were mostly pillagers. They'd wait till our smacks had done a rescue and then when the breeze eased down a bit they'd be off to strip everything they could lay hands on.

The Southenders and the Leighmen had all the Maplins down to the Blacktail and Foulness, but most of their pickings were off the Nore, right opposite their front door, though they had to share that with the Kentish men. The Leigh chaps used to go off in their boats and hang on behind the Nore lightships, waiting for ships that wanted a river pilot. There was any amount of craft at that time of day driving up on the tide, turning to wind'ard or filling and backing, which is how the collier brigs did it when they couldn't come about, and banging into each other so much that the Trinity tried to bring in a rule that inward-bounders should keep to wind'ard of the Swin Middle light vessel and outward-bounders to lee-ward.

There was some smacks, or bawleys rather, up at Southend and Leigh. One of them, the *Lydia*, she put four hands aboard a schooner called *Brisk* that was flagging for help off the Maplins. They tried to get her ashore but she sinks on them with all hands including the Leighmen.

But mostly that was boat work there.

In my father's young days there wasn't no regulations about carrying passengers. That came in just before Clacton and Walton had urban councils. At first the old boys didn't take no notice, but one or two got had up and fined and they could see they couldn't carry on like that. So one day the Clacton chaps all left their boats alone and they put up big chalk notices along the beach at different places saying, 'No boatmen will leave the pier or beach today. All gone to the Union.' That meant the Tendring Union, or workhouse, and the visitors was thinking, 'Oh dear! Poor old fellows!'

What they done was they marched up to the meeting of the Board of Guardians that were responsible for such things before they had the councils. They asked for certificates and the Guardians hadn't no idea what to do, as they were all farmers and didn't know stem from stern in a boat. But their engineer, Mr Saas, had a bit of sense and he went out to the boatmen and told them the Guardians were in as big a funk as they were. Nobody knew what to do next till Mr Saas suggested asking Jefferies, the Lloyd's agent at Brightlingsea, to take it on, and they shouted out that was the right idea. So he came over and examined the men and he looked at the boats and he gave the number of passengers each might carry and that had to be painted on her.

Then he done the same thing at Walton. He was getting on alright there, putting about a score of them through their examination till one he'd already passed started piping up. Jefferies was examining another chap when this first one makes a remark that surely he'll never pass him. So Jefferies says to the first chap, 'I think I could have made a mistake over you.' Then he asks him a few more questions about the mariner's compass and how he'd steer in case of thick fog coming down when he was off in the Wallet, and this chap couldn't answer, so he never got no certificate and Jefferies never had no more trouble.

The beach boats got plenty of jobs from the shore. A yawl called the *Queen of the Ocean* took off an anchor for a Maldon ketch called the *Sylphide*, when she drove ashore at Holland Low, just by Frinton Cliffs. Her owner, Henry Britton, and his crew of six said they had an agreement for £60 but when that came to court it was reduced to £30.

But their best chances were on the Gunfleet, right opposite their beaches. That sand lies between the Wallet, the inshore channel, and the Swin, which was still the great gateway to London that time of day. There's nothing much but coasters up and down Swin nowadays, but in those days it was packed with craft, some of them just colliers and such, but lots of them foreign-going craft. Most of the London traffic used the Swin and had to get past that Gunfleet, inward-bound with the flood tide setting right on to the sand, and outward-bound with the ebb setting off it.

Well, this same Jefferies got a wire one morning that there was a steamer ashore on the Gunfleet and the master and crew were being landed, so he jumps into a trap and gets himself down to Clacton, having told a couple of Brightlingsea smacks to meet him there. When he gets there he finds the captain making his deposition to the coastguard, and his two smacks already laying off the pier. The ship was the *Kronprincess Louise*, a mail boat belonging to Wigram and Co. That was a fine August day with a fresh westerly wind. The crew of twenty-three was also ashore by then.

Jefferies tells the captain and chief officer they ought to be aboard, and after some reluctance they agree. When they get there they find all the boat-men in Clacton helping themselves to anything they can, without any thought for getting the ship off. They were taking the bearings from the engine, using the ship's spanners to do it, and smashing the cabin doors to get the brasses. They'd taken the compasses and put them in their boats alongside.

Jefferies puts one of his smack skippers at each gangway and he reads them the riot act. He says this is plunder, not salvaging, and they'd have to answer for this disorderly wrecking, worse than being on the coast of Barbary in the olden days. That's the words he used, though I don't know what was made of them.

After a bit they leave off and go to the gangways, but there they get stopped by these old Brightlingsea skippers. Jefferies says to take the names of all the boats, so they unload what they'd taken and off they go.

That afternoon John Glover comes along in the *Increase* and another of our scropers with him, and Jefferies and the captain put the salvage in his hands. Then Jefferies goes off to get in touch with Lloyds and the owners. When he comes back next day Glover has rigged his patent pump and is using the crews of some of the other smacks he's engaged to get rid of coal to lighten her. She had about 120 tons, mostly on deck, and Jefferies tells the smacksmen to take as much as they can for £1. That seemed more sense than chucking it all overboard.

While they were working on the *Kronprincess Louise* they had one bad southerly blow. That came up in the afternoon. Some of the men got to their smacks in the Swin but others couldn't, and stayed aboard the wreck all night with Jefferies and the captain. Jefferies said they thought she was going to break up, she bumped so terrible all the high water. The mast was all tilted aft, with the stays and shrouds carried away by the straining. They were all in the deckhouse and Jefferies learned something about human nature that night. Some was praying and some wasn't, not by no means. Some was smoking and one old skipper found himself a bunk and slept through it all.

All the smacks had run for Colne or Harwich except Glover. He kept riding there all night. One old Rowhedger said, 'If we last the night Glover will be after us in the morning.' Next day that came a bit finer and at the low water Glover took them all off and landed them on Clacton pier. The people at the Royal Hotel knew what was up and had a good breakfast ready for them. All the boats that didn't get away were sunk astern of the wreck and there they stayed till the smacks came back for them.

By the time the tides began to make they'd got her lightened, so Jefferies went ashore and sent a wire for the tug *Harwich*. He wanted to let Glover know, but couldn't get back aboard as that was a flat calm and only sailing boats available, so he got the coastguards to row him off in their four-oar galley. The *Harwich* came along soon after and on the next high water she shifted the wreck out of the bed she'd made. But they decided to leave her on the sand and look at her on the low water, when they found a lot of her bottom busted in. They patched that up and stopped the leaks with some of the tricks them old salvagers knew, and then they towed her to the Colne and put her on the mud above Brightlingsea creek.

Later she was put ashore just below Brightlingsea Hard and lay there a long time while the salvage was settled. In the end she was sold by auction at Brightlingsea and bought by some people who speculated in derelicts. They took out her engines, using dynamite charges, and paid a tug £75 to tow her to the Tyne where she was made into a three-masted schooner.

Jefferies had to give evidence at the Board of Trade inquiry at Greenwich. It lasted a week. There were five QCs representing the different interests and one of them said to Jefferies, 'You said in the fore part of your evidence that the compasses had been taken out of the steamer and placed in the boats alongside for removal. Now if that was so, how was it you could give the position as about two miles from the west buoy of the gunfleet, bearing WSW?' 'From knowledge and experience, being accustomed to cruising about those parts the best part of my life,' said Jefferies, and the old judge nodded. The QC left off and afterwards he sees Jefferies and says, 'You had me that time, old fellow.'

On the way home he gets in a railway carriage at Liverpool Street and finds the two men who'd bought the wreck. He's just lighting his pipe when one of them says, 'Please don't smoke as we have about twenty-five pounds of dynamite in that bag under your seat. I don't think anything will happen but we don't want to take no risks.' These Johnnies had been all the way to Newcastle to get this dynamite and bring it back as personal baggage.

Next thing Jefferies has to settle with the Clacton boatmen. He wired to their leader to meet him in the Royal Hotel. When he got there he found the big taproom at the back full of boatmen. Jefferies inquires what they're asking to settle their claim, if they have one, and they say £200. With that he leaves them, telling them to think up something more sensible, or they could fight it out in the law courts. After half an hour they send for him and offer to settle for £100. Jefferies reminds them they'd done wrong in persuading the captain and crew to leave the vessel in such fine summer weather and then setting about breaking her up. After another half hour he went back and said 'Look, I am tired of this, I will make you an offer of £20.' They tried for £50 but in the end with a lot of grumbling they had to settle for £25.

One of the softest jobs them Clacton chaps had was when a great old steamship got up on much the same part of the Gunfleet. She was the *Crystal*[1] of Newcastle. She was outward-bound from London with a pilot on board when somehow she got on the Gunfleet one Thursday about midnight. They never got her off till the Sunday, and for three days them Clacton boats was around her, some of them trying to lighten her and some of them just sightseeing.

There was tons and tons of good tobacco thrown in the sea, and the people taking no more notice of it than if it was cheese. Some boats full of excursion folks loaded themselves so much the old boatmen made them throw everything overboard for fear of sinking. It was reckoned that boats of all kinds fetched ashore 300 hundredweight sacks of American Heather Bloom flour, and they sold twelve tons of Old Virginia tobacco in Brightlingsea, only them as bought it found they had to pay 3s 6d a pound duty on it.

---

1. A 2,000-tonner, bound from New York to Leith with a call at Deptford.

CHAPTER NINE

The Wreck of the Deutschland

All the time I was at school, it made me proud to be a scroper's son. We used to argue and scrap between ourselves all according to which type of craft our fathers shipped in.

When the codmen came home from Iceland in the autumn there would be boys full of tales of icebergs and grampuses and how the sun never set all night, but just gets down to about three feet off the water and then begins to rise again. That was the time the ketch barges were being built, and a launch was a big day. All us boys would play truant from school to see one go down the ways and the skipper would let his son stand on deck and be launched with her. Then he was cock of the classroom for a week, I can tell you. But when my dad had been out to a wreck and brought a

Wreck of the Deutschland, *1875, showing on right the tug* Liverpool *which saved 155. More than 60 lives were lost.*

crew ashore and then maybe gone out again next day and brought the vessel in, or got a load of salvage off her, I was like a dog with two tails. The scropers were the real heroes of Harwich, and I made the most of it.

Then, when I was coming up towards leaving school, things began to go sour. That started when a German steamship called the *Deutschland* got herself on the Kentish Knock. She was a 3,000-ton North German Lloyd liner, and she sailed from Bremen on a Saturday night with 123 passengers, mostly emigrants for New York, travelling steerage. As I've told you, them German emigrant ships had a horrible reputation, but the North German Lloyd always claimed they'd never lost one passenger since they started.[1]

But that seem a funny thing, she hadn't got a patent log aboard to tell the distance run. And though she carried two pilots, both were passengers in the North Sea, for one had finished his job when she cleared the Bremen River and the other wasn't to take over till she reached Southampton, her first port of call. And her boat davits weren't much good, but that was pretty common then.

Well, the *Deutschland* anchored in fog outside the Weser lightship for the Saturday night and got under way again on the Sunday morning with a blinding easterly gale with snow. The time was just before Christmas and the year was 1875 'cos it was my last year at school.

On the Sunday evening she was sounding with the lead every half hour. She got twenty-four fathoms and then next cast seventeen fathoms. The captain didn't fancy that, so he put her engines astern. The propellor broke off and before long she was ashore. Whether she got ashore first and sheared her shaft trying to get off, or whether the screw came adrift first they never knew.

They didn't think that night they was done for, and next day they had all the men passengers working the pumps and helping to throw cargo out of the forehold so she shouldn't slew round broadside to the seas. The Knock lightship had a flag in her rigging, and at least one steamship and one sailing vessel passed pretty close, so they reckoned at first they'd soon be reported and picked up.

But when no one came, they tried the boats. They only got two in the water and the rest were smashed up. One boat capsized and drowned nine people. The quartermaster and two passengers were in the other when she parted her painter. The quartermaster got a bit of sail on her, and she blew away before the gale till during the night he saw a light

---

1. The North German Lloyd was founded in 1856, had carried 540,000 emigrants to New York without loss.

which was on Sheerness. He runned her ashore there, more dead than alive, with the two passengers dead and blackened with cold. One of them only had a jacket and trousers.

They could see by now aboard the *Deutschland* that she was a goner, and they stopped lightening her and let go the anchor to stop her coming off into deep water and going down like a stone. When the next tide came she didn't lift. The seas broke all over her, carrying away the bulwarks, and all hands that could got up in the rigging. There must have been scores of them clinging on there all that Monday night. A lot of the women were down in the cabin and they found nineteen bodies there next day. There was several nuns among them. That weren't a very nice place for people like that to fetch up.

All day long the Knock lightship had been firing with her gun, but it's doubtful if she could be heard by the Sunk to windward. The *Deutschland* had a signalling gun as well, but the powder was wet and they couldn't fire it, and it don't seem likely anyone would have heard if it they had. When that was dark the lightship set about firing rockets, and in the end one was seen at Harwich. But all they done ashore was fire a rocket in reply, and if anyone of them poor devils aboard the *Deutschland* saw it and thought it meant anything that was the cruellest mistake of their lives.

Walter Watts, the owner of the tug *Liverpool*, and John Carrington, the skipper, they went round to the coastguards, but they reckoned they hadn't a hope in hell going to sea on a night like that. That did blow! When they had the inquest later they got the captain of the railway boat that crossed from Holland that night to give evidence, and he said he wouldn't have put to sea if he didn't have to, and though he heard a report of a ship in distress he wouldn't have risked his ship among the sandbanks, though he did also say that if he'd known what was up he might have cruised about till daylight to see what he could do.

So you couldn't expect the scropers to have a go under sail. Anyway they didn't muster. During the night Carrington discussed it with some of the bravest men in Harwich aboard the *Liverpool* and they all agreed they must wait till daylight. He got steam up and was away about five o'clock Tuesday morning. The mate of the *Liverpool* said later that if they had had a lifeboat to tow they would have started hours earlier, but Carrington stuck to his view that would have been useless, lifeboat or no lifeboat. That's true Carrington was nearer seventy than sixty at the time and maybe a younger man would have acted more foolhardy. But the real point is they didn't know there was hundreds of lives at stake. All they knew was someone was firing rockets.

Anyway, the *Liverpool* went and spoke the Cork lightship and they didn't know nothing, so she went on to ask the Sunk which sent her to the Longsand about five miles to the south-east, and still they couldn't find nothing, till they saw the Kentish Knock flying her signal, and that led them to the *Deutschland*. They anchored near the wreck in three fathoms and the mate and engineer made three trips in the boat, bringing off nine women and children each time. Then they begin to realise how many were there and Carrington takes her in right alongside, which wasn't a nice job with the steamer's bulwarks broken down and all jagged, even though the sea was easing. Before long there was upwards of 150 people crowding aboard that little tug. She must have looked more like an excursion tripper boat than anything else coming ashore.

Then all hell broke loose. There was a chap on the *Times* newspaper that knew just enough to be a bloody nuisance and not enough to be any proper help. What he wrote in that paper wasn't fit to put in a sandwich. Nothing he could think of to say about Harwich was too bad on account of its not having no lifeboat.

It was 'gross neglect on the part of an English seaport', it was 'cruel and criminal negligence and a disgrace upon the English name'. According to his ideas 'to provide a lifeboat is the obvious duty of any municipality which is in the least responsible for the safety of ships off the coast'.

What he didn't say is what he'd have done with his lifeboat that night and what he didn't seem to know was that anyway lifeboats aren't things town councils provide.

The Mayor wrote off to set things to rights, but that was no go; the old *Times* wouldn't let him get a word in edgeways. He said he read their criticisms with 'painful surprise' and the *Times* said that was nothing to the painful surprise of the nation that a wreck should be stranded off the English coast for thirty hours without aid. Then the Mayor pointed out that 'some years ago a lifeboat absolutely rotted to pieces without once being used, not because the seamen of Harwich were neglectful of their duty but simply from the fact she could not be got to sea in time to be of any use.' The *Times* come back, 'It seems there was a lifeboat and no tug; now there is a tug and no lifeboat.' Of course, they agreed, all sarcastic, that a lifeboat is no good unless you have both courage and common-sense, and they reckoned Harwich didn't have neither.

To make matters worse, by Wednesday, when the gale had blown itself out, there were twenty smacks and luggers all round the wreck and fifty or sixty men at work on deck or in the cabins. They were fishing up cargo, stripping the saloons and the cabins and, according to the newspapers, breaking open passengers' luggage. There were the *Cupid*, *Emperor* and *Increase* from Harwich, the *Qui Vive*, *Aquiline*, *Thomas and Mary*, *Prince of Orange*, *Faith*, *New Unity*, *Concord* and *New Blossom* from Rowhedge, the *Star* from Whitstable, and the *Violet* and *Wonder* from Woodbridge. They were all smacks, and besides them there was six luggers from Kent; the *Secret* and *Favourite* from Margate, and the *Eclipse*, RR223 and RR224 from Ramsgate.

When the Marine Salvage Association agent got there on the Thursday he found her stripped of all her running gear and he said there was hardly a rope yarn left. The *Times* chap he gave a pretty fair picture of the scropers' job, which is all they were doing, but he still had to say 'nothing can excuse their conduct in the case of the *Deutschland*'.

Before long there was tales of corpses being robbed and fingers cut off and bitten off to get gold rings. All the papers had taken it up, including the German ones, and they was soon asking questions in the German Parliament as well as ours.

When that came to the inquest at Harwich a juryman jumped up and said, 'Members of the German Parliament have talked about the Kentish Knock being three or four miles from Harwich. They and the newspapers do not seem to know as much about the facts as a monkey knows about a piano.' The coroner said that's nothing to do with us, but he had to let them have their say, they was so angry in Harwich. They brought in a verdict saying Carrington and his *Liverpool* was to be praised and not blamed at all.

Then the row seemed to die down like the gale had. After Christmas *The Times* was saying Harwich men had not been so black as they had been painted. The managing director of the North German Lloyd, he said he could see now there was nothing no one could have done any sooner. The Board of Trade inquiry was a proper whitewash. The lightships were absolved from any blame; any attempt at rescue on the Monday night would have resulted in failure; the smacksmen had done their duty well; no cases of robbing or mutilation had been proved.

As for the steamer that passed by in broad daylight on the Monday, they never even traced who she was. But the captain of the sailing vessel came forward like a man. Yes, he said, he could see the *Deutschland* was in distress, but he had his hands full to manage his own vessel and if he'd tried to go to her, he'd soon have been in trouble himself.

You'd think they could have seen the real point was nobody couldn't talk to nobody else, so nobody took no decisions. *The Times* had pointed out that 'If anyone had telegraphed Broadstairs where a lifeboat was ready for service, an attempt at least might have been made.' They weren't far out there, and they hit the nail on the head with another comment what it would have been better if they'd hammered home instead of trying to find fault with everyone they could think of. They said there ought to be a telegraph cable to the lightship, but the best the Board of Trade fellows could do in answer to that was, 'We doubt not that the Elder Brethren of Trinity, with that enlightened zeal which they have always evinced, will cheerfully adopt any suggestions you may be pleased to offer.'

CHAPTER TEN

The First Lifeboats

I don't know if you'd call it evincing enlightened zeal, but what the Trinity come up with was carrier pigeons.

So far they'd just given the lightship chaps guns and rockets, and all they could do was bang away day time and flare away night time. That didn't matter so much when the scropers and the Colne salvagers was cruising everywhere with eyes as sharp as hawks, for ten to one they'd see what was up before the lightships did and they didn't want no warning. But now we're getting to the time of steam tugs and lifeboats, and someone had to call them out.

So what happens? Why, there's a banging heard or a rocket seen and off they go. The Sunk will say the Knock was firing and by the time you get to the Knock he'll say that was just to warn a ship she was getting too near the sand, but he hauled her up and went clear. Or maybe, 'That was a little yacht standing into trouble, but he went right over the top of the sand.' Or the Sunk might say, 'No that weren't us. That was a steamer burning blue lights to say he wanted a pilot.' One time the Volunteers were practising firing guns at Landguard Fort, and the Cork hears them and thinks he'll join in, so they mustered the lifeboat for that. There weren't no system. Nothing meant anything in particular. You could be out twenty hours in bitter freezing weather hunting about for something that wasn't there in the first place.

As well as having to turn out for nothing, sometimes the lifeboat wouldn't come when it was needed. One of the Brightlingsea skilling smacks, the *Ostrea*[1] was bound home. She'd been a fortnight on the passage, and then she gets on the Gunfleet with 32,000 deep-sea oysters in her. With that load they thought she wasn't going to come off so they burned flares.

The Clacton lifeboat had seen enough of flares and would only answer

---

1. An Emsworth-owned ketch smack, registered at Portsmouth, but at this time Brightlingsea-crewed. Built at Emsworth 1890, 35 tons.

rockets, which they didn't have. So she didn't take no notice and they got in the boat and tried to row ashore. Presently in the blackness they make out the shape of a craft, which at first they take for a barge, but it don't give no answer to their hail. When they get near they find it's the old *Ostrea* come off on her own and jogging along on a course to go ashore again at Holland Low. So they scramble aboard and off into Colne they go. Some stowboaters see the flares and get their gear on deck but by the time they arrive of course there's nothing there. Nobody got hurt that time, but that wasn't often like that.

Well, the Trinity thought if they could train these pigeons to carry messages that might make a bit of sense. Eight years they messed about with that notion. They took the upper storey of the old high lighthouse, that wasn't used any more because the channel had altered and the old leading lights in line had come to be called the misleading lights and then given up. They turned it into a pigeon loft.

The first year they spent breeding young birds and teaching them to fly across the sea. The next summer they put some aboard the Cork lightship and some aboard the Sunk. Every time the sailing tender went off she took a basket, and they released one or two daily, weather permitting. They hadn't got the idea of fixing messages on their legs same as they do now; they just wrote the flag hoist code on their tail feathers with ink. But them birds only come home in fine weather. In gales or snow they got lost or just refused to leave the lightship. In the end they had to admit that they were useless, and they had an auction sale of 100 pigeons. But that took them eight years to find out and I don't know how many ships were lost in that time.

But I'm getting ahead of myself. If we are a-going to keep this yarn in order we'd best get back to Harwich at the time all hell was loose, after the *Deutschland* business.

While that row was still at its height, only a few days after the disaster, they had a meeting called by the mayor about a lifeboat. Captain Ward came down from the Institution, and he said we had such a splendid set of hobbling smacks always cruising about that when the Institution had asked whether a lifeboat was necessary the answer had always been in the negative. Moreover, the Kentish Knock was beyond the range of lifeboats, which were not usually employed more than five or six miles from the coast.

Oliver Williams, who besides being Lloyd's agent at Harwich was also

Vice-Consul for Germany, said, 'Nineteen years ago I gave my opinion against a lifeboat, since which time I have no recollection of a single instance where a lifeboat could have been made available in cases of ship-wreck off this port.'

That didn't seem possible at that time of day to have an open boat that would live in seas that was as much as the Revenue cutters and our big decked scroper smacks put up with.

Mind you, that wasn't for want of trying. Several times there was sub-scriptions got up, generally by people that was shocked by some wreck, but the boats they spent their money on didn't answer. There was a little thing at Bawdsey and a bit of a whaleboat at Landguard and a proper lifeboat called the *Braybrooke* in our harbour. Apart from not having no tug to take her about she never had a proper boarding boat so the crew couldn't get to her in a gale and they had to keep her ashore in winter. The upshot of that was a brig got sunk on the West Rocks and the crew hung on to the wreck in their boat till they got tired of waiting. They cast off and got picked up by a ship to leeward, and when this *Braybrooke* did get there they was gone.

Then there was another brig on the Roughs and they never launched, nor yet the Landguard and Bawdsey boats didn't either, on account of the soldiers at Landguard couldn't see her, though a Bawdsey boatman went off and saved the captain, who was the only one left alive. That *Braybrooke* did get credit for helping one vessel off the West Rocks, but she turned out to be a pretty useless article. She weren't no Swin Ranger.

After that one they had another try, about thirty years before the *Deutschland*. That come after a schooner called the *Hero* got wrecked on the Andrews.

Saxby was lying under the lee of Landguard in a gale in the *Scout*. He and his crew went ashore and got as close as they could, burning blue lights to show the chaps where to come. The lights showed up a man and boy on the bowsprit shouting out for a lifeboat, but that they didn't have nor yet rockets nor Manby's mortars, though they had them most other places. Saxby tried to get a line to her with an ordinary common rocket, but in the end two of the *Scout*'s men got through the surf with a line. They pulled one man in with that but he was the only survivor. The boy couldn't hold on no longer and he dropped off. The captain had tried earlier to get ashore wearing a life preserver, but that didn't help him and he was lost.

Captain Washington stirred things with the Admiralty. He got rockets and a mortar and within a couple of weeks they promised a lifeboat. That was built at Rotherhithe and they had a meeting whether to put her at Landguard or at Harwich, but that's all I know about it.

So that's why nobody reckoned a lifeboat was any use at Harwich. But now we'd got this tug *Liverpool* things were different. Actually she wasn't the first steam tug we see. There were three others at Ipswich, but they might as well have been in China for what chance there was of using them, and there was another one lying in the harbour called the *Robert Owen*,[1] but at the time of the *Deutschland* she was under arrest and not fit for sea.

With a tug to take her about, a lifeboat made a bit of sense, as Oliver Williams agreed. All sorts of people were falling over themselves to offer money, and they decided to accept £200 from a Miss Burmester for a boat and carriage. She lived in London but her brother was a parson at Oakley and a beak and such.

Within a week or two the Institution produced a little thirty-five foot self-righting boat called the *Springwell*. They showed her off in Regent's Canal Dock. They tipped her over with a crane and she came right way up and cleared herself of water in just twenty-five seconds. That was very nice in calm water in a dock with nobody in her, but them self-righters weren't so pretty at sea. They'd bob up alright, but what about the crew? There was generally at least one missing after they was flung out.

The Norfolk and Suffolk men wouldn't have them, but insisted on their own ideas and to hell with self-righting. They tried to get the Southwold chaps to try one of their big self-righters, but old Sam May, the cox'n, said, 'If the Institution be a-going to send a self-righting boat here they can send some self-righting people to go in her 'cos we shan't.' Maybe we ought to have spoke up like he done.

What's more, that *Springwell* would only blow to leeward. Even our Institution committee secretary after he'd been out in her said she was like a bung on the water. You'd think that would be no trouble to sail her round from London to Harwich, but they didn't even try it. She was too wide to go on the railway so they begged a free tow from a collier. The first one that tried it ran into bad weather and had to turn back at the Nore. With only four men in her instead of her regular crew of thirteen the *Springwell* was in trouble on her first voyage, and that wasn't the end of it, as I'll be telling you. However, another collier towed her round in the end.

---

1. An eighty-foot clinker-built paddler, built at North Shields in 1848 and employed at Yarmouth.

Of course the trouble with all these little self-righters was they were really only surf boats. They could anchor and veer down on wrecks ashore better than the scropers could, but they couldn't get there. The Institution didn't expect them to go more than five or six miles but that wasn't no good for the Burying Grounds twenty-five miles away. Perhaps if the chaps that had to use them had had more say in their design that might have been different.

Anyway, at Aldeburgh, where they never had a tug, they soon schemed up boats which would get about under sail and look after themselves, and soon after the time we are speaking of the Institution put a centreboard boat at Clacton. She was the first one that would get to windward in the Wallet without having to wait for a fair tide, which might mean a delay of anything up to six hours.

While they were waiting for the *Springwell*, the *Liverpool* was making some nice pickings on her own. She sometimes took half a dozen hands out of Lewis's *Volunteer* when she went scropering, and they didn't do badly.

Within a couple of months of the *Deutschland* Watts, her owner, brought a case claiming £400 for that Norwegian barque, the *Hunter*, that I've told you about, and £2,500 for getting a Genoese ship called the *Orto* off the Pye. She was ashore right opposite the Cliff Hotel at Dovercourt and the scropers threw her wheat overboard. All that winter the black geese came and fed on it till they couldn't move and you could pick them out of the water with your hands.

I don't know what the award was for the *Hunter*, but Watts was awarded £1,046 over the *Orto*, and it was mentioned at the hearing that the owners of a German timber barquentine, the *Cleopatra*, had paid £375 after the *Liverpool* had found her derelict on the Kentish Knock, got her off and towed her in. Round about the same time she got £800 for towing a vessel called the *Atlantic* off the Kentish Knock and into Ramsgate. So, whatever he said at the time, I reckon that *Liverpool* didn't owe Watts nothing time he went bust and she dropped out of things.

After that Vaux launched a new tug of his own called the *Harwich*. She was a fine thing, but she was built so heavy she wouldn't steam better than ten knots. Vaux treated her as what we call a hospital job, which meant working on her between urgent jobs such as he used to get plenty of with ships being brought in leaky from getting ashore and having to be unloaded and put on his slip before they could sail again.

I used to go climbing all over her, the years she was a-building, when I was a lad. After Vaux died Si Keeble, that was her skipper from the time she was launched, took the *Harwich* to the Tyne. The people that bought her thought it was worth taking some timber out of her so she was not so heavy.

CHAPTER ELEVEN

The Indian Chief

We hadn't had the *Springwell* long when there come another wreck that started the bands playing again. Yes, we had a repeat performance of all that music we'd heard when the *Deutschland* was lost, only this time that was worse because the Kent men came out of it best. That's something we couldn't hardly bear to think of at the time, and indeed I don't fancy having to tell the tale even now. My father said to me once, 'Never give way to a Kentish man, boy.' We was standing right across a Whitstable yawl. He was on starboard tack, and he sung out at us. 'Why not, father?' I says. ''Cos he won't never give way to you,' says father, and he didn't deign to acknowledge them Whistable chaps.

This time it was a big sailing ship, the *Indian Chief*.[1] She sailed from Middlesborough for Yokohama with general cargo at the New Year of 1881, so that was five years after the *Deutschland*. When she was four days out she picked up the Knock light around half past two in the morning. That should have showed up on the starboard bow, but blessed if they didn't see it on the port bow. Nobody hadn't thought to take a cast of the lead, which of course they should have done, though that would only have told them what they could see with their eyes, that they were right inside that light. They put the blame for that on the pilot when it came to the inquiry. Then to make matters worse the wind veered into the east and brought a squall of rain. That put the Knock Sand right under their lee.

She was under all plain sail, with the royals furled and the mainsail hanging in the buntlines. They put the helm down to come about, but that's not to be wondered at if there was a bit of a frap, seeing how things was. Anyway, the main braces fouled and before they could be cleared she had missed stays and was in irons. So they set to work to wear her, but there was a bit of confusion, with the ship laying over and everyone knowing the sands was close aboard. She paid off, and then the spanker

1. 1,238 tons.

sheet fouled the wheel. They got her round, but by the time the braces were belayed on the starboard track she struck. They let go sheets and braces but dursn't go aloft to stow up, for what with the ship beating on the sands and the sails thundering on the spars the masts looked like coming out of her any moment.

They sent up rockets and kindled a red flare, and it cheered them up to see the Knock and the Sunk lightships answering with rockets that roared up in the clear cold easterly night, bursting into smoke and sparks against the stars over their heads. They all knew the *Indian Chief* was likely to leave her bones on the sand, but that seemed as good as a promise that help would soon be on the way.

Lewis's *Albatross*, that was cruising near the Longsand, saw blue lights and found they were being shown by a steamer on the Lower Knock off the Sunk. She could not get near her in that wind and sea, but at day-break she saw the *Indian Chief*, and so did the Rowhedge *Aquiline*. They agreed the *Aquiline* should take one of the crew of the *Albatross* and go to Harwich and rouse out the tug and lifeboat. Cracking on in that breeze she sprung her boom and had to run into Walton backwaters. Her skipper, Harry Cook, scrambled ashore there and walked into Harwich to give the alarm around eleven o'clock.

They soon had the *Springwell* in the water, but they had trouble finding a regular crew and had to take three volunteers. They got their baptism alright and no mistake. John Tye the cox'n was away at his sister's funeral, so Bill Britton, who took over from Tye some years later, was in charge. John Vaux was in charge of his *Harwich* and Harry Cook went with him to help them find the wreck.

That took them two hours to tow out to the Sunk, and there they found the steamer under water with only her funnel and masts showing. That turned out later she was called the *Nymphaea*, but her crew had had the luck to launch their own boat and reach a steamer laying at anchor which later landed them at Gravesend.

As there was nothing to be done for her they went on towards the *Indian Chief* which they could see. But when they were only a few miles from her, what with the sea being such they couldn't steam above half-speed and that was coming on dark, and them still on the wrong side of the sand, they decided there wasn't nothing to be done before next day-light and they turned back. The rights and wrongs of that we'll come to later, but that's what they done.

They got in about five o'clock in the afternoon, and before they was alongside the pier the Sunk was rocketing again and the coastguard ashore was answering her. They asked Vaux if he'd turn the tug round for another go, but that he wouldn't, so they tried Daniel Howard, the Marine Superintendent of the Great Eastern steamboats, and he said the *Pacific*[1] could tow the lifeboat out when she sailed for Antwerp about half past nine.

There was a crowd on the pier to give them a cheer as they went, but as soon as they got outside that was terrible. They had to drive that ship to keep control of her, and soon she wasn't pulling that *Springwell* over the water, she was pulling her through it. Everyone in her was half drowned, and then John Tye, who'd got back and taken charge, he got a spark or a bit of red-hot coal out of the steamer's funnel in his eye. He was three parts blinded. Next thing was the tow rope parted. They couldn't turn the *Pacific* round to pick the *Springwell* up, not in that wind and sea, so they have to scrap that lifeboat in again for the second time.

That brought the time to half an hour before midnight. Next morning that started again. A Spanish barquentine called the *Rosita* had got under way from the harbour, and she ran ashore on the Holidays just outside. The *Springwell* could get that far on her own, and she got seven seamen and the captain's wife ashore by midday. Then she had to go again to get the captain, the second mate and one man who had refused to leave her. They got the *Rosita* off later and she sank in Walton backwaters. The Harbour Board tried to make the Spanish consul pay for clearing away the wreck.

While the *Springwell* was attending to the Spaniard, some of these pigeons from the Sunk came flapping in. The first arrived about half past ten and another about one o'clock, both marked JFC, meaning Send Lifeboat. That is according to the man in charge of the birds. The lightship keepers said they marked the first pigeon BDG and later when they could see the *Nymphaea* they sent some marked DVKG, meaning Steamer Ashore.[2] So they sent a telegram to Aldeburgh, asking them to launch the *George Hounsfield*. She was a proper sea-going lifeboat with a crew of eighteen.

The *Springwell* crew were still game to go if they could get there. In the afternoon they tried Vaux again, but he still wasn't having any more, and then they went to Captain D'Arcy Irvine, who was in command of the *Penelope*, an old up-funnel-and-down-screw warship that lay in the harbour. They asked him for a steam pinnace, but the best he could offer

1. Paddle steamer, 235 ft long, acquired by GER 1872, only in service about five years.
2. The International Code signals JFC and BDG mean 'Send Lifeboat' and 'A Vessel Ashore' respectively. DVKG is probably a mis-reporting for DVKQ which means 'Steamboat is Aground'.

was to telegraph the Admiralty for authority. I'm glad to say all the Navy captains weren't like that, for some years later after the *Penelope* had been replaced by HMS *Mersey* her captain saw the Cork signalling and sent his steam pinnace in to pick up the *Springwell* without even being asked.

During the evening the *George Hounsfield* came in to say she'd been to the *Indian Chief* but couldn't find no life aboard. At that moment there's a telegram from Southend saying there's a barque on the Maplins but they couldn't get there as they'd no tug, so the *George Hounsfield* went out again after that one. They never found nothing and got back to Aldeburgh next day, so they had thirty hours out.

Next, there's a telegram from Clacton to say their lifeboat *Albert Edward* was back, though it didn't say where she'd been. But that turned out she'd gone off the night before and got to the Longsand under sail. She sighted the wreck but couldn't get no further, not to weather of the sand, yet she wasn't for turning back. She anchored there for the night, but at half past two in the morning they saw the *Indian Chief*'s mast go by the board with the crew clinging to it. The lights aboard went out and that looked like the end of it, so they up-anchor and get back to Clacton after twenty-four hours at sea.

'To the Rescue', from a painting by George Mears, dated 1860.

Models of the tugs Harwich and Robert Owen, now in the Redoubt Museum at Harwich. They were, perhaps, made in the shipyard as toys for the children of J H Vaux.

Busy times for the paddle tugs in friendly weather and in less comfortable conditions. Above, the Great Eastern Railway tug Imperial tows a brig out of Lowestoft. Below, the United Services (built 1871) tows the Danish brigantine Anna (built 1849) into Yarmouth.

he lifeboat choice. The first Springwell *at Harwich was a thirty-five foot self-righter similar to
e* Covent Garden *at St Ives.*

he non-self-righting Norfolk and Suffolk type, such as the John Burch *of Yarmouth, was
referred by many lifeboatmen for its better sailing and sea-going qualities, but was resisted by the
RNLI because of the heavy losses when a capsize occurred.*

The tug Merrimac, *owned by Pauls, the Ipswich merchants, was active in salvage work as well as in towage and summer pleasure trips.*

The Walton volunteer lifeboat True to the Core II, *built at Rowhedge on the lines of the Aldeburgh lifeboat,* George Hounsfield. *She was forty feet long, carvel built (unlike the Sailors' Friend II, clinker built by Cann) and cost £473.*

CHAPTER TWELVE

Rescue from Ramsgate

At the time of all these goings on, we didn't know what Ramsgate was up to. Well, we soon heard, and that made us feel sick I can tell you, though we were glad to hear some of them chaps was saved, even if it was by Kentish men.

Of course I never see none of what I'm going to tell you now, but that was writ up wonderful in the *Daily Telegraph*. I kept that paper, and I daresay I've read it a score of times, so I can set this down as clear as if I'd seen it with my own eyes. They don't have newspapers like that no more.

Ramsgate had got some of the same troubles as we had. The French trawlers used great lights round the Goodwins and they used to get called out to them. Once or twice the flash of Calais light was taken for a ship's distress signal.

But they had something we didn't have, a tug called the *Vulcan* which was paid for by the Board of Trade whenever she towed their lifeboat, a forty-two-footer called the *Bradford* on account of she was paid for with £600 all collected in an hour on the Bradford exchange. And there was someone to take decisions and give orders – Captain Braine, the harbour-master.

They got the word at Ramsgate about the time we did in Harwich, and away they go. That's a little further from Ramsgate to the Longsand than from our place, and that was dead to windward. As soon as she cleared the old pier heads that tug was thrown up like a ball; you could see the starboard paddle revolving in the air high enough for a coach to pass under, and when she struck the hollow she dished a sea over her bows that left only the stern of her showing. The *Bradford* was towing on sixty fathoms of five-inch manilla. Every man aboard of her was soaked to the skin by the time they had the Ramsgate Sands abeam, and they knew what was ahead of them. They tried to rig a bit of tarpaulin round the mast for a shelter, but the sea soon washed it aft in rags.

When they cleared the North Foreland it was worse still, and when the

Vulcan slowed down they thought she was giving up. But she held on. Somewhere abreast of the Elbow Buoy a smack sheered over to speak to them. 'Vessel on the Longsand,' the skipper sang out. Then they met a collier called the *Fanny* running with her fore-topgallant yard gone, and she gave the lifeboat a cheer.

Round half past four they picked up the revolving light of the Kentish Knock lightship, and soon after five they were close to her. The way she pitched up and went out of sight and then ran up on the black heights of water gave them a better notion of the fearfulness of the sea than they got from watching the tug or from their own dancing. The cox'n hailed her, 'Have you seen the ship?' 'Yes.' 'How does she bear?' 'Nor'west by

Wreck of the Indian Chief, *1881. The Ramsgate lifeboat approaching the wreck (above) and making her rescue of survivors from the foremast (below).*

north.' 'Have you seen anything go to her?' The answer he caught was 'A lifeboat,' though the others heard it as 'A boat.'

They towed ahead and then after ten minutes the lightship burned a red signal. They turned and as the seas came abeam the boat filled twice and every man marvelled that they were not rolled over. This time there were six or seven men leaning over the lightship's bulwark. 'Did you see the Sunk lightship's rocket?' they all bawled together. 'Yes. Did you say you saw a boat?' 'No,' they answered. So they must have been mistaken the first time.

'Pull us round the Longsand Head buoy,' the cox'n shouted to the tug, and again the long plug began with rockets going aloft every now and again from the Sunk. Aboard both the tug and the lifeboat they burned hand flares. You fit them into a wooden tube and give a sort of hammer a smart blow and the light rushes out. Theirs were green ones, and the cox'n said that was a queer sight to see them all as green as leaves with their cork jackets swelling their bodies so as they scarcely looked like human beings.

But there was no reply from the wreck, and no sign of her. 'Vulcan ahoy!' they bawled. The tug slacked back alongside. 'What do you want?' 'There's nothing to be seen of the vessel. We'd best lie to for the night.' 'Very good,' he says, just like that, and without another word she goes slow ahead, her paddles turning just fast enough to keep from dropping astern, and the water pouring over her bows like cliffs.

They didn't know where the wreck was, nor yet whether there was anyone left aboard alive. They didn't know the Springwell had got nigh as far a few hours before and given up. And they didn't know the Clacton boat was lying on the other side of the sand.

They didn't know none of that aboard the Indian Chief either. The newspaper said later they must have seen the Harwich lifeboat, but none of them ever said they did. They don't seem to have seen the Clacton boat either. They did say they saw a lifeboat sail, but that was more likely the Albatross, or it could have been John Glover's Increase, which got within three-quarters of a mile of the wreck about half-past-eight in the morning, but he couldn't see no signals nor yet get an answer to the signals he made, so he sheered off about four o'clock in the afternoon.

During the afternoon they had tried to launch three boats. The second of them with two men in her went adrift and was swamped in a minute. The chaps in her vanished like you might blow out a light. The other two boats filled as soon as they touched the water so they had to give up.

Just before five, when the lifeboat was making the Knock, a huge sea swept the deck and left little but the uprights of the deck houses standing. Some of the men made for the fore rigging but the captain shouted to all hands to take to the mizzen as that in his opinion was the strongest. Seventeen men got over the mizzen top and started hacking out bits of rigging with their knives to use as body lashings. No one touched the mainmast for the ship had broken her back and everyone knew that mast was doomed.

The mate was in the mizzen, and the captain, who was encouraging the men and helping them lash themselves in, gave him his watch and chain along with messages for home. Below them the decks were ripping up, and over their heads the noise of the streaming canvas was like thunder.

All of a sudden that came into the mate's head that the foremast was safer than the mizzen, and he must get there. There was no hope of going on the deck so he swung himself from the crosstrees out on the stay to the maintop and then again went hand over hand down the topmast stay into the foretop. God knows how he did that. If he'd thought he'd never have tried. He found five men in the foretop huddled together and lashed in.

About three in the morning the mainmast went. As it fell it bore down on the mizzen. There was a crash of splintering wood and some shrieks, and when the next sea cleared the after deck all they could see was the stumps of two masts, the mizzen slanting over the bulwarks into the water and the men lashed to it drowning. That come ashore on Clacton beach in the end, that mast did. They put it over a sawpit and used it for gate-posts for the railway station.

When dawn began to break the foremast still stood. Aboard the lifeboat the crew lay in a heap huddled for warmth. The cox'n had looked for a bit of Fry's chocolate he always took with him, but found the locker awash and the chocolate nothing but paste, with some biscuits turned to pulp. 'Well,' he said later, 'we hadn't come to enjoy ourselves, so nothing was said.'

In the first grey glint of day as they rose on a crest they saw her – a single mast sticking up out of the water three miles away to the westward. 'Let slip the tow-rope. Up foresail!' came the word, and dead before the wind they headed into the broken water. First they saw a length of canvas streaming from the top and then at last they saw the men. There seemed such a huddle of bodies they thought at first it was the whole ship's company, and hopes were high as they let go the anchor fifteen fathoms from the wreck and veered cable while the half-frozen men unlashed themselves and dropped one by one into the lee rigging.

The cox'n shouted to them to hitch a bit of wood on a line and throw it overboard for them to get hold of. With that they hauled up under the ship's quarter away from the worst tangle of broken gear. Then they saw the dead bodies among the spars with the captain still lashed to the head of the mizzen. His head was upright with his eyes turned to them, and the seas moved him so that he seemed to be struggling to reach the lifeboat. The cox'n cried out to hand him in, but they said he had been dead for four or five hours. 'I can't hardly get those fixed eyes out of my sight,' the cox'n recalled. 'I lie awake for hours at night and so does Tom Cooper and others of us, seeing those bodies torn by the spars and bleeding, floating in the water alongside that miserable ship.'

Twelve men were got into the lifeboat alive, but the second mate died within half-an-hour. Fifteen had perished in the mizzen.

CHAPTER THIRTEEN

The Aftermath

As you can imagine, there was all hell let loose again in Harwich. The Board of Trade inquiry came out pretty blunt about them pigeons being useless, and how it was high time the Trinity found a way to get a telegraph cable to the lightships, specially seeing as they'd got an offer from the Telegraph Construction and Maintenance Company to do the job and maintain the wire for a year without charge.

So at last they took that offer up. The company put a cable down and kept it going for a year, all at their own risk. The Trinity took it over after they'd tested it every day, both telegraph and telephone.

Then the very next year the Board of Trade held an inquiry to decide if the result had justified the cost, and I suppose they reckoned it hadn't, for after another two years they hired one of Packard's Ipswich steamers to pick it up and then they sold it to somebody. I don't know what value they put on sailors' lives, but that can't have been much, because they were complaining that 'we have to pay the rent of a little room at a Post Office and have to pay wages for a man there.'

But we're talking about the *Indian Chief* report.

About the *Springwell* they asked the question, 'Whether every possible effort was made by the cox'n and crew of the Harwich lifeboat to reach the wreck.' And they gave the answer, 'Seeing what the Ramsgate and Clacton lifeboats did, the court was not prepared to say that the Harwich lifeboat might not have gone to the wreck.' But although they gave a great old report as long as your arm, with something to say on all and sundry, they never mentioned Vaux and the *Harwich*.

But the newspapers did. They got at him and no mistake. The *East Anglian* at Ipswich said, 'Whether the Mayor of Harwich is an especially gallant landsman we know not. The impression cannot but prevail that the gale which he ventured to face and which quenched his zeal might not have deterred a crew of sailors alone.'

Mark you, there wasn't no love lost between Ipswich and Harwich, for Ipswich was deepening its river and making its own docks to take the trade away from Harwich, and our *Harwich Free Press* always had something to say when a ship got ashore trying to get up there. But this time even our *Free Press* had to agree that 'a great weight of responsibility rests upon our present Mayor, the owner of the only tug in the port, who adopted such an extraordinary course. If it was not inhumanity we should like to know by what other name it should be called. It makes one's blood run cold to think what must have been the feelings of the crew of the wreck when they saw, as they must have seen, a tug and the lifeboat approach them within two miles and then go away again.'

Now I haven't got no particular regard for them newspaper chaps that have to come out with a verdict before they have had time enough to get a proper hang of what it was all about, nor yet for them Board of Trade courts. This one took time enough, for it was seven months before their report came out, and by that time the old *Springwell* was gone without their help. They were in the right about those damned pigeons and the need for the telegraph, but they never even come near the other real point, that you've got to have a tug and a lifeboat work together under somebody's orders.

Now, I done a lot of thinking over the years and this is how it seems to me. Vaux had to take the decision, and seeing he had the ebb tide to help him I still can't believe that tug couldn't have weathered the Longsand Head. But the master of the tug, Si Keeble, agreed with him. You may say he daren't go against his boss. But don't forget he had Harry Cook of the *Aquiline* aboard, too, and he was of the same mind. Of course he wasn't a steamboat man, and you may say he didn' t know just what the *Harwich* could have done. But he was a first-rate salvager and I lay he had the measure of things.

Bill Britton in charge of the lifeboat said he gave a signal to keep on, but then he said if they had he didn't think the tug could have got to the Longsand in safety, she was shipping so much water. So they asked, 'Then if you did not think it safe why did you signal the tug on?' And he said, 'I would not be the first to give up. I wanted to try to get round.' Then they wanted to know if he'd have tried if he'd been in charge of the tug and he said, 'Yes, I think I would have.'

If John Tye had been there he might have had his way, but I doubt it. At Ramsgate the lifeboat cox'n was the boss, but the way it was at Harwich, with nothing properly organised, the tug's skipper treated the lifeboat as just something he had in tow.

So I reckon it was Vaux's choice, and I allow he was wrong to get up in that position. One night he'd be at his council meetings or a mayor's banquet, or tending to his Freemason's ceremonies, for he was a big number in all that sort of thing. He had his shipyard to run, and with two hundred hands employed that was the biggest firm in Harwich after the railway, as well as having a coal merchant's business with it. He had hell and all of ships of his own to manage, and he had foreigners to look after, for he was Vice-Consul for France, Russia, Turkey, Uruguay, Portugal and God knows where else. He was chairman of the Barge Alliance, which was the insurance club, and a Commissioner of Taxes and he had to sit on the bench as a magistrate. So that didn't make no sense to turn out lifeboat towing the way he did.

But that was the kind of man he was. He didn't sit on his arse and leave things to other people. Each time he was mayor, which was seven times, he gave a dinner of roast beef and Christmas pudding to anyone who liked to apply. I ought to know because I went once. When one of his cod smacks came in from Iceland or the Dogger he'd go aboard and have dinner with the skipper.

He was a great big man and weighed twenty-two stone, though before he died, which he did when he was only fifty-two, he wasted away to a shadow and that brought tears to your eyes to look at him. He married a daughter of Pattrick what had the cement factory at Dovercourt, and they thought he wasn't good enough for her, for the Pattricks were a bit of a County family, but if they'd looked after their affairs the way Vaux did to his maybe they wouldn't have humbugged that trade out of existence. No, Vaux he was a man. Fancy having your fearnoughts and oilskin frock hanging in the cupboard alongside your aldermanic robe and your Masonic fal-de-lals!

He may have been wrong, but he weren't so wrong as them chaps in high places that kept writing each other letters and making reports and doing nothing about things that were urgent because there was men drowning all the while. And he never took no notice of all the unkind things that was said of him nor yet troubled to reply.

A few weeks after the *Indian Chief* job there was a steamer called the *Clytie*, with coals from Newcastle to Tarragona, got on the Longsand within half-a-mile of the same place and the *Harwich* towed the *Springwell* out to her. She had been reported by two Colchester salvagers, David Martin's *Concord* and William Cheek's *Faith*.

The *Springwell* didn't do no good, because by the time they got there the crew had managed to get across the breakers in their own boat to the *Concord* which brought them in and towed their boat as well. They must have been coming in the same time the tug and lifeboat was going out, and it's a funny thing they never saw nothing of each other.

But the really funny thing is that Vaux took the *Harwich* himself, after all that had been said and written about him. Perhaps that was his answer after all.

CHAPTER FOURTEEN

Capsize of the Springwell

Harwich soon had something to take its mind off the *Indian Chief*.

Towards the end of the month there came a January gale that was said to be the worst in forty years. That was more like a hurricane. To tell you what that was like they had to barricade the windows of the Great Eastern Hotel to prevent them being blown in, and when a boy had his hat blown off near the quay and he ran after it he couldn't stop himself and got blown right over into the water. One of the boatmen, a chap named Stonehouse Stuart, he went in after him and got him out. They got up a subscription for him and raised £50. He bought a new boat and called her *Reward*. After that he always done a wonderful good trade with the visitors.

While this little old breeze was piping, with blinding showers of sleet and snow, they saw a barque go ashore, and got the lifeboat out of her house for launching. When the wind is on the shore there, there is so much surf that can't be done, and they said later they wouldn't have tried if it hadn't have been for all the tales in the newspapers about Harwich men being cowards. As it was they ran her round to the continental pier and used the railway crane to get her into the water. While they were doing that they had a telegram from Woodbridge saying a vessel was sunk in the Haven, and they thought they could see the crew in the rigging. That turned out later she was a Whitby schooner called the *Deptford*, but what became of the crew I don't recall.

Well, they double-reefed the *Springwell*'s mainsail and reefed her mizzen and they give her a start. John Tye was away again. His wife was ill this time, and that was Britton in charge. She wasn't hardly clear of the pier, and still in the harbour, when a gust hit her and she went over, though they had let the sheets go. She turned bottom up but righted in thirty seconds with all bar two of her crew thrown out of her. It was lucky those two had clung on to the thwarts, for they were able to help the rest back aboard, all bar one man, William Wink. He was a stone man, and had a little smack called the *Matilda*.

A lot of boats went after them. The railway steamer *Claud Hamilton* soon had one in the water with eight men in her. The chief officer of another packet, the *Adelaide*, with five other men took a waterman's boat from the pier. He was first away, but he was overtaken by the lifeboat cutter from HMS *Penelope* with about fourteen hands. The cutter got Wink after he'd drifted over two miles on the tide, but he was too far gone and he died soon after they had him aboard.

Most of them boats managed to reach some craft lying in the harbour, though a lot of the men never got home before midnight. The boat from the *Claud Hamilton* couldn't find nothing to catch hold of and she blew right up to Mistley and only took an hour to do it. They came home by train. The lifeboat herself drove close to a cod smack called the *Ranger* which got a rope aboard. She was lying to two anchors, but with the weight of the lifeboat she broke one chain and dragged off into the tideway. The ice killed the cod in her fish well.

In the end the lifeboat drove up to Parkeston, and the crew walked home. They reached Harwich about seven in the evening and came into one end of the town just as Wink's body was being brought ashore from the *Penelope*'s cutter at the other. That was the first they knew he was gone.

That day there was a schooner called the *Marie* drove ashore in Dovercourt Bay, firing rockets and burning a tar barrel, and a brigantine over by Walton Naze. In the harbour the railway steamer *Rotterdam* parted from her moorings at the pier, and all the *Penelope*'s boats, including the steam pinnace, were swamped alongside her. Groom's shrimper *Saucy Jack* was smashed up against the walls of the Angel Gate battery and so Fairchild's *Gratitude* would have been, only he gave old Blower Brown a quid to go off with a maul and knock a hole in her bottom so she sank before she hit the wall. Next morning the beach was all wreckage from one end to the other.

That was a Tuesday, and on the following Thursday evening those same chaps were called out again. They didn't have no tug but rowed and sailed to the Swin where they met the *Albatross* about three o'clock in the morning. She told them there was a steamer on the Sunk, and she towed them that way for an hour or so under sail. They found the wreck about five, but when Britton sung out to know if anyone was alive there was no answer bar moaning. But as the light made they could see seven fellows in the rigging. They had a job to get them with the tide ebbing and the steamer all broken iron spikes and stanchions.

On the way back they fell in with the Lowestoft tug and lifeboat, the

Despatch and *Samuel Plimsoll*, coming back from another wreck, so at least they gets a tow in from the Cork. The steamer was the Dutch fish carrier *Ingerid* bound from Bergen to Naples, and she'd been ashore there since early on the Monday morning. They'd made two attempts to launch boats and lost a man each time. Then they'd been in the rigging since Tuesday.

That so happened Captain Nepean, the district inspector of lifeboats, was in Harwich over the recent troubles, so he had a trip to the *Ingerid*. He and Britton both got silver medals and a vellum and the crew £4 each. Those in the capsize got thirty shillings each for that, extra to the ten shillings they'd been paid for the launch. But the Lowestoft cox'n got told off good and proper.

What happened was this. The Great Eastern steamer *Avalon*[1] saw a big Italian barque dismasted and lying to two anchors near the Shipwash. The captain thought he'd better try something, so he sent a boat off but it couldn't reach her. They got the steamer close enough to the barque to get lines aboard but they broke and they couldn't do nothing. Then getting her own boat, the *Avalon* rolled so much she hit the bosun in the boat and cut his head. He was trying to get a rope fast to himself, when the next lurch she gives over he goes and they never see no more of him.

So after lying-by till nine o'clock in the evening, the *Avalon* comes into Harwich and tells Captain Howard, the marine superintendent. Knowing what a hell of a state the *Springwell* is in he telegraphs Lowestoft where the harbourmaster sends the *Samuel Plimsoll* and the *Despatch*. When they get to the Shipwash they find the Italian in charge of one of Hewett's fish carriers which ultimately tows her into Harwich.

The Collector of Customs at Lowestoft wrote off to the Institution wanting to know what the hell the tug and lifeboat were up to when they might have been wanted at home. They had to have a special meeting, and though nothing came of it that made you think you couldn't do much without someone finding fault with you.

The little *Springwell* only did one or two more jobs after that.

In October the same year she went under sail to the Cork to a big Swedish timber barque called the *Iris* ashore there. She couldn't get her off but brought the twelve hands ashore. On the way in a smack hailed them that there was a French fisherman ashore on the Gunfleet. So they turned out again, behind the *Harwich* this time, but found the Frenchman abandoned.

1. Paddler, 613 tons, 230 feet long, commissioned 1864, sold in 1880s.

She was called the *Madeline*, and the Clacton boat had got the crew out of her.

Next day the *Springwell*'s crew thought they'd go back to the *Iris* and do themselves a bit of good, but the Institution wouldn't allow it. They said, 'We are supposed to be a-saving of lives. There ain't no harm in your doing yourselves a bit of good on the side so long as we make out it ain't no concern of ours, but you can't go taking the Red White and Blue off to a wreck where there ain't nobody left to be saved. The people we look to for the money, they might start asking questions.'

So when the Sunk starts banging again soon after this our chaps muster at the lifeboat house but they refuse to launch. What riled them was the tug and the scropers was making a lot of money and all the lifeboatmen got was ten bob for a daylight launch and a quid at night. That was worth more than it sounds today, when we've got fishermen in Harwich earning £5 a week and sleeping in their beds every night, but that wasn't nothing to what the salvagers sometimes fell in for.

So you can understand that made them swear when the *Harwich* and the *Volunteer* and the *Reindeer* fetched that *Iris* in the very same day they was refused.

CHAPTER FIFTEEN

The Second Springwell

About a year after the old *Springwell* had capsized we got a bigger boat at last. In fact she was one of the biggest in the service, forty-five feet long and eleven feet beam, pulling ten oars as well as having sails. She was another self-righter and she was another gift from Miss Burmester, so they give her the same name, *Springwell*.

She was too big to keep ashore so she had a mooring in the Pound. Admiral Ward, the Inspector of Lifeboats, tried to blame it on Vaux that we hadn't had a bigger boat before. He said he had tried for a berth in Vaux's yard but Vaux wouldn't have it. So he had to choose the site to keep the boat and then had the boat built to suit the site. If he was really that silly it explains a lot, and he never said why he didn't ask the harbour-master for a berth in the Pound in the first place. He did say that you couldn't keep a lifeboat nice if it was exposed to all sorts of weather, so she was up on Vaux's slip for a paint-up for two months every summer.

That didn't matter so much now they'd got the boats at Walton and Clacton; in fact once when they sent for her to go to a dismasted Norwegian barque called the *Roma* on the Gunfleet and she couldn't launch off the slip, the Clacton boat done the job alright and brought in her crew of thirteen and the English pilot. But that started the old yapping again, with the *East Anglian* saying, 'The Harwich lifeboat appears ready to go out sometimes, the Clacton lifeboat always.' What there was between Vaux and the Institution over that berth I don't know, because Vaux never deigned to answer that sort of talk.

The second *Springwell* reigned eight years and she done some good jobs. But salvaging now was getting competitive for scropers and for lifeboats, as I'll come to explaining in a minute, and this new boat had a lot of disappointments because they still didn't sort out no proper scheme with the tug.

Back at the time of the *Deutschland* they'd been saying Harwich was first a place that had a lifeboat and no tug and then it had a tug and no lifeboat. Since then it had been a place with a tug and a death-trap of a life-boat, and now at last it had a decent lifeboat you'd think they have seen it needed some idea better than hoping the tug would oblige.

After we'd had the new *Springwell* about a year, which was just about the time Britton retired as cox'n and Tyrrell took over, Vaux had a go. 'Look,' he says, 'the *Harwich* will do the towing if you'll pay for the coal and insure her for £5,000 for the six winter months. If I get anything from salvage there'll be no charge, and I'll contribute five per cent of what I get towards the cost of the insurance.' He wasn't insured at all at the time of the *Indian Chief*, and maybe that's another reason why he didn't fancy risking her.

But the Institution wouldn't look at it. They reckoned tugs wasn't their department. And you might think it was the Harbour Conservancy that should have taken some responsibility. Then the whole outfit might have been controlled by the Harbourmaster, but for some reason no one never seemed to get on to them about it.

Anyway, for a year or two the second *Springwell* had to make the best of it on her own, and the result is when she went as far as the Burying Grounds the Ramsgate boat had generally done the job before she got there. One time they had twenty hours' rowing to the Kentish Knock, and as Ramsgate had already been they had to row home again. Our *Free Press* said, 'If the Institution will not accede to the fair terms offered by Mr Vaux or arrange for a tug to tow the lifeboat out it would be better she should remain at her moorings. As without a tug she is not the slightest use.'

So after that she didn't go much on the longer trips, which is what she was provided to do. She done some jobs on the Gunfleet and as far as the Sunk, though.

One time she went to the Sunk to an Aberdeen barque called the *Mirford and Trubey*. She got three men out of the main rigging and one out of the mizzen. They'd been there forty-six hours and were so far gone they couldn't wait to cut the captain's dead body down from the mizzen rigging. They'd lost one man and the cook in attempting to launch the boat. It was forty hours before anyone ashore knew there was a ship in trouble, all because they were still relying on pigeons and rockets. John Mills, the second cox'n, couldn't bear to think about the captain's body still hanging there, so he and eight other chaps went off next day in a bawley. Four of them made three attempts in their foot boat and at last they got him. He was hanging by his ankles. They say he left a wife and fourteen children.

So they did manage some good jobs without a tug, saved some lives and made some money, like when they got £90 for fetching in a Rochester barge called the *Jessie* abandoned on the Heaps. The reason I recall that is that the only thing they found alive aboard of her was a mouse in a trap.

Vaux's *Harwich* was off on her own now, or working with the scropers or with the *Bobbie Owen*. That was the tug that was under arrest at the time of the *Indian Chief*, but later Vaux bought her. She was West Country built. We called her the *Bobown*. I've already told you about some of the jobs they done off Suffolk and I'll tell you some yarns presently.

Yes, I reckon them tugs done alright, time they didn't have to mess about towing a lifeboat. They weren't always lucky though. One time there was a Liverpool ship called the *Lathom* on the Longsand. She was bound home from Calcutta and worth something. The *Harwich* and Cheek's smack *Faith* had a go at her, but they could not get near her. When the *Harwich* went again two days later she was all a wreck.

CHAPTER SIXTEEN

Clacton and Walton Join In

Apart from having no tug, another trouble the second *Springwell* had in working the Gunfleet and such was that the Walton and Clacton boats had a head start of her.

The first Clacton lifeboat, called *Albert Edward*, was a little self-righter like our first *Springwell*. She done remarkably well to get to the Longsand at all over the *Indian Chief*, but some years later they launched her in a nor'west gale and over she went just like ours did. She righted in two minutes but they lost the second cox'n and Tom Cattermole, what everyone knew because in the summer he kept the donkeys on the beach.

The Institution subbed up £250 for one widow with six children and £200 for the other who had three children, and they sent a new thirty-nine foot *Albert Edward*, with twelve oars and a centreboard. With that she'd really go to windward, and all the lifeboat crews was soon wanting them. What's more they made two wooden slipways so she could be launched from either side of the pier. That was a good fit-out and gave her an advantage.

She had a funny thing happen on her first voyage. About a year before, just three days after her capsize, the first *Albert Edward* had gone to a steamer called the *Hawthorn* ashore on the Gunfleet. They wired Harwich for a tug but there wasn't one there, so a London tug came and got her off. Well, the new *Albert Edward*'s first launch was to a Faversham brigantine called the *Elizabeth Blaxland*. She wasn't needed as it happened, but as she was bound home along comes a steamer and offers her a pluck. Blowed if wasn't the *Hawthorn*. Both them crews made quite a party of that tow, as much as they could, seeing the weather was just about as coarse as when the old boat capsized, and they'd been out in it thirteen hours.

A year or so before they had this centreboard boat at Clacton they got a boat at Walton. She was a thirty-seven-foot self-righter, paid for by the Honourable Artillery Company. The Duke of Portland done the handover ceremony for the Institution. He said he hoped the boat would be 'most useful in saving life and that it would add to the prosperity of Walton-on-the-Naze'. That gives you an idea of how such things were regarded then.

The first cox'n was Henry Britton, who had been apprenticed in a Colne smack and was part-owner of a great old beach boat called *Skylark*. He carried on for thirty years and only missed one service in all that time.

This *Honourable Artillery Company* had a bad start. The first day they had her they took a party of ladies and gentlemen out for a sail and stove her in coming alongside the slipway. But she made up for that on her first service when she went to a big German full-rigged ship, the *Deike Rickmers*, on the Longsand. They got the word around dinner time on Christmas Day, but they didn't settle to go till the evening, and then it took them an hour and a half to get her out of her house, down the pier and on to the slipway. That blew north-east, so they fetched across the top of the Gunfleet and brought up to windward of the wreck to wait for dawn.

When they finally veered down under her bowsprit they found there was twenty-five men aboard. The German captain didn't reckon he could take them all, but Britton sings out 'I shan't leave till I have all of you'. So down they come, the captain's dog first, and the captain last. The wind the way it was they couldn't weather the end of the Longsand, and they had to lay for four hours with forty men and a dog in that little thirty-seven footer before the tide was high enough for them to get across and fetch back to Walton at seven in the evening.

That slip was an awkward thing. They had this idea that a lifeboat must have a little house ashore to live in, but even when things were right that took twenty-five minutes to get the boat in the water. They had to run her out on her carriage and then check the carriage down the slip with drag-ropes. The end of it was that it killed one of the crew. They had the usual rush for the belts and them as didn't get a belt stayed to help with the launch. One of them, Darkie Downes, never let go his rope in time and he got dragged under one of the carriage wheels and crushed to death.

After that they left her on a mooring off the pier and used a boarding boat and to hell with the paintwork. The Clacton boat, all the time I can remember, done a running launch off her slip, without no carriage under her, though they used to keep the first boat in a house ashore. Of course these pier-head slipways wasn't no good to come back to, not with the wind on shore, but the Walton boat could always use Harwich and the Clacton boat go into Brightlingsea.

After the *Honourable Artillery Company* had reigned about ten years there came a quarrel among her crew. Some of them left and bought a lifeboat of their own. They called her *True to the Core*. She was a Norfolk and Suffolk type that could leave the *Honourable Artillery Company* standing when that came to a race, which it did most times they launched. At first she lay in the Backwaters, round the back of the Naze, but before long she was put off the pier as well.

Them two boats used to scrap something terrible. One time the volunteer chaps said the *Honourable Artillery Company*'s fifteen-man crew included two bricklayer's labourers, a fitter, a foundry-man and a turner. One of the Institution chaps retorted that if he was a bricklayer's labourer that was better than 'lounging about against the hotel corners as some prefer to do', and he said the *True to the Core*'s crew was made up of a fishmonger, a painter, a paper-hanger, an insurance agent, a Limehouse docker, a tobacconist, three bricklayer's labourers, a stage super, a baker, an oil merchant, two sons of clergymen and a barman.

To make matters worse, the *True to the Core* chaps had only themselves to please, and they could go off salvaging whenever they fancied, instead of having to wait for orders like the *Honourable Artillery Company* had to do. That irked the Institution men. They said the volunteer crew hadn't got no right to collect donations from the holiday visitors.

The Institution were pretty fair-minded, and made awards to the *True to the Core* same as they did to their own crew, but at first the coastguards would only pass messages from the Gunfleet to the *Honourable Artillery Company*. The MP wrote to the Admiralty about this and it was ordered that all messages should be put on a notice board, with a Blue Peter flag hoisted by day and a light shown at night as a sign that news had been received. An Institution man going to his boat met a volunteer man taking news from the coastguard station to the *True to the Core*. He set about him and got had up for assault.

That sort of squabbling went on for twenty years. The *True to the Core* was an old boat when they had her. Her mizzen rigging failed the first year and she had to be towed into Harwich. So they set about raising money and had a new boat. They went to Houston at Rowhedge and told him they wanted one as near as possible like the Aldeburgh boat. The new *True to the Core* was the third lifeboat copied from that *George Hounsfield*.

The *Honourable Artillery Company* reigned for sixteen years and when that came the time for a new boat the crew would not have a self-righter.

They insisted on a Norfolk and Suffolk, much like the *True to the Core*, but a bit bigger. She was forty-three feet long and twelve feet beam, and had two centreboards, which meant you could use the forward one to hold her head up going to windward, and the aft one to steady her running. She was called the *James Stevens*.

These two kept teasing each other right up to the time the *James Stevens* was one of the first lifeboats to have a motor, and the *True to the Core* had to have a bigger one, so then they was racing each other with all sails set and motors going.

That *James Stevens* was the only time the Institution gave way on our coast over self-righters. That was something argued over wherever lifeboat men met. The rights and wrongs of it were never settled and they never will be now.

CHAPTER SEVENTEEN

Paddle Tugs' Heyday

I can't tell you much more about them Clacton and Walton chaps, nor yet about the volunteer lifeboat off the beach at Frinton. That was started by a Lowestoft beachman, David Cook, who was one of several came to those parts around the turn of the century to work beach boats and bathing machines. The Suffolk beach companies was finished then, you see, and these Essex seaside holiday places was on the way up, with the railways running cheap excursions and the old *Woolwich Belle* and *Koh-i-Noor* and such paddle steamers landing people from London on the piers every day.

Three of David Cook's sons were in the *True to the Core*, and one of them bought an old thirty-two-foot lugsail boat called *Godsend* that was kept for a bit of salvaging in the winter, but her main work was summer visitors' trips. He renamed her *Sailors Friend* and then he replaced her with another *Sailors Friend* that was a proper forty-foot Norfolk and Suffolk lifeboat, built a-purpose for him by Cann at Harwich, with a Society to manage her. She went off once with the Clacton boat to a Russian schooner on the Blacktail, and when they were lowering the mainsail to speak the Swin Middle light vessel for directions, one of her crew, Cecil Bambridge, was knocked overboard and lost.

But this yarn is about Harwich, and I'm only telling you about these other places to show you how we didn't have the Gunfleet and the Burying Grounds to ourselves no more, us and the Colne men.

In fact, by the time we had all this lot of lifeboats, which was the middle of the 1880s, the old-time scropers had seen their best days. It wasn't just that the lifeboats and the tugs put them out of business, though they might have done that anyway. Other things was altering, too. There was fewer ships and more of them were steamers, which used to get into trouble, but not so regular as the old sailing vessels.

They made a lot of trouble for other people too, the way they kept going in fog. There was plenty of craft run down by sailing ships, but that was generally in a breeze of wind when they couldn't handle them.

But with steamers about you wasn't safe even when you did the proper thing in fog, which was to bring up and keep your bell ringing.

Once we had steam I reckon as many craft were run down as got wrecked. A lot of the smacks went that way.

The *Energy* was stowboating when she was hit, and so I believe was the *Weigh*. I allow them chaps did bring up and shove their gear in anywhere in the tideway, fog and all, and they was taking risks. But the *Two Sisters* and the *Orion* and the *Aid* and the *Greyhound* were all under way when these steamboats just come into them. There was ten lives lost in a few years in those four mishaps, just chaps going about their business in their own home waters, carrying fish to Billingsgate and such like.

The *Greyhound* had been to Whitstable with brood oysters. She started home and just disappeared. A Whistable diver found the wreck with the stern all smashed up and the boat with it, so it looks like they were trying to get in it when she was hit. Charlie Barber had two sons with him. His eldest son and his son-in-law had both been lost in the skilling disaster the year before, so his wife was in the position she'd lost two husbands, three sons and a son-in-law.

That wasn't the only time the steamer never stopped. That was wicked the way they kept a-going, though they could be had up if they were caught, or fined £20 for not giving their name, but they never took no notice. When the *Osprey* of Burnham was sunk in Long Reach, turning up to Billingsgate, they charged the pilot of the steamship with manslaughter, but they let him off.

Tom Barnard's son, William, in the *New Unity*, he see a steamer flying a jack for a pilot somewhere between the Gunfleet and the Sunk. So his brother Daniel and two other hands go off in the boat to her, and the next thing they notice from the smack is the steamer's crew all pointing down at the water and their boat not to be seen nowhere. Barnard gybes over in a hurry, and being short-handed he busts his gaff. While he's lying there half disabled he sees this damned steamboat go off on her way without so much as lowering a boat. She was called the *Tiger*, bound from Hamburg to London, and I hope they went for her when she got there, though I never heard of it.

Round about the same time there was a Boston schooner called the *Success* brought up in fog one night by the Gunfleet light. Soon after midnight along comes a steamboat. She heard their bell and went astern, but she still comes into them. 'For God's sake don't leave us. We are sinking,' the skipper sings out. 'It's only a bit of bulwark broken,' he hears someone aboard the steamboat say, and she backs off and away she goes. The three hands got in the boat with some clothes and blankets and a few bits of biscuit and the schooner sank in less than an hour.

The *Reindeer* found them seven hours later and brought them in. They were lodged in a boarding house and sent home by the Fishermen's and Mariners' Royal Benevolent Society, which is how such things were done at that time of day. John Vaux was the honorary agent. He used to look after that among other things.

One of the General Steam Navigation boats, the *Seamew*, left Parkeston one night and ran down something off the Cork. She lowers a boat but can't find nothing so she humbugs off to Hamburg with part of this craft's mast still on her focs'le head. The lifeboat and two tugs were out all night in blinding snow, and they find the horn of a gaff and another bit of a mast. Next day the Trinity yacht *Satellite* finds some sails and spars, enough to show she was a ketch that had her sails set when she was hit.

That was another month before the *Satellite* found her stern frame. She was a little Goole billy-boy called the *Rose in June*. The owner said his son and two other chaps were aboard. She was a hundred years old.[1]

What with one thing and another, them steamships made some jobs for the salvagers, if that's how you like to look at it, but they took some away too, because they could do a bit of salvaging themselves.

You could see that happen when Paul's, the Ipswich merchants, started steam barges. The first one they had was a 170-tonner called the *Swift*. They reckoned she'd do London docks to Ipswich in ten or twelve hours, compared with two or three days by sailing barges. In the end that didn't answer. They built the barges bigger and faster and they paid better. Folk ashore always have the idea steam must beat sail but that didn't always. Of course now they're getting these little motor craft that's different. They do hell and all of freights and don't cost nothing to run.

But while Paul's had these steam barges they were up and down Swin every day and they'd pick up a salvage job before we knew it was there. Ernest Tovee was skipper of the *Swift* and after her of the *Speedwell*. He gloried in a bit of salvage. That broke the monotony of banging up and down Swin I daresay, apart from his share of the rewards.

The first winter he had her, the *Swift* found a foreign ship called the *Antonia* on the Gunfleet and comes into Harwich with her alongside.

Then a few years later he's on his way up Swin when he finds a sailing barge bottom upwards hear the North East Maplin buoy. She was the

1. Built at Ipswich in 1798

Formosa, a famous racing barge. She was only ten years old and worth £600. They get hold of her and tow her four and a half miles into the shoal water, which took seven hours' pulling. Then Tovee humbugs off up to London to get his freight and leaves his mate with the barge. That was April time, but a capsized barge seems a funny place to spend a night. I suppose they left the foot-boat for him to sit in.

Tovee gets back about eleven o'clock next morning and they set to work trying to get that barge right way up. It took them till the afternoon to turn her over, and then they reckoned they had to bail out sixty tons of water before they could take her in tow. But apart from her gear and rigging she was hardly damaged.

The next year Paul's had a new *Speedwell* that was built as a trawler. That made her a beautiful thing for salvaging, and blessed if she didn't pick up a prize on her first voyage – a barge that had broken her mast in collision with a barque.

They had some games, them steam barges. One time the *Speedwell* tries her hand towing a Nova Scotia barque called the *Georgia*, bound the same way as she was, which was London to Ipswich. Doing that she burns all her coal and has to bring up in the East Swin. That was December time and thick weather. Along comes the *Swift* and finds them there, so she picks them both up and tows the pair of them up into the Ipswich river as far as Pin Mill, where the *Georgia* gets picked up by the *Little England*.

That *Little England* was one of Paul's river tugs. She was for everlasting sinking. I don't know how many times that little thing tried to drown herself before they got rid of her. The other one they had in the river was the *Era*, but they weren't really fit for salvaging at sea or lifeboat towing.

Then at last they replaced that *Little England* with something very different – a beautiful great thing that put you in mind of the Great Eastern Ipswich–Harwich river boats, only she had a better promenade deck than they did. She was much the size of the *Harwich*, nearly 100 feet long, and she was called the *Merrimac*. She'd been working a daily passenger service between Bristol and Penrith, and could take 172 passengers. Nowadays passenger packets and tugboats are as different as chalk and cheese, but in the paddle days the same craft would do for both. They worked excursions in the summer and salvaging in the winter.

Tovee shifted over to the *Merrimac*, and she did a lot of lifeboat towing as well as salvage jobs on her own. Vaux had made it up with the Institution by now; I don't know if he came to some terms or just felt he couldn't keep on passing the *Springwell* and leaving her to struggle as best she could. So as often as not the *Harwich* would take the *Springwell*, or the reserve lifeboat that replaced her for a while, and the *Merrimac* would pick up the Walton boat.

Within a month of her coming to Ipswich the *Merrimac* picked up £50 by agreement for a service to the *Achilles*, a steamship that got on the Shipwash. The *Harwich* and our lifeboat were on that job too. They took their claim to court and got £560. Between them they helped to throw 300 tons of railway sleepers overboard and then they towed her in.

Any God's amount of jobs Tovee done with one of the lifeboats or on his own, as many as any lifeboat, I reckon. He was often down as far as Aldeburgh.

He pulled a schooner called *Aire* off the ground near there and claimed £300. The owners put in a counterclaim against him for £40. They said he'd negligently slipped their anchor chains and prevented their crew getting back aboard. In the end the old judge gave £50 to the *Merrimac* and said £30 ought to go to the owners, £15 to three members of the crew who jumped aboard the ship, and the other £5 to the rest of them.

A few years before that he'd been to a four-masted barque called the *Glencairn*, ashore at Thorpeness just north of Aldeburgh. Sixteen beachmen relieved the barque's crew, who were exhausted, but that was a proper tugs' tea party. The three Great Eastern Railway tugs from Lowestoft were there, with three more from Yarmouth, three of Watkins' from London and one called the *Gleaner*, as well as the *Merrimac*. They pulled her off and took her to Gravesend. They put the value of the barque at £9,000 and her cargo at £7,410, and they gave £2,175 salvage. The *Merrimac* got £225 and the beachmen £400.

All three of our Harwich tugs had a job getting a steamer called the *Brighton* off the Gunfleet. The *Harwich* got £200, the *Merrimac* £175 and the *Robert Owen* £150, and they gave £150 between the crews of the Walton lifeboat *Honourable Artillery Company* and a yawl called the *Dogger Bank*.

Another time Tovee got a commendation for towing the *Springwell* out to a Russian Finn barque called the *St Olaf* which had parted from her anchor and gone on the Longsand. They fetched the crew ashore and left her for a total wreck, but blessed if she didn't float off a week later. The Trinity House yacht *Irene* found her near the Sunk and towed her in with her masts gone and six inches of freeboard.

Later on Tovee got a Royal Humane Society testimonial for lifesaving, but that was nothing. He was coming alongside the quay at Slaughden one Bank Holiday with the *Merrimac* when he sees someone fall in the water and pulls him out. I allow he'd done the same thing two years before opposite the Lock Tavern at Ipswich but that seem a funny thing to make a fuss of that alongside some of the jobs at sea that meant some risk. But people will always pay more heed to something they can see than something that happens where they haven't been and couldn't imagine. And Ernest took care that anything he done was in the *Free Press* next Friday.

Yes, he was for everlasting in the news. One time his house caught fire and he got a paragraph to say he burnt his hand a-putting of it out. After the *Merrimac* he took the *Spray* and sold some old rope off her to the sailmaker. He told the beaks that wasn't Paul's rope but bits he'd picked up at sea, or broken ends from towing foreign vessels, and he got away with that. Another time they had him up for being drunk in charge of a horse and cart. He said he wasn't in charge, only driving, and they let him off that one too.

I was trying to tell you how if you wanted plenty of applause that paid to have a good audience.

The most medals I recall given out was when a schooner called the *Rose*[1] ran ashore against the coastguard station at Felixstowe. She was an old thing that belonged to William Scarf at Ipswich, and he'd always sailed her himself up to this last voyage. The coastguards had two tries at her with their galley but each time they got washed back and capsized. The Harwich lifeboat[2] got a line aboard and got three hands off her, with one hurt when he fell between the lifeboat and the schooner. Next day she shoved her bow up the beach with three foot of water over her deck at high water. The beach men stripped her on the ebb.

All the lifeboat crew were given medals at the Ipswich Grand Nautical Fair, and then the Board of Trade gave medals to six of their boatmen. I don't disallow they earned them, but they only got them because there was hundreds of people looking on and cheering and several Suffolk gentlemen getting their feet wet and their names in the paper helping to shove the galley off. If that had been away on the Burying Ground with twice the danger and no one to see it that would never have been noticed.

1. Built at Dundee 1828, 97 tons.
2. *City of Glasgow*. See Chapter 19.

CHAPTER EIGHTEEN

Railway Boats and Royal Yacht

To get back to my yarn, I'm just trying to make you understand there was plenty of steam craft about now to have a go at the jobs that used to give my father his living. That wasn't only little things like the *Speedwell* and the *Merrimac* that would pick up the plums. The railway steamers weren't above a bit on the side either.

The *Claud Hamilton*[1] was on her Antwerp run when she sees an iron barque called the *George Bewley* in trouble off the North Hinder lightship. She gets a rope on her but that parts, so she uses chains and tows her into Flushing. When she sails again for Harwich she leaves her chief officer aboard the prize to make sure of her rights. In my time in the railway boats if we'd been humbugging about in the North Sea for half a day, so as all the passengers missed their trains, there'd soon have been some of them round the office wanting their money back, but when the *Claud Hamilton*

The *Great Eastern North Sea packet* Adelaide, *which several times interrupted a voyage to perform a salvage. In December, 1882, she reached Harwich seven hours late, towing a disabled Norwegian barque* Kong Sverre, *and three months later she tried to take in tow the German ss* Carl Woerman.

1. Paddle steamer with two funnels and two masts. The first GER ship to be built on the Clyde, and the pride of the fleet. Sold in 1897.

got in all the passengers signed a testimonial praising the captain. That was thought the right thing to do.

A week afterwards the *Richard Young*[1] came across a steamer called the *Ben Avon* of Aberdeen. Her skipper had a bit of a go but seeing there was nothing he could do he went on his way. She didn't come to no harm and was soon picked up by a tug from London, but that caused so much criticism leaving her after only one attempt that the captain had to write a letter to our *Free Press* saying as how he went round the disabled steamer twice and slacked away lifebuoys, the sea being too rough to lower boats.

All around the same time the *Adelaide*[2] came into Harwich seven hours late with a Norwegian barque called the *Kong Sverre* behind her, and again the passengers according to our *Free Press*, 'spoke in terms of the warmest praise of the brave manner in which all aboard did their duty'. Later that winter the *Adelaide* tried to tow a German steamer called the *Carl Woerman*, but she parted her ropes and they had to leave her at anchor just to the south'ard of the Kentish Knock. The Germans sent the ss *Livonia* to Dover to get two tugs and they towed her to London.

Once when the *Harwich*[3] (the railway boat, not the tug) didn't arrive they thought she must be lost at sea, but what happened was she'd picked up a derelict and turned round and towed it to Rotterdam. Another time, on her homeward run, she picked up a schooner and brought it into Harwich.

You never knew what you were in for when you bought a ticket to Holland that time of day. The *Adelaide* busted her low pressure piston forty miles off Harwich. Nowadays someone would send out a salvage tug. But Captain Howard just orders the *Ipswich*[4] to get ready to go out. Then in comes the *Brandon* with news that she's been laying by all day, so he turns her round and goes off in her and tows the *Adelaide* in. Another of them old craft smashed up one paddle, so they got some canvas on her and come in in fine style under full sail and one paddle.

Remembering how they got on to the captain of the *Richard Young* for abandoning the *Ben Avon* reminds me how the Duke of Edinburgh done a lot worse. He came to Harwich to inspect the old HMS *Penelope*, which was just back from Egypt where she'd been bombarding Alexandria and

1. Paddle steamer converted to screw and renamed *Brandon*. Sold in 1905.
2. Paddle steamer built 1880, sold 1896. Popular with passengers on the Antwerp service.
3. Started 1864 as cattle and cargo carrier. Converted to screw and sold 1907.
4. Built by Earle's of Hull 1883, first of a class familiar for 25 years. Twin screw, two funnels, reciprocating engines. Sold 1907.

done more damage to herself than she did to Alexandria by all accounts.

He was supposed to inspect the coastguards as well, but he never did. Instead he humbugs off in a hurry in his Admiralty yacht for Sheerness. When he gets to the North East Gunfleet there is a German barque called *Wodan* ashore there, with Lewis's diving smack *Cupid* attending to her. The *Cupid* signals to the Royal yacht to stop, but what does he do? He alters course so as not to be spoken to. The Germans were in the rigging and the skipper of the *Cupid* said you could hear them hollering.

When he gets to Sheerness His Royal Highness sends a telegram to Harwich saying this barque is in need of assistance, but by this time ten of the crew had been washed out of the mizzen rigging. The captain was lucky. He had gone forward to get some rowlocks, and he saw them go. The *Cupid* and the *Faith* brought in him, and three other survivors. The lifeboat got the Duke's message around three o'clock in the afternoon and went out, but by then there was nothing to see bar wreckage.

The *Free Press* let fly. 'It would have been more use if the noble Duke had returned to Harwich and towed the lifeboat out or attempted to render assistance' is what they printed. Mr Bigger, MP, got on his hind legs in Parliament, but seeing the Duke was one of the Royal family and not just a Harwich lifeboatman they gave him a whitewash. 'The course adopted by the Duke had received the approval of the Admiralty' come the reply.

CHAPTER NINETEEN

The Steam Lifeboats

What with thing having reached the state I've just described, rowing and towing seemed to be getting a bit old-fashioned, and a lot of them in Harwich were saying a steam lifeboat was the only thing would answer.

So presently, in 1890, the Institution come up with one called the *Duke of Northumberland*.[1] That was the first time they'd tried steam, and the thing about her was they didn't like to have a propellor on account of it getting fouled up in a tangle of wreckage, so she kind of sucked the water in through her bottom and blew it out through her sides to make her go ahead or astern or even sideways.

What a lot of people in Harwich hoped was that she'd be a cruising lifeboat, and be out and about in bad weather, keeping an eye on such places as the Burying Ground, like the scropers had always done. The lifeboats in Norway do that; they go cruising with the fishing fleet, same as the Bethel boats do among the smacks on the Dogger, though souls is what they're after salvaging which they do by singing a lot of Sankey and Moody and giving them tracts and bibles to keep their minds off the Schnapps gin the Dutch copers are offering them.

That seemed to me the right idea but they never tried it. No, she just lay in the harbour and when she was called she towed the *Springwell* behind her. She was designed to go all in alongside of wrecks but they dursn't. For one thing there was an engineer and two stokers battened down under the deck with a damn great fire and boiler, and if anything had happened to her there wasn't nothing to be done for them.

So they just used her for a tug, which the *Harwich* or *Merrimac* could do just as well or better, seeing that for getting through the water a pair of paddles was better than all this sucking and blowing.

But the main trouble was that after all these years there was still no way

---

1. Fifty-footer, 12 foot beam or 14 ft 3 ins including her padding, 21 tons, 170 h.p., steel-built. She drew three foot three inches loaded with three tons of coal, her crew and thirty passengers.

of calling her out. Six years after they'd taken up the Sunk cable there was a Royal Commission report that recommended cables to five lightships – the North Goodwin, the Kentish Knock, the Shipwash, Haisborough, and Scarweather. That was going to cost around £2,000 for the Shipwash, which they done not long after, but at the time nobody done nothing because they said all the money for that year was spent.

That same year, which was the worst Lloyd's had ever had for casualties, they put a cable from the shore to the Gunfleet lighthouse, and they said that in moderate weather signals from the Kentish Knock could be seen by the Longsand and from there seen by the Gunfleet. I don't know if they thought ships got wrecked in moderate weather. There was more sense talked in the *Brightlingsea Parish Magazine* than what there was by the Board of Trade and the Trinity. The old rector wrote there, 'Recent wrecks on the Longsand and Kentish Knock might have been prevented had there existed communication such as was at one time established between Walton and the Sunk.'

There was an English ship called the *Enterkin* got on the Galloper. That's a long way out in the North Sea, well beyond the Burying Grounds, best part of half way to Holland.

Well, this vessel made the Galloper lightship about half past five in the evening but didn't give herself room enough to wear. She struck and fell over in the night when the tide ebbed. A Ramsgate smack got an apprentice and two hands, but the other twenty-eight were all lost. There was the usual firework display, with the Galloper rockets repeated by the Longsand and then by the Sunk and then by the Cork.

At last the *Duke of Northumberland* did get out and had to go from lightship to lightship bawling out to the crews. When she finally got there there was nothing to be done. The Shipwash never picked up the signals; if she had, the Aldeburgh lifeboat could have been there in two and a half hours with the flood tide. The *Free Press* said we hadn't learned nothing since the *Deutschland* seventeen years before. They said we was actually worse off than in the wars with Bonaparte, when there was a system of signals all round the coast, which were kept for a while against smuggling and then done away with.

Besides Aldeburgh, there was two lifeboats in Harwich, two more at Walton and one at Clacton, all idle and ignorant while those twenty-eight chaps drowned, all because the Trinity wouldn't pay for a man in a room at a post office. Not long after this they put the cable to the Sunk back again and then that was alright for the lifeboats to lay and wait to be called, but in the time when there weren't no scropers cruising nor yet no proper

way for the lightships to call the shore, it would have been better to have
had fewer lifeboats and kept one of them at sea, to my thinking.

But that wasn't the way of it. The different places liked to have their
own boats. They took a pride in them and they reckoned they was good
for the places that had them. The Institution wouldn't never touch
government money for fear of interference, and when you consider how
much they talked in Parliament and the Board of Trade and how little
they done you can see what they meant. The fact remains there was still
a hell of a lot of chaps getting drowned at sea and a hell of a lot of people
ashore writing each other letters and reports saying there was nothing
they could do about it.

I don't want to suggest the *Duke of Northumberland* didn't do no good.
She done several good jobs the two years we had her.

The *Achilles* I've mentioned already. A year after that she towed the
reserve lifeboat out to the Longsand to a three-masted schooner called the
Mercury, bound from Grangemouth to Buenos Aires with coal, and got
the twelve hands out of her. They were lucky, for she'd been on the sand
for twenty-six hours and the Sunk had been firing all day, but no one
couldn't hear on account of the wind being a gale from the north-west.

Some of the lifeboat crew went out next day in the smack *Kitty* to see
if there was anything worth salvaging. They got a few sails and spars, but
the vessel was sanding up so fast she was pretty well buried. Maybe that
was called the Burying Ground because that buried ships as well as men.

Then the *Duke of Northumberland* went away to New Brighton and later
to Holyhead, and we had another called the *City of Glasgow*, because that's
where most of the money was raised, and they had to take her all the way
there to be christened. She had a foot more beam, and she had her steam
capstan on the engine house instead of the fo'c'sle. She was another sucker
and blower but her machinery was different. She had two vertical pumps
working through two inlets on her skin driven by a 200 horse-power
compound engine. They reckoned she could use what they called lateral
propulsion to stop herself being dashed against a ship's side. She had a
crew of seven with an engineer and two stokers. The *Free Press* said the
crew were to be employed full-time 'so the boat would always be ready
and possibly will often be cruising about among the dangerous sands on
the East Coast', but again that never come about.

She wasn't much improvement on the *Duke of Northumberland*. The
Institution tried to transfer her for six months to Gorleston, but they gave
her one trial in a breeze of wind and wouldn't have nothing to do with

Harwich steam lifeboats. The Duke of Northumberland (above and left) was the RNLI's first use of steam in 1891. She was followed in 1894 by the City of Glasgow (below). Both were 'jet-propelled', pumping water in through holes in the bottom and out through holes in the sides. Screws and paddles were thought too vulnerable, but the idea was not a success.

Wreck of the Berlin, seen (above) shortly before the disaster in 1907. Right: The broken hull revealing one of the boilers. Below: Showing the lattice light tower and the rails down which a cart was pushed to recover the last bodies.

her, so we had to have her back. She done half-a-dozen jobs in the six years she was here.

The biggest was when a German barque called the *Pampa* was on the Maplins. The Aldeburgh boat was in Harwich after landing a shipwrecked crew, so she went along with her, and the *True to the Core* was there too. Between them they helped throw overboard 1,260 barrels of cement weighing 300 tons, but they couldn't shift her. Then a Watkins tug came and got her off with the help of one of Paul's Ipswich tugs, the *Spray*.

On her way home the Aldeburgh boat found a Norwegian ice barque called the *Magdimenta* on the Heaps and took sixteen men out of her. The Institution gave a reward for that, but left the *Pampa* as a salvage claim, she being nearly new and worth something. The tugs got the best of it with £550 to the Londoner and £300 to the *Spray*. The three lifeboats got £450 between them.

They could see by now this patent propulsion wasn't no good, so they built a second *City of Glasgow* which had a screw in a tunnel like they still have, and she reigned right up to the War. She could work on her own, but they seemed to think they had to have a second boat, same as they always had. So after the second *Springwell* was scrapped they sent another pulling and sailing boat, the *Ann Fawcett*. She was a forty-three-foot Watson type, but she never done much.

Now the lifeboats are all done away with at Harwich like a lot of other things.[1]

1. For the restoration of the lifeboat since the time of this yarn, see Preface.

CHAPTER TWENTY

The End of the Scropers

Now we're a-coming to the end of this yarn, and to finish it I'll have to go back to the beginning.

Time I was at school I always thought I'd be a scroper same as my father, but when that came to getting a job I began to see things different. Several times I shipped in one of the smacks, both fishing and salvaging, but that was only when I couldn't get a job ashore, and I never settled into it regular. I daresay I wasn't the man my father was. That's what he thought anyway.

But I could see things was changing, and not for the better in Harwich. All the old trades seemed to be finishing and nothing coming in to replace them.

The old stone men were over and done with before my time, so I can only just recall the last of them, and as I began to look around nearly all the cod smacks were going to Grimsby and them as was left couldn't get no price for the fish, though they was still bringing them in. I reckon Harwich made Grimsby and humbugged itself up in the process.

Besides that, the new dock at Ipswich was taking a lot of ships that we'd got used to unloading in our harbour. Colonel Tomline what owned half Felixstowe took it into his head to build a dock there, too. He was a proud sort of fellow and when he got beat in an election he said he'd make the grass grow in the streets of Harwich. That did too, though it wasn't all his doing.

Worst of all, we lost the railway boats when the Great Eastern built a new port for them at Parkeston, same as I've already told you. So what with one thing and another there wasn't nothing to do in Harwich. Things were as bad as they had been after the wars with Bonaparte, when the Navy building finished and the old Post Office packets moved away to Dover.

The salvaging died out about the same time as the cod fishing. The old craft are forgotten now, though I often think of them.

The *Reindeer*, she got on the Gunfleet, and Tom Daniels had to leave her there. He and his five hands were nine hours in their boat rowing ashore to Felixstowe. That was the year after she took the crew out of that Boston schooner *Success*, and not far from the place she sank.

The *Aurora's Increase* was run down and sunk, and so was the *Aid*, same as I've told you. Tom Barnard's *New Unity* was wrecked on the Grain Spit, trying to run into the Medway in a gale of wind and snow.[1]

The *Faith* got wrecked on the Cork. William Cheek was stowboating with her, and he went out early one morning and mistook the buoys. If a man of his experience could do that it's no wonder so many strangers got into trouble. Our smack *Secret* got the crew in and they stripped her gear where she lay.

The *Cupid* was sold away and finished up in Ramsgate, and the *Albatross* was sold to Hull around the same time. The *Emblem* and *Thought* were sold to Iceland and sailed out there by Brightlingsea crews.

The *Volunteer* reigned a good many years at Brightlingsea under different owners right up to the War. She done some more salvaging there, in fact some of the yarns of her I've told you, such as when she got the *Ornan* off the Gunfleet, were when she was working out of Colne. But she wasn't so much a salvager at the end as the *Faith* and the *Emily* were. The *Volunteer* was mostly stowboating or down Channel in the winter on the oyster and scallop dredging off Havre and in Eat Apple Bay.[2] That's where they used to go, them Brightlingsea dredging chaps, there and to the skilling.

The skilling was the worst trade of all, I reckon. Half the craft that went there came back smashed up, bulwarks gone and all, and a lot of the others never come back at all. In one year[3] they lost five smacks and over thirty hands in the North Sea. The old rector wrote in his magazine, 'In that vast cemetery we have buried twice as many men as in the old churchyard at home.' He called it madness and folly, but they still kept a-going. They had some of our old Harwich cod smacks, the *Leith* and the *Hawthorn* and the *Swift*, for that, and though they'd been used to going to Iceland they never got so knocked about as what they did in the skilling.

They kept up the old ways longer at Brightlingsea than we did at Harwich. They had the yachting for the summer, and that brought in a bit of money to put into the smacks and meant a lot of hands were wanting jobs in the winter, so they had to go in for their deep-sea dredging. Some of them was coasting, too, mostly the new potato trade from St Malo or

1. See *Last Stronghold of Sail*.
2. Etaples.
3. 1883–1884.

the Channel Islands, or fish-carrying, salmon from Scotland to London or Sligo to Liverpool, right round the top of Ireland, or herring from Yarmouth to Bruges and Ghent or even from Stornoway to the Baltic. They'd try anything. The *Vanduara* got ashore in the Scheldt loaded with dynamite for Antwerp, which don't sound the sort of cargo you'd choose to have, not banging about on the sands there.

They got the fish-carrying because they were so fast. As I've told you, they were like yachts, but for speed and for handling dredges they were terribly low in the water, and that's why so many of them got clean swept, and lost gear and hands if they didn't lose the craft in the Channel gales.

When I think of what happened to a lot of them, perhaps it ain't such a bad thing we did have the railway boats and the Trinity to turn to, even if it did mean the end of the old ways in Harwich.

Back here, the *Agenoria* just died of old age on the mud off the Bathside. John Glover that had the *Increase* kept on working for the Trinity, landing pilots. He lived to be eighty-two, and when he died they reckoned that in sixty-two years knocking about in the Swin he'd saved 300 lives. Of course you can soon make a high score if you count everyone brought ashore as a life saved, same as the lifeboats do.

The *Increase* was one of several craft the Trinity hired for pilot landing. First they closed down the stations at Yarmouth and Southwold and told the pilots to move to Harwich, which was a hardship to them to leave their homes, and in fact some never did. That was because the old sailing ships from Norway and Sweden and Finland and Russia was gone off the Suffolk coast.

Then they decided to have just two cutters at the Sunk station and two at the Shipwash, and they employed our scropers to tend on them and land the down pilots. John Glover done that to the end. But that weren't much of a success. Scropers wasn't used to regular work, and as soon as there was a smell of a vessel ashore they'd humbug off and to hell with the Trinity. So in the end the Trinity said to hell with them and they used their own steam cutters.

Some of the others turned to a bit of fishing, going whitn'n[1] down Channel in summer and stowboating for sprats or laying a few cod lines along the shore in the winter. The whelk trotting and mussel dredging both died out same as the oyster fishing had, but the lobster hooping kept up and so did the shrimpering.

1. Fishing for whiting.

In fact the only trade that did look up in my time was the shrimpering. The railway made that. Thousands of gallons they send up to London now. In my father's time they boiled them ashore in big old coppers in the Navy Yard where they used to boil lobsters as well. They packed them in peds[1] where now they just put them in bags. Then they took to having boilers in the bawley and cooking them alive. That makes the shrimps tastier. They go red and curl up. When they were cooked ashore they stayed white and straight. Yes, I've seen 118 shrimping bawleys sail out of Harwich in a tide. Of course they didn't all belong to Harwich.

But I hadn't no heart to be a fisherman. My father, he said to go to Grimsby, that's where the future is, he said, but Grimsby ain't a place anyone would go to without they had to. No, what with nothing seeming to have no future to it, I reckoned to go for a regular job with a wage. That made my father snort, but I'd seen enough of him always waiting for something to turn up, and I reckoned I wasn't going to have my wife placed as my old mother had been, having to manage for weeks on hopes for housekeeping.

If I'd known what the sailing barges was going to come to then I think I might have went in then. But at the time of day I'm speaking of there was the boomsail ketches knocking about down Channel and anywhere between Antwerp and the Tyne, and I liked to be home sometimes, seeing I was courting then. Or there was a few little things mostly loading stacks up and muck back, with a lot of poking and shoving up such places as the Backwaters behind Walton, and no money at the end of it.

After Vaux died and McLearon took the old Navy Yard he and John Cann set about building beautiful things, like yachts, they were. They chased steam barges like the *Speedwell* off the water. I liked to see them building and go to the launch days, and later on whenever I was ashore I'd take my opera glasses down to the harbour and see another new one come in. But there weren't a lot of them about when I had to make my mind up.

So that was a choice between the Trinity and the railway boats. A lot of the codmen went into the lightships and some done well, finishing as master and such, but I didn't fancy chucking about off the Galloper for a couple of months on end with only my mates for company. So I went stewarding in the railway boats. I didn't mind being civil to people, that was one thing I could do that my father couldn't. He wouldn't have lasted many trips a-stewarding. He'd have given them a bit of his mind.

Now I'm getting past usefulness myself. My eyes are dim and my blood

1. Wicker baskets.

is thin, and I do more thinking about the old days than these strange times we live in now. My old dad what had nothing got on alright because he had to. I don't know you'd say he was happy, but he was content. My grandson that's at college, learning to be a schoolteacher, he wouldn't have no comprehension about what I've been telling you nor be able to understand it if he tried to take an interest, which he don't. He's got everything and nothing seem good enough for him.

But there I go, that sound just like how my father used to carry on about me.

CHAPTER TWENTY-ONE

Wreck of the Berlin

So I reckon the time has come to clew up on this yarn, but first I'll have to tell you just one more tale.

I've told you I went for a regular sort of life, and that's how it was, back and forth between Parkeston and Antwerp and Rotterdam, and then later on it was the Hook of Holland in the *Harwich* and the *Roulers*, and in my last few years to Zeebrugge in the train ferries which put me ashore nearer my home in Harwich.

I was in the *Harwich* after she was changed from paddle to screws, the time she picked up the derelict and humbugged off to Holland with it. The passengers thought that was an adventure, but I could see it was going to do me out of a night home. I thought if there was a bit of salvage I might hear something, but I never.

That was nothing, but a few years later I got mixed up in something that was something. Yes, that's a funny thing, but I got a bellyfull of just what I reckoned to keep clear of.

I'd had a fancy to get into one of three sister ships that were my favourites in our fleet – the *Amsterdam*, *Berlin* and *Vienna*. They weren't quite so big as our *Dresden*, but they were pretty things, proper little liners, with two funnels and two masts, built a-purpose for our Hook of Holland night run.[1] I went for the *Berlin* because she'd got a good old skipper, Captain Precious,[2] that come of a family owning smacks in my grandfather's time, but that weren't a lucky choice.

The night I want to tell you of, which was a Wednesday in February,

1. Built by Earle's of Hull in 1894, 1,745 tons gross, 302 × 26 × 15, speed 18 knots from two triple-expansion engines driving twin screws. They were designed for the 110-mile Harwich–Hook of Holland service with sleeping accommodation for about 300 passengers. They originally had navigation bridges level with the boat deck but were later fitted with flying bridges. The *Amsterdam* and *Vienna* were both taken over by the Navy in the 1914–18 War, the latter being renamed *Antwerp*, and on her return to the GER after the War again renamed as *Roulers*. She served in the Belgian service till 1930; the *Amsterdam* till 1928.

2. See Book Three, 1823 and 1825.

we sailed usual time, ten o'clock. That blew a gale of wind north-westerly and we knew it was going to be a funny old night. She did roll!

We only had eighty passengers and I was glad of it, with three-parts of them sick. There was a company of German opera singers that had been performing in London, and the captain and second mate of a Blue Funnel liner[1] going to join her in Amsterdam, and a little old German boy, only five years old, travelling all on his own, so he was put in the special charge of my chief steward, W J Moore.

Around five o'clock on the Thursday morning they blew the bugles to tell the passengers to get their baggage up and be ready to disembark in half an hour, and then just as we was coming into the Hook she gave a hell of a lurch and sort of screwed round, and then she rolled again fit to chuck everything all over the place and then she hit with such a God Almighty crunch as I don't want never to hear again.

You must understand this Hook of Holland is an artificial entrance they'd made to save humbugging about over the Brielle Bar at Hellevoet-sluis, same as they used to do, and that had great piers a mile long running out to sea to protect it. The north pier was just a long run of great stone blocks and spikes, with a lattice light tower near the end of it.

There was a lot of tide setting to the nor'ard on to this place, and as luck would have it the *Berlin*, running in with the wind and sea dead astern, got caught by a swell under her port quarter that slewed her round to the nor'ard so she was going for the end of the rocks. She answered her helm and straightened up, but then another huge ground swell caught her on the starboard beam. She may have lost steerage way; anyhow, she was washed right up on to them lumps of granite.

I've heard arguments over which was the hardest sand to hit, the Shipwash or the Gunfleet or the Longsand, and my father saying that anyone of them you might hit so hard you'd be thrown off your heels and down on your back on deck.

But this place was worse than that. That might have been made to tear a ship to pieces. That's what it done anyway, just ripped the bottom out of the *Berlin*. I'd seen some poor old collier brigs and such stand up to a fair hammering, and I never thought to see a fine ship like her go to pieces in half an hour, but that's how long it took.

By half past five she'd broken her back. The people ashore saw the lights go out, and they could see the two masts go all askew across each other, being on the two different halves of the ship that had come apart. They put her engines astern when she touched, but within a few minutes

1. Captain G W Parkinson of the *Myrmidon*.

the engineers came up to say the stokeholds was flooded and the fires out.

The steam lifeboat *President van Heel* came out of the Berghaven Basin. She put me in mind of our *Duke of Northumberland*, and in fact the Dutch lifeboat people had been to Harwich and built this one after the same model. The passengers could see her so there wasn't anything what you might call panic. But she couldn't get alongside, so she tried shooting lines. In the end our chaps caught one of them, and just then a hell of a sea chucked the lifeboat back and parted her anchor rope. She didn't have no spare anchor and had to go back to get one.

While she was gone, about ten to eight, the fore part, with both funnels on it, slid slowly off the north pier into the channel. Just the top of the foremast was left sticking out of the water, still showing the two black balls that was the distress signal. If the lifeboat had been there she might have picked up some more of the people; as it was when she came back she had to cruise round looking at bodies to see if any was alive.

All around the same time our cargo steamer *Clacton* came in. She stood by outside for a bit, but couldn't do nothing and had to go on into her berth.

The captain of the Blue Funnel liner was in the water clinging on to a bit of wreckage and sung out to her as she went by. Then the lifeboat got him. He'd gone up on the bridge with Captain Precious and the Dutch pilot and the chief officer when she struck. He said to the chief, 'This is going to be a bad job', and he just answered, 'It is', which was about the last words he spoke. This Blue Funnel captain was the first to be picked up by the lifeboat. He went on to join his ship at Amsterdam, but he never see no more of his second mate.

The Dutch pilot was aboard all the while, because at that time of day the pilots made the whole crossing, and he took charge at the Maas lightship, but Captain Precious had to be given the blame afterwards for trying to get in at all and then not allowing enough for wind and tide. That's what you get for being a captain.

His son was serving as a seaman aboard the *Clacton*. He could see all that was going on and so could the crews of lots of ships entering and leaving, all passing close by, for there wouldn't have been no advantage in closing the harbour. After it was all over young Precious gave up the sea. I can't blame him. I might have done the same, only by then I wasn't of an age for a new start.

All that Thursday and through the next night such things happened in the stern half of the *Berlin* as made me understand some of my father's tales. Some of the people died on deck from exposure and some were washed overboard. The breakers were sweeping her deck and they couldn't cling on to the rails and stanchions. Ashore at the railway station they'd got thirty-three bodies laid out in the Holland Amerika Line's warehouse, either washed ashore or picked up.

Next morning that weren't no better. Prince Hendrik of the Netherlands had come down to the Hook now and he was dodging about in the pilot cutter *Jan Spaniard* and a bigger steam pilot boat, *Hellevoetsluis*. The first chance was around one o'clock, which was low water. We see the lifeboat come again, followed by two tugs and the *Hellevoetsluis*. The only way to reach us was to land on the north pier and get a line from the light tower to the *Berlin*. They anchored the *Hellevoetsluis* and the two tugs bow to stern so as to help the lifeboat get some of her crew ashore. One of them did land, but he had to get back out of it. That was still blowing a full gale, with breakers sweeping over the pier and snow squalls shutting everything out.

Then blessed if four chaps from one of the pilot cutters didn't have a go, using a boat the lifeboat had towed out. We could see them standing in the breakers with a rope, but they couldn't do no more and were in danger of being washed off. So the skipper of the *Hellevoetsluis* calls for volunteers, and six pilot apprentices man their boat to join the four ashore. Them ten chaps come wriggling and crawling down to the light tower, sometimes flat on their faces to get a handhold, but when they get there there's no one aboard the *Berlin* got strength enough to take their rope.

So one of them sees a boat's davit fall hanging from our side and he gets through the water somehow and makes fast to it. The other end they fixed to the light tower about twenty feet up. I come down that rope, though I don't remember much about doing it, and so did six passengers, two of our firemen, one seaman and a fifteen-year-old deck boy, Farthing his name was. One of those opera singers could not hold on and fell in the water, and them Dutchmen went right in and got her out unconscious. They got us aboard the lifeboat and then the Prince said to come aboard the *Hellevoetsluis* and by half past five we was in the Berghaven. We was all brought in on stretchers, though young Farthing, he wanted to light a cigar and walk up. He was light-headed.

By this time there was forty-four bodies in the warehouse and three more women still left aboard. They made several plans for the night low water. One was for the lifeboat to take the same men and the same boat that had got us off that afternoon. Another was to get a cart on to some rails that ran down the pier and take ladders on it. But that was done in the end by a Dutch salvager, Martin Sperling, who was skipper of a salvage craft called *Van der Tak*. He was a famous diver and life-saver, just as well known in his parts as Lewis and Glover back home, so I was told. He'd been out for a look that afternoon, and he got a big paddle tug called the *Wodan* to tow his yawl down around midnight.[1]

He and three mates got aboard by the same boat's fall and found these three women still alive and sitting on the promenade deck with a dozen bodies scattered around them. One of them was another of these opera singers with her sixteen-year-old maid servant, and the third was a German woman with her dead baby still in her lap. Her husband had been drowned. Sperling dragged them aboard somehow and when they was landed that was the lot.

They pushed that cart down on next day's ebb and brought back fifteen more bodies on it. There was only fifteen passengers saved, six women and nine men, and five of us out of the crew. Eighty passengers had gone and forty-eight of the crew, including all the officers.

We all came home in the *Clacton*. Her tween-decks was all coffins everywhere, with Union Jacks draped over them. I forgot to mention, they picked up the body of my chief steward Moore with that little old German boy's body still in his stiff arms.

I couldn't get them German opera women out of my mind for a long time after that, same as them Ramsgate chaps said they kept on seeing the captain of the *Indian Chief* looking like he was trying to reach them and him drowned hours ago. They put me in mind of them damned nuns washing around in the *Deutschland*'s cabin; in fact, I thought of the *Deutschland* several times that awful Thursday night, and how nothing hadn't changed much, though here we were in sight of safety and everyone trying to get at us and they were miles from anywhere and no-one knowing nothing.

I can see them still sometimes, but now I'm older they get blurred in my mind and mixed up with other things, like that skipper of the *Mirford and Trubey* they had to leave hanging in the rigging, and I can see now why John Mills couldn't help but go back for him next day, or that load of kids drowned lying in that *Rochford* barge's boat, same as their mother had been, or that little old skipper of the *Arrival* that they got into Woodbridge river and left thinking he was alright now, and then he hangs himself under his own cabin skylight because he wasn't.

Yes, nothing never seemed quite the same, not after that *Berlin*. Before

1. Built of iron in 1833 at Kinderdyk for the famous firm of L Smit and Co., 272 tons gross, 132×24.

that, when I was younger, that all seemed just like a boy's adventure story, but now, if you get my drift, I sometimes wonder about spinning so many yarns about such hellish happenings. Still, that serve to clear such things out of my memory, and now I'm rid of these tales I hope the old boys I've been telling you of will lie a bit quieter in my mind.

Who, what, when and where

BOOK THREE

Who, what, when and where

Most of the incidents in the foregoing chapters will be found below in chronological order with a note of the source, which usually indicates a date.

There are also many references to incidents for which there was no space in the text. Even so, I have had to omit as many incidents as I have been able to include, for the full list I have noted would have been impossibly lengthy.

I have included only a selection of important dates up to 1812 from which period I have culled local newspaper files. The standard of reporting varied from period to period and from paper to paper, for which reason too many conclusions should not be drawn from the fact that some years seem so much more eventful than others.

A comparison with the lifeboat service records (conveniently published in Malster's *Wreck and Rescue on the Essex Coast*) will reveal a number of services which I have not included, usually because they were not significant in the context of this story. Indeed, one could probably go on indefinitely discovering new tales of drama and adventure. Nevertheless I hope and trust that those I have told, supported by the references which follow, provide a reasonably balanced and comprehensive account of a stirring century.

The references are:

BPM Brightlingsea Parish Magazine
ChCh Chelmsford Chronicle (now Essex Chronicle)
CG Colchester Gazette (now Evening Gazette)
ES Essex Standard (now Essex County Standard)
FWS Memories of a Retired Pilot, Mr F W Smith (unpublished)
HD Harwich and Dovercourt Free Press (later Standard, now Harwich & Manningtree Standard)
IJ Ipswich Journal
JG Notes of the late Doctor J L Groom, including Harwich Customs Letterbook, JG/LB (unpublished)

K&EM   Kent and Essex Mercury
LSS   Benham: Last Stronghold of Sail
OPT   Benham: Once Upon a Tide
SC   Suffolk Chronicle
SWSC   Cooper: Storm Warriors of the Suffolk Coast
S from S   Malster: Saved from the Sea
WR   Malster: Wreck and Rescue on the Essex Coast

Files of the *Essex Standard* and *Ipswich Journal* are available at Public Libraries or the Essex Record Office, but the back numbers of the *Harwich and Dovercourt Free Press* have not been micro-filmed and are not available for public access. Most of the items will, however, probably also be found in the *Essex Standard* files.

The *Brightlingsea Parish Magazine* was, in the words of my old friend, 'as good as the *Shipping Gazette*' from 1872 to 1917 when the Rev (later Canon) Arthur Pertwee was rector and wrote a feature, 'Gossip from the Hard'. He went to sea in the smacks, making a number of oyster-dredging voyages to Terschelling, and was responsible for the memorial tablets around Brightlingsea church commemorating lives lost at sea. (See *Last Stronghold of Sail* and Wakeling: *Stories Behind the Tiles*, 1973). The magazines are in the Library of Essex Archaeological Society at Colchester.

The account of the Clacton boatmen and the *Kronprincess Louise* is from the unpublished memories of A A Jefferies, a Brightlingsea Lloyd's agent. The date is not mentioned.

The encounter between the Brightlingsea and Harwich stone dredgers is from the ms of a story sent by Mr Jefferies in 1908 to the *Wide World* Magazine, under the title 'A Nautical Tournament'. He states that the incident occurred 'about fifty-five years ago', that is in 1853, in which year there was a skirmish with strike-breakers. I do not know if the story was published.

Albert Aldous Jefferies was related by marriage to the Brightlingsea ship-building family, as his name shows. (A boat-builder member of the family returned the compliment with the name Albert Jefferies Aldous.) He refers to the Brightlingsea participant as 'Tommy', and adds a note that the case came to court, but 'The magistrates let 'Tommy' off with a caution and a small fine.' I have not succeeded in finding the report of the case, but from other hints I suspect 'Tommy' may have been his father, appointed Water Bailiff in 1824.

The account of the boarding of a Russian barque on the Shipwash by a Bawdsey salvager is from an article by 'Kentish Knock' in the *Yachting Monthly*, December, 1912.

The details of the stone trade are from many sources, including Dr Groom's transcripts of account books kept between 1840 and 1848 by George Monger, who worked several boats, including *Good Intent*, *Mineral* and *Two Brothers*. Sometimes he only values stone at 1s 6d a ton, possibly when he was only taking a share from another owner's boat. For a fuller history of the trade see *Victoria History of Essex*, Vol II.

Mr J W Wood's ideas for training schemes and life rafts were in a paper read to the Society of Arts in 1870 (ES March 25).

Some minor discrepancies will be noted. For example, the smacks *Ranger* and *Violet* are described in 1859 as 'both of Ipswich', whereas I think the former belonged to Harwich and the latter to Woodbridge. Six years later the *Violet* is 'of Aldeburgh'. In 1890 the *Alpha* 'of Aldeburgh' is concerned in a salvage, but the following year the claim is made by the *Alpha* 'of Harwich'. Apart from possible errors in contemporary reporting, these discrepancies easily arise from referring sometimes to a smack's port of registry and sometimes to her home port. Aldeburgh was not a port of registry, and many of its smacks were registered at Woodbridge. Ipswich, like Colchester, was a port of registry without a fleet of smacks in the town itself, and 'of Ipswich' usually (though not necessarily) refers to Pin Mill, which was in practice more closely associated with Harwich.

I have therefore not attempted to reconcile such apparent contradictions, nor have I always corrected the sometimes picturesque spelling of the names of foreign places and ships. I have, however, occasionally quoted a reference within inverted commas to indicate it is either quaint or questionable.

1671
Great storm destroys seventy-five ships on the East Coast. 'The sea is so full of wreckage on these coasts that those at sea are forced to look out sharp to steer clear of it.' **OPT.**

1692
One hundred and fifty of a fleet of 200 light coasters wrecked on the North Norfolk coast, together with fifty ships outward bound from the Wash – a total destruction in one night of 200 ships and over 1,000 lives. **OPT.**

1744
Colchester (50 guns) wrecked 'between Kentish Knock and Longsand.' Scuttled 'to prevent sinking' (in deep water presumably). Fired 140 guns, answered by warship at the Nore, which could not assist due to contrary wind. Long boat lost with thirteen men. Another boat sent to Harwich and returned with six smacks which saved 365 men. 'The sick all perish'd, which were 16 in number. In all we lost about 40 Men and one Lieutenant.' Letter from surgeon's mate printed in cutting (from unidentified source) pasted in author's interleaved copy of *Harwich Guide* (1808) in Colchester Public Library.

1770
Great gale of December 18, with thirty vessels wrecked off Lowestoft and (according to tradition) twenty on Longsand. Followed by proposal for lifeboat at Lowestoft. **OPT** and **S from S.**

1789
Great gale of October 30. Ten ships ashore at Yarmouth, forty between Yarmouth and

1789—*cont.*

Southwold, eighty fishing boats lost on Norfolk coast, 120 bodies ashore. Followed by Trinity House lightship at Newarp Sand and lighthouse at Happisburgh. **S from S.**

Roman or Aquatic Cement patented by James Parker at Northfleet, Kent. *Victoria History of Essex* (Vol 2).

1807

Great February gale. Many wrecks including Revenue cutter *Hunter* at Happisburgh and gun brig *Snipe* at Yarmouth. Followed by invention of George Manby's mortar. **S from S.**

1808

John and Jane of Rowhedge (Robert Prestney) broke from anchor while salvaging brig ashore on Foulness. Drove ashore and wrecked on Sheerness with loss of two lads left aboard, one of them Prestney's son. **OPT.**

1812

Sale of gear including four carriage guns from snow *Thetis* of South Shields (230 tons) 'lately lost near Landguard Fort.' **SC May 9.**

Unnamed brig, about 130 tons, lost on 'East Burners' (? Burrows). Crew feared lost. Cutter *Maria* saving materials. **SC Sept 5.**

Sale at Wivenhoe of *See Einhorn*, 351 tons, nearly new, built for Greenland Whale Fishery. Had been ashore on West Barrow. **SC Dec 5.**

Prussian ship *Curier* (300 tons) wrecked on Shipwash. Salvage supervised by privateer *Courier*. Followed by warning to owners and masters to hand in cargo and materials from Prussian ship *Courier* (sic). **OPT** and **SC Dec 12.**

1813

'Life-saving bed or mattress' exhibited in Harwich harbour by 'a man named Goodwin of the Alien Office boat'. His body remained 'erect about one-third out of the water.' **IJ Mar 6.**

Sale at Orford of butter and cheese from Prussian ship *Curier*. **IJ Apr 3.**

Sale at Harwich of rum and other cargo from ship *Atlas* from Jamaica 'wrecked on the Kentish Knock in 1811.' **SC Apr 3.**

Transport *Euphemia* of London lost or Sunk. Crew saved. Dutch vessel lost in same place on same day. **SC Jan 15.**

Essex Vice-Admiralty publish warnings about anchors, cables, cordage, etc., concealed and fraudulently disposed of. **CG Oct 8.**

Sale of wreckage at Brightlingsea including sixty-four-foot mast. **CG Nov 26.**

'Signal stations on Essex coast now all discontinued and Lieutenants who commanded them discharged.' (But see also September 2, 1815.) **CG Dec 17.**

Sale at Harwich from ship *Maria and Francisca*, 250 tons, 'wrecked on her voyage from Hamburg to Porto Rico', including 'the larboard side and stem of the said ship.' **CG Dec 24.**

1815

Loss of Howard's Manningtree smacks. **CG May 6.**

Boat of Revenue cutter *Fox* of Colchester meets armed smuggling lugger. Four killed, including officer and his brother. Three wounded. Only one unhurt. Two smugglers (Gilham and Brock) hanged at Execution Dock. **CG Aug 12** and **Dec 9**, and **Feb 3, 1816.**

Signal posts around coast 'to be kept up during the peace on an improved system. They are to use telegraphic signs. The purpose is to prevent smuggling.' **CG Sept 2.**

Brig *Planter* (Petersburg to London, tallow) ashore on Ridge, towed in by Revenue cutter *Hawke* and three smacks. Twenty casks tallow on board – rest thrown overboard near Smith's Knoll (which suggests the stranding was not on the Essex Ridge). **CG Sept 23.**

Crew of *Hercules*, 'lately wrecked on the Sunk', sent home in the Colchester-Ostend packet *Success*. **CG Oct 7.**

Dutch hoy *Ouvermagh* (Amsterdam to London, apples, cheese and silk) founders in Harwich Rolling Grounds. Crew saved. **CG Oct 28.**

D O Blyth of Colchester appointed Deputy of Cinque Ports jurisdiction. Publishes warning as to concealing 'direlict [sic] property, whether flotson, jetson, lagan or otherwise.' (The references are respectively to material found afloat, material washed ashore, and material sunk – particularly buoyed with a view to recovery, a practice increasing at this time.) **CG Nov 11.**

Sale from brig *Friendship*, wrecked on Knoll. **CG Dec 16.**

Brig *Palemon* (Zante to Hull, fruit) on Andrews, Thursday night. Two men in boat belonging to Heselton and Billingsley get aboard, losing boat. Then could not be reached till Saturday. Captain with broken leg hoisted to tops each tide. **CG Dec 16.**

Sale of part wreck and cargo of ship *Adrof* (Jacobstadt to London, tar) wrecked in Swin. **CG Dec 23.**

1816
Sale of *Johanna Sophia* of Rotterdam (60 tons) 'as she now lies on the Bathside' and snow *Minerva* of North Shields (190 tons) with 200 chaldrons of coals 'as she now lies sunk near the breakwater.' **CG Feb 10.**

Lease of Harwich lighthouse renewed to Major General Rebow on condition he 'rebuilds them on a given plan and exhibits lights upon an improved mode.' **CG Jul 20.**

Vice-Admiralty advertise warning about concealment and disposal of salvage 'despite my warning of October 1814.' **CG Oct 12.**

Brig *Exmouth* (Aberdeen to Sheerness, stone) lost on West Rocks. Crew saved. **CG Nov 2.**

Warning following pillaging of sloop *Two Brothers* (Manningtree to London) ashore on Nore. **CG Nov 9.**

Good Intent of Yarmouth (from Liverpool, slates) wrecked on Shipwash. Crew saved. **CG Dec 14.**

1817
Revenue cutter *Ranger* of Yarmouth has three killed, seven wounded in fight with smuggling lugger, thirty-six men, twelve nine-pounders. Two men and boy seized, rest escape. Cargo worth £80,000. **CG Mar 29.**

Boat belonging to Revenue cutter *Viper* of Harwich 'employed on the newly-adopted system for the prevention of smuggling' lost at sea with all hands, all inhabitants of Harwich. **CG Dec 6.**

1818
Boat belonging to *Rose* cutter of Harwich lost with five men, including Samuel Dunnage, pilot. **CG Jan 17.**

Sales of rice, cotton and 'munject' from East Indiaman *Marquis of Wellington* (653 tons) 'as she lies on the Mouse Sand.' Followed by repeated warnings to salvagers. **CG Mar 21, 28, May 2, Nov 14 and 28.**

Brig *Maria* of North Shields lost on Shipwash. Crew into Harwich. **CG Apr 11.**

Sloop *Industry* (Gainsborough to London) wrecked on Sunk. Captain drowned, crew into Harwich. Cargo (earthenware) into Wivenhoe. **CG Apr 25.**

'Ship' *Eliza* (Memel to Bristol) lost on Kentish Knock. Timber into Harwich. **CG Aug 15.**

Snow *Alert* of Whitby (Newcastle to Maldon, coals) on Knoll, then sinks in two-and-a-half fathoms. Cargo out and 'expected ship will be weighed.' **CG Aug 15.**

Playing cards (432 packs) seized by Revenue cutter *Eagle* burned at Harwich by 'Commissioners of Her Majesty's Stamp Office.' **CG Dec 26.**

1819
Brig *Hartley* of Dundee (oats) wrecked in Spitway. Crew in by *Good Intent* of Brightlingsea. **CG Mar 6.**

Trinity House start licensing pilots in Colne. **CG Aug 15.**

'Large foreign built ship' *Susannah* of London (from Archangel, tar and tallow) brought into Harwich by two Barking smacks. Found abandoned and full of water off Lowestoft. **CG Sept 25.**

Revenue cutter *Eagle* brings in *Huzza* lugger of Boulogne (crew twenty-three, eleven French, twelve English) after 'desperate resistance.' **CG Nov 24.**

1820
'A Scotch trader having on board about 200 men, women and children belonging to the Veteran Battalion, bound to Chatham, struck on the Cork and knocked her rudder off.' Got off without casualties. **CG Jan 1.**

Sale of *Phoenix* of London (145 tons) 'on the beach at Walton-on-the-Naze where she lies.' **CG Mar 18.**

Many ships on Gunfleet full of water, including *Curlew* and *Boyne*. *Ann* of Whitby on the Main at back of Landguard. **CG Oct 28.**

Vice-Admiralty Court warning about wagons carrying mahogany from ship *Robert*. **CG Nov 4.**

Schooner wrecked on Cork with loss of all nine hands. Leading to campaign to provide lifeboats at Harwich and Brightlingsea and formation of Essex Life Boat Association 'the preservation of lives to be the sole object.' Trinity House contributes 100 guineas. **CG Nov 28, Dec 2 and 30 and Jan 13, 1821.**

Sale at Colchester of '2500 gallons of the finest Hollands Geneva ever imported, saved from the *Maria* of Dover, lately stranded on the Burrows Sand.' **OPT.**

1821
W Brasted of Brightlingsea, master of smack

1821—*cont.*

Friendship, brought from Portsmouth to 'the public office Union Hall' to answer charge of stealing collier's anchor and chain sold by him to Rotherhithe anchorsmith for £33. Result not found. **CG Mar 10.**

Life-saving air jacket shown at Harwich. Plans for society to supply it to 'such persons as may go to vessels in distress in the proportion of one to every three men.' **CG May 5.**

Advertisement of launch of 'Essex Life Boat.' (Postponed to September 11.) **CG Aug 4.**

Sale of timber cargo from *Friede*, of and from Hamburg. **CG Oct 13.**

Experiments to signal ships in distress from Landguard. Two blue lights and guns at night, two flags by day, adopted. **CG Oct 20.**

'In view of impractibility of crew reaching (Harwich) lifeboat on present moorings which would have required at least two hours to fit her for service . . . should be placed on truck and kept in the jetty battery or cement mill yard during winter months.' **CG Nov 17.**

Friendship of Sunderland sinks in deep water after having struck a sand. **CG Dec 29.**

1822

Brig *Ann* (South Shields to London) wrecked on 'Neaps' (? Heaps) Sand. Crew and most materials into Brightlingsea. Essex Life Boat Association award 20 guineas to *Providence* (Matthews). Four of crew go off in coble at Corton to seek passage home. Ship picks up boat but tows it under with loss of three of *Ann*'s men. Later *Ann* of South Shields reported assisted into Gothenburg, dismasted. **CG Jan 12** and **Apr 6,** and **S from S.**

Brig *Westmorland* in distress off Lowestoft in hands of salvagers, who cut adrift Lowestoft lifeboat. **CG Jan 26** and **S from S.**

Sale at Harwich of materials from brig *Mary* of Sunderland (188 tons). **CG Feb 3.**

Brig *Elegant* of Sunderland wrecked on the Roughs Sand. All lost bar captain, saved by Bawdsey salvager J Watts. 'Leads us to ask why the Essex Lifeboat was not used and may throw some discredit on that establishment.' Governor accepts some neglect by Landguard garrison for failure to launch lifeboat there. **CG Mar 16.**

Haabet 'of Scheen, a fine Norway vessel' (350 tons) lost on Gunfleet 'though a branch pilot was in charge.' Crew into Harwich. **CG May 4.**

Vessel for London got off West Rocks by *Braybrooke* in easterly gales. **CG Jun 7.**

Fourteen vessels on Gunfleet in gale. 'All will come off except two which are sunk' – *Vigilant* (Hamburg to London, wool) and *Ebor* of Hull. No lives lost. Crew of *Vigilant* after eight hours 'taken up by a collier also foundering.' Sloop *Dove* of Berwick wrecked on Buxey. Crew, and later sloop, into Brightlingsea, followed by sale of materials. Crew of brig *Hertford* on Gunfleet saved by *Good Intent* (Underwood). **CG Dec 14** and **Jan 4** and **18, 1823.**

Spea Nova (Christiania to London, deals) into Harwich after nine-week voyage, out of all provisions bar a little bread. (Usual voyage four days.) **CG Dec 28.**

1823

West and Cliff Foot rocks, Harwich, reduced by dredging for cement stone. Upwards of thirty vessels produce £70 a week. Stone from old Harwich Church sold for £230 for cement making – 'assistance which the pious Duke of Norfolk, who raised the first one, little calculated upon.' **CG Jun 7.**

Four Brothers of Harwich (T Precious) sunk by brig while on lobster voyage with loss of four lives including 'two brothers Lewes' (sic). **CG Jun 14.**

Prince Coburg of Brightlingsea sails with other smacks to assist ships in distress. Reaching Spitway finds ship dismasted. Tries to board but fails. In returning, boat upset with loss of Joseph Thorpe, master, R Frost and J Garrett. (See also May 20, 1831.) **CG Nov 8.**

Braybrooke awarded £10 for assistance to HM cutter *Surly*. **S from S.**

1824

Brig *Malvina* (Newcastle to Southampton, coals) got off Platters with loss of mate. Assisted by Landguard lifeboat *Ipswich*. **CG Feb 29** and **S from S.**

Colville of Lynn, new ship, rigged with jury masts, driving on to Sunk. Crew take to boat and lie at anchor. Picked up next day by *Ino* of Colchester, thirteen exhausted, one dead. Ship beats over and taken into Ramsgate. **CG Mar 13.**

Wreck and part cargo of *Britannia* brought in from Gunfleet. **CG Mar 13.**

Smack *Friendship's Increase* (Pittick) wrecked on Gunfleet with mackerel for London. Crew saved. **CG Jun 5.**

Revenue cruisers test sailing qualities by race from Cork round Kentish Knock to Margate. Result: *Scout* 1, *Fly* 2, *New Charter* 3, *Lively* 4.

Eagle, Sea Lark and *Desmond* several miles astern. **CG Jul 24** and **Aug 21**.

Thomas Jefferies of Brightlingsea appointed Water Bailiff at Colne Admiralty Court. **CG Aug 14**.

Brig with coals 'upset in the Wallet and all on board perished.' **CG Nov 27**.

1825

Sale from brig *Industry* of Sunderland, wrecked on Gunfleet. **CG Jan 8**.

Smack *John and Elizabeth* of Harwich (John Gane master and owner) lost off Heligoland, hired as Hamburg and Bremen Post Office Packet. Crew and mails saved. **CG Jan 8**.

Aurora (E Lewis) leaves two men in boat lying to ship's anchor. *Hope* of Rowhedge (John Allen) claims salvage job. Anchors close by and upsets boat, drowning both men. 'Nearly twenty minutes in water' without rescue. Allen committed to Newgate on trial for manslaughter at Admiralty Court. Result not found. **CG Feb 5** and **26**.

Smack *Ebenezer* (Thomas Precious) towed in damaged off 'Marples Sand' (? Maplins). **CG Mar 12**.

Brig *Northumberland* of Sunderland (coals) on West Rocks. Lifeboat *Braybrooke* got out 'as soon as possible' but finds brig sunk and abandoned. Crew had laid to wreck in their boat, but despairing of rescue cast off and were picked up by another vessel. **CG Nov 5** and **12**.

Utility (of and from Sunderland, coals) wrecked on Sunk. Crew and one passenger, 'a felon heavily ironed', reach Harwich in own boat. **CG Nov 5**.

Smack *London* (Arbroath to London) lost on Shipwash. Crew and part cargo saved. **CG Nov 19**.

1826

Eliza and Jane (of and from Sunderland) lost on West Rocks. Crew saved. **IJ Jan 7**.

Two ships found sunk SE of Whiting Sand. 'Appear to have struck each other.' No news of crews. **IJ Jan 14**.

Mentor of South Shields brought in by salvage smacks after being seen to drive past Harwich and being found abandoned outside Deben Bar. Rewards of 10s 6d each to sixteen persons for attempting to save crew made by Suffolk Association for Preserving Lives of Shipwrecked Seamen. **IJ Feb 10** and **Apr 22**.

Bruce of Aberdeen (Brazil to Hamburg, tobacco, sugar and cotton) wrecked on Longsand. Crew saved. **IJ Jun 3**.

1827

Sale at Brightlingsea of brig *Goole* of Hull (153 tons) 'lately wrecked on East Barrowes.' **SC Feb 10**.

Neptune of Rochester sinks in squall while stone dredging. Crew saved. **SC Jun 29**.

Two Brothers of Altona (Hamburg to Cadiz, linen) wrecked off Harwich. Crew in by own longboat. **SC Oct 27**.

Brothers of Bridlington and *Vesta* of Sunderland (both St Petersburg to London) 'are lying on the Gunfleet. Hopes are entertained of getting them both off.' (See also July 25, 1828.) **SC Dec 29**.

1828

Admiralty removes supplies depot from Harwich to Woolwich. **ChCh Jan 4**.

Admiralty Court upholds Colchester magistrates' awards against 'ship' *Brothers* (St Petersburg to London) and brig *Vesta* (from Memel, timber and grain) ashore on Gunfleet on Dec 17 and 18, 1828, respectively. For *Brothers*, cargo valued £10,000, award £28 each to sixty-four men, crews of fourteen vessels engaged for fourteen days and 'suffered numberless privations.' For *Vesta*, salvors saved property worth £1,000. Award £400. **ChCh Jul 25, K&EM Jul 22**.

Russian ship *Suomi* (Finland to Cadiz, tar, pitch, deals) brought in by Revenue cutters *Scout* and *Charlotte* and smacks. Driven back into North Sea after reaching English Channel, then ashore on Lemon Sand off Yarmouth, losing rudder, foretopmast, main topgallant mast and sails. Six months under repair at Navy Yard. **K&EM Sept 30** and **Mar 17, 1829**.

1829

John Cook loses his hat, his dog, his peter-boat and a ton of cement stone. (See Introduction.) **K&EM Feb 10**.

Sale on Wivenhoe Quay of 300 casks of butter from *Vrouw Maria* 'lately lost on Cork.' **K&EM Feb 10**.

'Large sale of ship's timbers lately lost on Gunfleet' advertised to be held on cliffs of Frinton and Little Holland. **K&EM Mar 10**.

Sale at Harwich including seven anchors of five to twenty-one cwt with 'twenty-two fathoms of three-inch junk,' and eighty anchors one to nineteen cwt. **K&EM Mar 24**.

1829—cont.

Death at Malta of Captain J Cook, RN, for six years Commander of Revenue cutter *Scout*. **K&EM Apr 1.**

Smack *Superb* (Aberdeen to London, stone) lost on Shipwash. Crew in rigging forty-four hours. Two fall in sea, captain and two others remain lashed in, unconscious. Boat from smack *Paul Pry* of London boards but is smashed and crew also take to rigging. Then all saved by *Lively* of Ipswich. **K&EM Apr 8.**

Revenue cutters to be refitted at Harwich Navy Yard following an outcry that they were being sent to Cowes. **K&EM Jun 12** and **Sept 30, 1828.**

Wreck buoy placed over Humber keel sunk on Eagle Sand. **K&EM Aug 11.**

John Cook sues Seamen's Friendly Society for sick pay refused in July 1828. **K&EM Sept 1.**

Barque *Fanny* (London to Newcastle) lost on Shipwash. Crew saved. **K&EM Oct 20.**

Sale of salvage at Brightlingsea from ship *Wavertree* (250 tons, Hamburg to Liverpool) lost on Longsand and brig *Agenor* 'lately lost on Gunfleet.' **K&EM Oct 27.**

Concordia (of and from Hamburg) assisted in off Cork. **K&EM Nov 11.**

'We exceedingly regret that no appeal – however frequent, however sincere, however importunate – appears to reach the hearts of the gentlemen of Essex respecting the neglected, the disgracefully neglected, state of the Essex lifeboat called the *Lord Braybrooke* (sic) and now lying here rotting and breaking as fast as time and thieves can destroy it.' **K&EM Dec 22.**

1830

Sale at Harwich of brig *Francis* of Sunderland 'now lying on shore near the breakwater.' **K&EM Jan 12.**

Vivett of Newcastle wrecked on Shipwash. Crew in by *Pearl* of Ipswich. **SC Feb 6.**

Brancepeth Castle of Shields on Naze, full of water. **SC Feb 6.**

'One of vessels lost on Heaps on 30th ult. was *Elizabeth and Mary*' (Shields to London). **SC Feb 6.**

Schooner *Lively* (Yarmouth to London, malt) 'upset' off Bawdsey. Assisted in by Revenue cutter *Scout*. **SC Apr 24.**

Admiralty sale at Woodbridge of galleas *De Dde Brodre* (72 tons). **SC Jun 5.**

Brig *Liberty* of Plymouth lost on Shipwash. Crew in by *Pearl* of Ipswich (Jennings). **SC Oct 30.**

Bales of goods washed ashore. Boy from *Helena Theresa* of Altona (Hamburg to Havannah) picked up by *John* of Colchester after thirty hours lashed to spar. **SC Dec 4.**

1831

RC *Scout* captures smack *Emerald* of Colchester with forty-eight half-ankers of spirits and finds fifty more sunk. J Barber and three others discharged by magistrates. **ES Jan 7 and 14.**

Prince Coburg lost on rocks entering Bangor with oysters. Crew saved. Owned and formerly commanded by Joseph Underwood who had 'snatched from a watery grave at various times nearly 100 brave men.' (See Nov 8, 1823.) His widow rendered destitute by loss. **ES May 20.**

Brig *Betsey* of Yarmouth (London to Antwerp) lost on Gunfleet. Crew and materials into Wivenhoe by lugger *Aid*. **ES Sept 24.**

Brunswick (of and from London to Hamburg) in with crew of *Brunswick* of Yarmouth (Hamburg to London) which ran foul of her at sea. (This report suggests a journalistic as well as a navigational confusion.) **ES Oct 8.**

Ann of Ipswich seized with small boat and twenty-two tubs of spirits. **ES Oct 8.**

Two brigs lost on Gunfleet. *Maria* of Scarborough (coals and glass, Newcastle to Sheerness) crew into Wivenhoe. *Three Friends* (wheat and barley, Wells to London) crew into Harwich. **ES Oct 15.**

1832

Claim against brig *Triton* of Yarmouth (coals) ashore on Buxey by *Ann and Maria* (J Demperton) and *Fair Traveller* (B. Wade.) Value £420. Award £84. **ES Jan 28.**

Adventure of Hull (about 50 tons, flagstones and Epsom salts) got off Gunfleet but sinks in six fathoms. Crew in by *Princess Royal* of Ipswich 'Pumpstand being of iron supposed to have affected compass.' **ES Feb 18.**

Faithful of Sunderland (coals to London) on Cork. Three apprentices lost taking boat contrary to instructions of master who wished to wait for ebb. Other boat lost. Five remaining crew taken off by *Spy* of Ipswich (Jennings) with loss of boy overboard. 'Jennings has rescued twenty-three in past eighteen months.' **ES Mar 10.**

Claim by *Matilda* (R Godfrey) for value of goods salvaged from brig *Helena Theresa* on Gunfleet in 1830. Linen valued at £43. **ES Mar 17.**

Brig *Wharfinger* of Sunderland (230 tons) on Gunfleet. Crew in by *Spy* of Ipswich (Jennings.) Followed by sale of wreckage. **ES Dec 22 and Jan 12, 1833.**

Smack *Betsey*, lately purchased by J Easter, crossing from Barrow Deep into Swin strikes wreck (it is supposed) and sinks. Subscription raises £360. **ES Dec 29 and OPT.**

1833

Collier brig *Eslington* (230 tons) on Gunfleet. Boarded by two boats which leave without chance of salvage. In getting through breakers one boat upset with loss of William Mudd, master of *Samuel* of Ipswich, two of his crew and three of brig's crew. Remainder saved by other boat. Mudd had Silver Medal of Royal National Institution for Preservation of Life from Shipwreck and had saved many lives. **ES Jan 5.**

Sale of wreckage from snow *Robert* of Bridlington (210 tons) wrecked on Gunfleet. **ES Oct 5.**

Brig *Malvina* of Shields (241 tons, Archangel to London) wrecked on Mouse. Followed by claim by *Liberty* (T Allen) and *Endeavour* (J Clark) and other Colchester smacks. Crews of 'upwards of thirty smacks of this port' (Colchester) saved 1,480 barrels of tar worth 10s 9d a barrel. Award £300. **ES Oct 19 and 26.**

'Ship' *Ellill* (241 tons, Newcastle to London, coals) struck wreck on Heaps and had to be run ashore on Maplins. Crew into Wivenhoe by *Liberty* (Allen). **ES Oct 19.**

Claim against barque *Eugenee* of New Bedford (400 tons, only six months old) by *Indefatigable*, *Henry and Elizabeth*, *Friends Goodwill*, *Lively*, *Pearl*, *Snowdrop*, *Aurora* and *Pheasant*, all of Colchester. Got off Gunfleet and into Wivenhoe. Value £422. Award £200. Followed by sale at Wivenhoe of 'a large quantity of the best material ever sold in this place' including 'a beautiful carved stern; device – a female reclining on a couch with her hand upon the globe, watching the progress of a ship in full sail, bales of goods and navigation books in the foreground, and a cornucopia on each side with scroll and fiddle head.' **ES Nov 16 and Jun 14, 1834.**

Claim against sloop *Lord Brougham* of Wells (73 tons) found dismasted between Gunfleet and Sunk by Barking smack *Richard and John* which

towed into Harwich. £100 agreed in court without adjudication. **ES Nov 16.**

International incident over seizure of Brightlingsea smacks oyster dredging off French coast, including *Hebe*, *Globe*, *Martha*, *Royal George*, *Penelope*, *Prosperous* and *Fair Traveller*. **ES Dec 7 and 21.**

Brig *Priscilla* of Aberdovey parts from anchor in Nob Channel and drives ashore on West Barrow. Crew, bar one, reach Harwich in own boat. Boarded by salvagers 'who were fishing.' R Murrells, R Shed and R Levett drowned in boat upset. Others find remaining crew member dead under windlass with arm broken in two places and other injuries. They pump brig dry but have to leave her due to gale threat and she sinks in night. **ES Dec 28.**

1834

Brig *Juno* of South Shields (159 tons, coals) parts from two anchors in the Nob Channel and loses a third on the Cork. Boarded and brought in by *Pearl* of Ipswich (J Cracknell.) Agreement £85. **ES Jan 11.**

Claim against *Horatio* (420 tons) homeward-bound from India with cargo worth about £30,000. Struck on 'Martland Sands' (? Maplin) then on Knock, then on Blyth. Got off after fifty hours' work by two Colchester smacks and three Southend galleys, in all twenty-two men. Award £150 – £30 to Southend galleys, £120 to Colchester smacks. **ES Jan 25.**

Claim against *Britannia*, found abandoned by Harwich smacks. Valued by owners at £800, by salvors at £1,700. Award 'moiety of the whole value.' **ES Jan 25.**

Brig *Britannia* of Newcastle (about 200 tons, to London, coals) seen to strike Cork by *Pearl* and *Tryal* of Ipswich. Crew about to leave but brig got in. Agreement £82 10s. (It is not clear whether these two items refer to the same *Britannia*.) **ES Feb 22.**

Claim against brig *Downe Castle* by *John and Eliza* and *Dory* of London, *Rumley* and *Abeona* of Ipswich, and yawl *Aid* of Colchester. Got off Gunfleet. Value £800. Award £300. **ES Mar 22.**

Brig *Triad* of South Shields lost on Heaps. Master and two men into Burnham in own boat. Fate of other boat with eight men unknown. **ES May 29.**

Harwich coastguards capture 'boat called a centipede' with spirits, tobacco and snuff. **ES Jun 28.**

1834—*cont.*

Philip Sainty bankrupt. Wivenhoe shipyard for sale. **ES Jul 19.**

Marquis Huntley (sic) (564 tons, coppered, Leith to London, crew 33) on Heaps with troops and Government stores thick weather, wind ENE. Rowhedge smacksmen throw overboard 4,000 muskets and refloat after few hours. Three lost from boat, including two brothers Cook, after volunteering to go to Port Admiral at Sheerness. See also May 8, 1835. **CG Nov 21.**

1835

Sale of brig *Ebba Charlotha* of Copenhagen (129 tons, built at Berwick 1812) 'competent of removal to any place at an easy expense.' Followed by sale of materials of the brig 'now breaking up', and of wreckage of schooner *Confidence* (129 tons) 'lately lost on the Gunfleet.' **CG Feb 14** and **Mar 12.**

Claim by thirty Lowestoft smacksmen against snow *Melona* of South Shields (250 tons, coals) ashore off Corton on maiden voyage. Value £1,650, 'insured with the Northern Clubs.' Award £417 (one quarter). **ES May 27.**

Claim against *Marquis of Huntley* (see Nov 21, 1834) by eight smacks of Wivenhoe and Brightlingsea, from twenty-one to twenty-nine tons, total crews thirty-seven. Smacksmen claimed ship given over to them. 'Was this credible with 45 men on board, an old and experienced commander, a lieutenant in the Navy and a licensed pilot?' Owners of vessel (value £1,500) tendered £400. Board of Ordnance (owners of cargo) referred claim to Admiralty which failed to appear at hearings in May and June. Finally in November further award £900, making £1,300 in all – £150 to each of eight smacks and £100 each to families of three men lost. **ES May 8, Jun 13, Nov 20.**

Friends of North Shields (227 tons) sailed from London 9 am. Next daybreak off Dudgeon, 5 pm off Orford Ness, 9 pm struck Gunfleet in north-east gale. Skiff washed away. Crew left in longboat with only two oars. At midnight and again at 5 am in breakers. At 8 am failed to attract notice of passing brig. At 11 am picked up by another, thirteen hours adrift, and landed at Dover. **ES Oct 23.**

Sale of salvage including 700 bottles of eau-de-cologne from wrecks including *Aurora* 'lately stranded on Gunfleet.' **ES Nov 27.**

1836

Henry Powell, a respected Rowhedge smack-owner aged over seventy, charged with having an anchor lost by the Sunderland brig *Adeline* on the West Rocks in December 1835 with her 'name at full length upon it.' Acquitted at Assizes on ground of insufficient evidence. Evidence by Deputy Serjeant of the Cinque Ports (J G Chamberlain) and the Agent for the Sunderland Policies (J Clay). **ES Mar 11** and **Jul 15.**

Advertisement for sale at Wivenhoe of ship's stores from the *Clingard* (120 tons), wrecked on Gunfleet on passage Goole to London. **ES Mar 25.**

Claim by Harwich salvors, unnamed, against *Ebenezer* (London to Sunderland) which parted from anchor off Lowestoft and was brought into Harwich. Value £400. Tenders £5 and £10 refused. Award £40. 'Court should never lose sight of the importance of rewarding such cases as encouragement to parties on the coast to render assistance to vessels in distress.' **ES May 13.**

Joseph Brown, master and owner of *Good Intent* of Wivenhoe, charged with possessing two jibs from Barking smack *Jane* wrecked on Maplins on October 12 and 'next day completely stripped,' according to her owner, James Morgan. Committed to Sessions and hearing not found. **ES Nov 18.**

Sloop *Susannah* of Colchester wrecked. Alleged smacksmen offered receipt for £400 if paid £200 and on this being refused tried to hole vessel. **OPT.**

1837

Claim against brig *Quebec* of South Shields (233 tons, Newcastle to London) on Gunfleet December 4, 1836, by *Prosperous* (Barnabas Wasp), *Martha* (Woods), *Laurel*, *Gipsy*, *Hope* and *Friends*, all of Colchester. *Prosperous* and *Martha* boarded in westerly gale, but skipper would not engage them till half-hour before high water. They rigged ninety-fathom ropes to each smack's capstan but failed to haul off. Other smacks arrived and crews threw out twenty tons of coal as well as pumping all day. Next tide, with sail set and ropes to smacks, brig moved thirty fathoms. Following tide hauled off into four fathoms with anchor of *Prosperous* on eighty-fathom rope. Finally got into Harwich. Claimed for brig, 'could have been got off first tide. Smacksmen slacked own rope to avoid breaking it and refused to use brig's rope.' For salvors claimed, 'rope only slacked to avoid smack breaking from anchor. Brig's rope not used because tide had ebbed.' Verdict, vessel in great danger. Great exertions. Entitled to liberal recompense. Award £400. **ES Jan 23.**

Death of Captain G Munnings of Thorpe Cottage, ex-master of privateer *Courier*. Found dead on floor of cabriolet after being taken to his lodgings at Peel's Hotel. **ES Feb 17.**

Great gale N to NNW. Many ships in Swin part from anchors. *St Lawrence* of North Shields (240 tons) total wreck on Middle, dismantled and stores into Wivenhoe next day. *Medora* of North Shields (nearly 300 tons) 'taken in arms of eight smacks,' all of Wivenhoe, to Sheerness. *John Hunter* of North Shields (260 tons) got off and brought up in Swin but to avoid sinking run ashore on East Barrow. Crew twenty hours in rigging fearing mast would go, vessel on side with lower and topsail yards in water. Saved by *Elizabeth* (J Pennick) and *Robert* (Robert Tracey). One man drowned from longboat. Followed by letter of thanks signed by master, mate, four seamen and two boys. **ES Mar 3 and 10.**

Claim by two boats (unnamed) against *Oscar* (260 tons, Gothenburg to London, iron and wood) on Lemon. Unshipped rudder. Claimed 'only needed pilot.' Counter claim 'Must have suffered damage as passengers had to pump.' Value £1,800. Award £80. **ES Mar 12.**

Two stone boats upset in squalls. One crew rescued. Other lost two men. **ES Mar 19.**

Norwegian ship 'some days on West Rocks' brought in. **ES Jul 29.**

1838

Pipes of sherry landed at Cinque Port warehouse, Brightlingsea, 'supposed to be from a vessel wrecked on the Gunfleet six weeks ago.' **ES Feb 2.**

ss *London*, arriving at Harwich from Dundee, reports brigs ashore on Shipwash and on Gunfleet. Crew of former landed by smack at Gravesend; of latter, *Brunswick* of Sunderland, at Wivenhoe. **ES Feb 23.**

Sale of wreckage including 'pan boat' from *Betsey* of Whitby (70 tons) wrecked on Blacktail. **ES Mar 29.**

Sale of wreckage from *Moscow* of Hull (421 tons). No details. **ES Oct 12.**

Smack *Robert* of Colchester (Robert Tracey, owner and master) founders off Scarborough, bound Shields to Brightlingsea, coal. Crew picked up by Barking smack after five hours in boat. Built at Brightlingsea 1835 and 'fitted out at an expense of nearly £700.' This 'humane and enterprising young mariner' had saved

many lives including those (wrongly stated as eleven) rescued from rigging of brig *John Hunter*. (See March 3, 1837.) **ES Nov 16.**

Diana of Sunderland lost on Gunfleet. Crew in by smack. **ES Nov 23.**

Hutchison of Sunderland wrecked on the Gunfleet. Captain Thomas Hutchison, part-owner, and crew ashore in own boat. John Crickmore charged with receiving a boat sail; discharged. His son Henry charged with stealing a tiller; committed for trial. Daniel Taylor and Barnabas Wasp charged with stealing doors. Henry Crickmore of *Blue Eyed Maid* was in partnership with Samuel Harris of *Prosperous* 'who has absconded.' Protests in court at triviality of charges, met by chairman's warning that 'even concealing the most trifling items is an offence in law.' **ES Nov 16 and 23.**

Five vessels lost in two days. On Saturday schooner *Ocean* of Sunderland (126 tons) on Middle – a complete wreck; crew into Wivenhoe by *Beulah*. Also *Leda* of Scarborough (221 tons) on Shipwash. On Sunday *Mantura* of Scarborough (210 tons), *Science* of Scarborough (232 tons) and *Medway* of Sunderland (about same tonnage); crews landed at Harwich, Brightlingsea and Wivenhoe respectively. Total loss near £15,000. All three Sunderland ships belonged to same owner. Followed by sale of stores. **ES Nov 30.**

Brig *Vigilant* of London cut down and sunk by brig *Teasdale* of Stockton (from St Petersburg). Crew saved except two boys in bunks – one so wedged in by broken timber that his father could not free him. **ES Nov 30.**

1839

Sales advertised of sloop *Friendship* of Hull and items from her, *Panhope*, *West Kent* and other vessels. **ES Jan 4.**

William and Henry of Sunderland, blown from anchorage in Humber, loses anchors, cables and sails. Masts cut away. Picked up by ss *London* and towed into Harwich, tow ropes parting four times on passage. **ES Jan 18.**

Claim against *Ceres* of North Shields by *Maria and Ann* (Hedgthorn) and *William and Eliza* (Peggs), both of Colchester, *Britannia* of Maldon and two smacks of Southend, totalling 149 tons and twenty-five hands. Got off Nore, November 1838. Tender £100. Award £170. **ES Jan 15 and 22.**

Claim by *Fame*, *North Star* and *Two Brothers* (in all twenty-one hands) against *Hero* of Stockton, got off Whiting December 26, 1838 after

1839—*cont.*

twenty-nine hours' work. Smacks specially fitted for North Sea fishing worth £1,000 each and so cannot afford salvaging unless well rewarded. Value £2,300. Tender £150. Award £200. **ES Apr 19.**

Scotch sloop or smack of about 70 tons is sunk in 'Goldeman's Gatt.' Sail marked P Gavin, Leith. **ES Apr 26.**

Claim against Prussian barque *Mercure* of Memel ashore in November, 1838. Magistrates had awarded £140 to three smacks but refused claim by *Endeavour*. Admiralty Court accept some doubt whether *Endeavour* was engaged, but award £20. **ES May 10.**

Fair Traveller, returning from Harwich, falls in with Dutch schuyt on Gunfleet with three men in rigging. Captain Robert Wardley tries to row to her but boat swamped. Man and boy left aboard smack see mast fall and Dutchmen go, then sail back to Colne. Appeal for Wardley's family mentions previous rescue from French barque on Mouse. £15 donation from Lloyds. **ES May 17** and **Aug 8.**

Egeria of Sunderland (Archangel to London, oats) wrecked on Gunfleet. **ES Aug 8.**

Brig *Severn* of Gainsborough abandoned on Gunfleet but salvaged by five smacks. Followed by application by J Lawrence of *Martha* for compensation for life salvage of crew. **ES Aug 8** and **Sept 20.**

Claim against *Possidone* of Odessa (281 tons, Antwerp to Naples) by *Good Agreement* (J Brown), William Cranfield (one of crew of *Phoenix*) and Samuel Taylor of *Rumley*. Seen on Longsand on broadside. Thought he was off French coast. *Good Agreement* got alongside and took off two 1,600 lb casks. Then kedged off. Claimed 'nothing done but relieve by five tons.' Value £6,460. Award £525. **ES Sept 7.**

Claim against schooner *Don Juan* of Liverpool (163 tons, Hamburg to Newfoundland) by *Elizabeth* of Harwich and *George and Eliza* of Colchester, lying on lookout at West Barrow. At dawn saw *Don Juan* on Mouse 'very close to where *Malvina* was lost some years before.' (See Oct 19, 1833.) Deck casks emptied and 175 bags of biscuits transferred to smacks. Kedged off hour before high water. Award £75, to be shared equally. **ES Dec 3.**

Claim against *William and Anne* (250 tons, Newcastle to London, coals) by *Gipsy* (Levett), *Eagle* (W Easter), *Elizabeth* (J Bragg) and *Adamant* (W Holding.) Lightened and got off using *Gipsy* and five boats to handle twelve-cwt

anchor and ninety-three fathoms chain. Award £240. **ES Dec 20.**

1840

Ringdove of Sunderland lost on Gunfleet. Wreck set alight by fire lit on cabin floor. Vessel lying a-dry with a brig and two smacks alongside. Later got off. Award £350 to R C *Desmond* (Saxby) with letter of thanks from captain published. **ES Jan 31, Feb 14** and **OPT**

Friends Adventure of Mistley, only nine months old, with sixteen keels of coals, wrecked on Gunfleet. Colchester corn dealer fined £20 for receiving sails. **ES Jan 31** and **OPT**

Reports of 'large ship with copper bottom and painted ports, supposed a West Indiaman,' on Knock Sand above Blacktail, and 'another large ship' on Maplins. **ES Jan 31.**

Mary Ann of Greenwich (J Wright) brings in crews of brigs *Dunn* of Ipswich and *Prospect* of Sunderland (267 tons, only two years old). Both foundered on Dogger. **ES Feb 7.**

Industry awarded £30 for assistance to *Ebenezer*. (No details. If arising out of salvage of May 13, 1836 the delay is unusual.) **ES Feb 21.**

Schooner *Fruiterer* (coals) assisted in from Hollesley Bay by Wivenhoe and Barking smacks, including *Sarah*. **ES Feb 28** and **OPT.**

Prussian schooner *Iris* (Stettin to London, 1300 quarters barley) picked up off Cromer by *Mary Ann* of Aldeburgh and towed for three days into Harwich. Award £500. **ES Apr 3** and **OPT.**

Brig *Thomas* assisted in off Shipwash by *Superb* of Greenwich and *Pearl* of Ipswich. **ES May 15.**

Brig *Two Brothers* assisted in off Gunfleet by 'mackerel steam tug' *Queen*. **ES Jul 10.**

Now 180 boats dredging cement stone, earning nearly £400 a week. 'The competition between members of this industrious little fleet for the first turn to deliver stone gives a daily illustration of the excitement of a regatta.' **ES Aug 7.**

Hope of Sunderland wrecked on Gunfleet. Crew saved. **ES Aug 21.**

Brig *Isabella* of Weymouth lost on Kentish Knock. Seven of crew gallantly saved by crew of Kentish Knock light vessel and brought in by RC *Desmond*. Captain, one man and boy lost. **ES Sept 25.**

American schooner *Forrester* (cargo and thirty-five emigrants) assisted in off Longsand by RC *Scout* and cruiser *Flying Fish*. Award £225. **ES Oct 2** and **Nov 13.**

'Two fishing smacks which a few days since brought in the *Two Brothers* (London to Amsterdam, and not the vessel of the same name referred to under July 10) with loss of mainmast, on putting to sea again fell in with the hull of a Dutch fishing boat, about 40 tons, the greater part under water. They took her in tow and with great difficulty got in to port. On getting her ashore Mr Stiles, the harbourmaster, went on board and discovered a drowned man in the net. 'The fate of the rest of the crew is unknown, but from her bows and stern being stove-in she is supposed to have been run down by some vessel at sea.' **ES Oct 16.**

Claim by three Colchester smacks, un-named (total tonnage ninety-eight, total crews fifteen) against collier brig *Premium* on Gunfleet in June. Value £1,700. Tender £75 upheld. 'No great danger.' **ES Oct 27.**

George Pozzey washed overboard and lost from *Aurora's Increase* (then only a few months old) riding in Spitway. 'At same time a schooner drove ashore, fell over and every soul perished.' **ES Nov 20.**

Sunk lightship driven off station by gales. Eight ships wrecked with loss of about twenty-five lives – *Mary* of Newcastle (whose captain swam to another ship), *Vesper* of Newcastle, *Pericles* of Sunderland, *Sarah* of Whitby, *William* of Shields, *Thomas* of Newcastle, *Sally* of Shields and a schooner un-named. **ES Nov 27.**

HMS *Fairy* sails from Harwich and disappears. **ES Nov 27.**

Hebe of Whitby lost on Gunfleet. Crew saved by RC *Desmond* – her third rescue in a few months. **ES Dec 11.**

Laurel of Greenwich brings in boat and ship's company of Danish vessel wrecked on Goodwins. Eight crew, captain, his wife and twelve-year-old daughter picked up in Swin fifteen hours adrift 'with scarce any covering.' 'The females of the party had to remain on board the smack till some clothing was sent off to enable them to come ashore.' **ES Dec 11.**

Norwegian schooner laden with deals driven into Harwich harbour with no one aboard. Crew had been landed at Deal. **ES Dec 18.**

Isabella wrecked on Gunfleet. Two days later *Friends Regard* of Whitby wrecked on Gunfleet. *Jarrow* also ashore but bumped over and sank in deep water. 'Another wreck, if not two, took place on the Gunfleet last night.' **ES Dec 25.**

1841

Brig *Merchant* of Sunderland, abandoned on

Gunfleet, brought in by nine smacks 'mostly of Colchester.' Award £280. **ES Jan 31** and **Feb 19.**

Claim by *Endeavour* against *Brutus*, towed in off West Rocks. Value £1,000. Tender £15. Award £65. **ES Feb 12.**

Ardwell of Newcastle found abandoned and brought in by HMS *Blazer*. Later sold by auction. **ES Mar 5** and **26.**

Smack *Friends* of Ipswich seized with fifty-five tubs of gin by RC *Scout*. Crew of four sentenced to six months, passenger acquitted. **ES Mar 12.**

Claim by RC *Defence* against Russian barque *Theodor Hendrik*, brought in on November 15, 1840. Tender £200. Award £300. **ES Mar 19.**

Brig *Persevere* assisted in off Cork by *Aurora's Increase* and *Romney* (perhaps *Rumley*?) of Harwich, and *Agenoria* of Ipswich. **ES Apr 2.**

Moses of Sunderland on Blacktail assisted into Sheerness by *Britannia* and *Perseverance* of Milton and *New Dart* of Southend. **ES Apr 2.**

Smack *Rosabella* of Ipswich seized by RC *Scout* with '80 to 90 packages of dry stuff, including tobacco, snuff and spices.' Two men sentenced to six months, two boys discharged. **ES May 1.**

Barque *Olivia* of Danzig ashore on Goodwins. Off leaky and ashore again between Landguard and Felixstowe. Assisted in by smacks' crews. **ES May 14.**

Wilsons (Newcastle to London) got off Blacktail and into Wivenhoe after throwing out 200 tons of coals. **ES Jun 4.**

French schooner *Marie Louise* of Nantes ashore on Shipwash then on Longsand. Assisted in by RC *Scout*, *Aurora's Increase* and *Atalanta*. Award £130. **ES Jul 31** and **Aug 20.**

Cottingham's pump tested at Navy Yard. 'Worked by eight men, throws three tons a minute. Impossible to choke and very portable.' **ES Aug 6.**

Captain Saxby of RC *Desmond* reports seeing wreck of foreign galiot on Longsand, apparently lost the previous night. Could distinguish word *Othello* on stern. **ES Aug 13.**

Large Russian barque *Triton* assisted in off Shipwash by *Aurora's Increase* and *Sarah* of Barking. **ES Sept 17.**

Large Prussian barque *Neptune* assisted in off Longsand by several smacks with loss of rudder. **ES Sept 24.**

'The wreck lately fell in with and reported to the Admiralty by Captain Washington of HMS

1841—*cont.*
Shearwater, which has been drifting along the coast to the great danger of navigators, has now drove ashore near Southwould.' **ES Nov 28.**

Brig *Catherine* of Sunderland wrecked on Gunfleet. Crew and part stores landed at Wivenhoe. Coals and other stores into Harwich by stone boats. 'Two other vessels have been on shore near the same place but got off without assistance.' **ES Dec 3.**

Claim by smack *Sea Mew* for saving lives of fourteen of crew of barque *Union* of London, wrecked on Sunk. Twenty-four hours' effort to save ship failed with loss of boat, oars, kedge and cable. Award £45. **ES Dec 17.**

Lapwing of London towed in to Wivenhoe abandoned and full of water. 'Crew supposed to be drowned.' **ES Dec 17.**

Claim by *Hero* and *Aurora's Increase* against *Normanby* (Stockton to Chatham, coals). Got off Cutler and towed in. Tender £50. Claim £250. Tender upheld with £10 expenses. **ES Dec 24.**

1842
Customs provide bonded warehouse at Colchester for tea, sugar and coffee. **ES Jan 14.**

Samuel Woolvet, smack-owner of Brightlingsea, charged with possessing spelter from *Alarm*, wrecked May 1841. Bench 'obliged' to exact full penalty of treble duty (£11 15s). **ES Jan 14.**

Thames of Goole lost on Gunfleet. Boat washed off deck but remained alongside. Crew leave in it without oars and picked up by *New Blossom* of Wivenhoe (Mills). **ES Jan 14.**

Smack *New Maria* wrecked on Longsand. Distress signal (flag with handkerchief attached) not seen by Sunk lightship but ultimately seen at greater distance by *Endeavour* (Lewis) which finds two dead after twenty hours in rigging but saves three, frost-bitten. Later returns for bodies but finds one gone. 'It is inferred that sufficient look out is not kept' (by lightship). **ES Jan 21.**

Company formed to provide patent slip at Wivenhoe. Barque *William and Maria* had to go to Harwich – 'a disgrace.' **ES Jan 21.**

Claim by *Atalanta* against *Neptune* (Danzig to London, oats. See Sept 24, 1841) dismissed on grounds she was at fault in making *Neptune* wear and go on Kentish Knock and Longsand. 'Should have gone to southward on larboard tack, wind south-east.' Claim by other smacks for lightening allowed, over-ruling previous decision by Trinity Masters that they had partici-

pated in original error. Award to them £200. **ES Jan 21.**

Claim by *Success* against brig *Ark* (355 tons) got off Gunfleet October 16, 1841. Value £1,900. Tender £60. Award £85. **ES Jan 21.**

Schooner seen flying distress signals off Leigh 'just below the lighthouse.' *Lydia* of Leigh put four hands aboard, slipped cable and ran for north shore, but waterlogged schooner sank with crew of seven, a woman and child and the four Leighmen. *Lydia* following saw 'punt' drawn alongside and men get into it. Diver later brought up boat showing schooner to be *Brisk* of London (coals). **ES Mar 18.**

Coronation Medal awarded to Capt G Manby of Yarmouth, inventor of line-throwing mortar. **ES Apr 8.**

Sails and spars from *Brunswick*, wrecked on Sunk, handed in at Harwich to Deputy Serjeant of the Cinque Ports (Francis Hales). **ES Apr 15.**

Claim against Spanish ship *Independiente* (Hamburg to Havannah) on West Rocks, by *Friends Goodwill* (S. Wisbey) of Colchester, *Celerity* (J Manning), *Aurora's Increase* (Lewis) of Harwich, and ss *Brocklebank* of Colchester. Mate pointed to Walton Naze, thinking it was South Foreland, and he was on Goodwins. Wisbey loosed fores'l and topsail and set jib and vessel dragged off into 'Gullet Channel' where anchored afloat with rudder unshipped and hoisted on tackle to save stern frame. *Aurora's Increase* lost sixteen-foot boat alongside and narrowly escaped destruction lying astern when ship's cable stopper cut. Next day into Colne with help of RC *Desmond* (Saxby) and towed to Wivenhoe by *Brocklebank*. Saxby 'considered West Rocks the most dangerous part of the coast, more so than any of the sands.' Value of cargo £20,000. 'If allowed to become derelict would have got one third. Asking for one-sixth or one-seventh.' Award £450 which 'appeared to cause much surprise it being supposed a much larger sum would be given.' Salvors threaten to appeal to Admiralty Court but owners offer extra £100 which they accept. **ES Apr 15** and **Jun 24.**

Claim by *Sea Mew* and *Rumley* of Harwich and *Good Intent* of Colchester against *Leocadie* of Dieppe (Sunderland to Rouen, coals) got off Longsand May 20, 1841. Value £400. Award £80. Vessel then sailed from Harwich. **ES Jun 10** and **17.**

Schooner *Good Design* of Arbroath (Danzig to London) ashore on Buxey and then sank in deep water, raised and brought in. Cargo discharged. **ES Jul 8.**

Lewis Cottingham undertakes to remove 'small shoal' discovered in entrance to Harwich. Harbour. **ES Jul 15.**

Schooner *Water Nymph* (Newcastle to Dunkirk, coals) on Longsand. Crew saved. **ES Oct 28.**

Gannet of Newcastle wrecked on Whitaker. Crew saved. **ES Nov 18.**

Hamilton of London (300 tons) wrecked on Gunfleet in gale. Crew of ten in rigging. Next day *Endeavour* (John Lewis) sees mast go overboard with crew. One survivor. **ES Nov 18.**

Schooner *Progress* (London to Goole) capsizes and sinks near Gunfleet beacon. Crew saved. **ES Nov 11.**

Self-righting tide gauge erected on Glatton breakwater, Harwich, by HMS *Shearwater*. Lewis Cottingham to be in charge of it. **ES Dec 17.**

RC *Scout*, cruising off Kentish Knock, seizes stone boat *Princess Charlotte* with one and a half tons of tobacco and twenty-six boxes of cigars. John Martin and Henry Simmons sentenced to six months in Colchester Gaol – Martin with hard labour. **ES Dec 31.**

1843

Schooner *Julia* assisted off West Rocks. *Jemima* and schooner *Jane* off Gunfleet. **ES Jan 6.**

Russian Finn brig *Oberon* assisted off Shipwash by RC *Desmond* (Saxby) – his third salvage job in a month. **ES Jan 6.**

Brig *Esk*, 'a Newcastle trader', blown off the land by gales. 'When nearly a wreck fell in with HMRC *Defence*, which being a powerful vessel got her into port.' **ES Jan 13.**

William and Ann and *Euston*, both of Sunderland, wrecked on Gunfleet. Crews saved. **ES Jan 13.**

Brig *Mary* of Ipswich abandoned, dismasted, in North Sea, got in by smacks *Elizabeth* of Ipswich and *Star of Brunswick* of Deptford. **ES Jan 27.**

HMS *Shearwater* replaced at Harwich by HMS *Blazer*. **ES Feb 3.**

Thomas Barnard of Rowhedge charged with stealing lanyard chain from Blacktail beacon. As he took trouble to replace it, lenient sentence of one week's imprisonment. **ES Feb 10.**

Four of crew of smack *Resolution* of Barking in collision with brig off Shipwash brought in by *Dolphin* of Greenwich. Fate of three others unknown. **ES Feb 24.**

Brig *Traveller* (Hartlepool to London) on Gunfleet. Seen at dawn by *New Gipsy* and *Atalanta*

of Colchester which could only stand by all day and all night. Next day all crew in rigging saved by smacks' boats – six by *New Gipsy* and four by *Atalanta*. *New Gipsy* ran to leeward into Wallet; *Atalanta* to windward into Swin, where ss *Gazelle* lay to and took survivors. **ES Mar 3.**

Captain Isaac Saxby appointed from RC *Desmond* to RC *Scout*. **ES Apr 7.**

Schooner *Delft* of Whitehaven brought in by *Scout* 'with bitts carried away and (windlass) pawl upset.' **ES May 5.**

Stone dredgers strike and obtain better price. Some smacks still working boarded and turned back. 'Now upwards of 120 vessels, including many large ones with four hands.' **ES May 26 and Jun 9.**

French brig *Pere Hitet* (coals) assisted in by *Eagle*, *Lord Howe* and *Friends Goodwill*, all of Colchester. **ES Jun 16.**

Claim against *True Blue* (93 tons, cargo 'anchors etc', Aberdeen to London) by *Sylvan* (Cooke), *Aurora's Increase* (Lewis) and four others, ashore on West Rocks. Claimed other smacks not engaged. Tender £6 to smacks named upheld. 'Any claim should be against the smacks that engaged them.' **ES Jul 20.**

Trinity House to place floating light on Cork ledge to enable ships to run in at night, 'particularly those that had lost anchors in Yarmouth and Lowestoft Roads.' 'Ought to have been placed before.' **ES Sept 1.**

Schooner *Ann Creighton* of Arbroath (St Petersburg to Cork, tallow and hides) assisted in by *Endeavour* (Lewis). **ES Sept 1.**

Samuel Billingsley, shipowner and merchant of Harwich, bankrupt. **ES Sept 22.**

Smack *Olive Branch* of London (54 tons) caught by *Scout* thirty-five miles off Orford Ness with 124 bales of tobacco, and twenty-three boxes of cigars, 'in all about three tons.' Crew of seven sentenced to six months in Colchester Gaol. **ES Sept 22.**

Cygnet (Stockton to London) wrecked on Gunfleet. Crew saved. **ES Nov 3.**

1844

Smack *Ariel* of Grimsby lost on Cork. Crew saved. **ES Jan 19.**

Claim by RC *Scout* and smack *Fox* against *Sheridan Grange*, assisted off Shipwash, December 1843. Award £160. **ES Feb 9.**

Brig *William and Nancy* of Leith on Sunk in gale. Got off but sank in deep water. **ES Feb 23.**

1844—*cont.*

Lewis Cottingham undertakes boring for water in Harwich with equipment borrowed from Admiralty. And uses his patent pump to free the well. **ES Mar 1** and **22.**

Schooner *Aquatic* (of and from Hull to London) assisted off Cutler by smack *Fiz* of Ipswich. **ES Mar 1.**

Schooner *Peace* assisted in by Barking smack *Despatch* and *Rose in June* of Harwich. **ES Mar 8.**

Brig *Sappharas* of Whitby assisted in by *Success* and *Fox.* **ES Mar 15.**

Brig *Alpha* of Sunderland, arriving in Colne, reports she saw brig nearby capsize and sink in five minutes near Sunk. Saw crew of seven clinging to her side. Some of crew say 'Scarborough' seen on stern. **ES Mar 22.**

Smack *Martha* of Colchester brought in by RC *Scout* with eleven half-ankers of spirits 'stated to have been picked up floating.' Crowded court cleared after objections, and three men including Thomas Death, master, sentenced to six months in Colchester House of Correction. **ES May 24.**

Six large stone boats put to work deepening entrance to Harwich harbour. **ES May 24.**

Claim by *Friends Goodwill* of Colchester and *Prosperous* of Faversham against sloop *Major Nanney* of Pwllelli (Bangor to Ipswich, slates) in danger off Barrow. Value of ship £300, of cargo £200. Eight hours' work but no danger. Award £80. **ES May 31.**

Stone boat *Saucy Jack* lost on West Rocks with boy of fourteen. **ES Jun 21.**

Schooner *Coronation* assisted in leaky off Gunfleet, saved by Cottingham's 'two-man pump.' Sold by auction for £385. **ES Jul 5, 12** and **26,**

Prussian brig *Caroline* (Memel to Rotterdam), ashore on Lemon, brought into Harwich by four smacks after master and crew landed at Yarmouth. Later advertised for sale. **ES Aug 9** and **Oct 4.**

Chasse-marée *Le Jeune Edward* (Hartlepool to Bordeaux, coals) wrecked on Longsand. Crew landed and sent home. **ES Oct 28.**

Schooner *Matilda* of Nyestad, cargo iron, 'to Harwich for orders,' ashore on Felixstowe Main, and is expected will become total wreck. **ES Nov 1.**

Danish schooner 'in charge of branch pilot from Lowestoft on fine moonlit evening after having passed close to Cork light vessel deliber-ately ran upon the Main and the vessel became a total wreck. The only excuse we have heard was that the pilot was very old.' **ES Dec 13.**

Wreck of schooner *Hero* (London to Amsterdam trader) on Cork with all hands bar one man rescued by crew of RC *Scout.* Followed by offer of Admiralty lifeboat. **ES Dec 20** and **27.**

Claim against *Ruby* of South Shields (188 tons) on Gunfleet. Seen at dawn by eleven smacks, five from Harwich, six from Colchester. Crews all day throwing out coal. Following day got off with two anchors and into Harwich. Value with cargo £800–£900. According to owners, 'chiefly labour. Local knowledge not needed.' According to salvors, 'meritorious service. Took forty hours. All would have been lost.' Award £160. **ES Dec 27.**

1845

Barque *Governor Harcourt* of London (Honduras to Newcastle) brought in off Barnard Sand, leaky. Proceeds on voyage with six extra hands to help at pumps. **ES Jan 10.**

Captain Saxby of *Scout* reports falling in with wreck of large vessel inside the Galloper Sand – topmasts, top-gallants and yards floating alongside. **ES Feb 14.**

Claim against American ship *Cumberland* (400 tons, Bremen to New Orleans with 153 emigrants). Found on November 1, 1844, thirty-five miles off course, between Longsand and Sunk, when supposed to be in English Channel. Conducted into Harwich. Value £2,278. Claim £80. Tender £30. Award £50. **ES Mar 7.**

Lady Stuart (Perth to London, potatoes) wrecked on Gunfleet. Crew landed at Wivenhoe (many other vessels in with damage). **ES Mar 14.**

Upwards of 300 sail taking refuge in Harwich. **ES Mar 21.**

Claim against *Endymion* of Newcastle (277 tons, Newcastle to London, coals) assisted off Gunfleet by *Friends Goodwill, Mary* and *Beulah* of Colchester; *Rose in June* and *Endeavour* of Harwich; and *British Queen* of Rochester – in all thirty-seven hands. Value of cargo agreed at £117, but disagreement as to value of vessel. Richard Hales, superintendent of the dockyard at Harwich, for owners, valued at £546. Mr Sainty, shipbuilder of Colchester, for the salvors, at £694. Compromise fixed at £625. Compensation to salvors £200. **ES May 9.**

Swedish brig *Riso* assisted in by four smacks off Sunk, leaky, and with loss of anchors and chains. **ES May 16.**

Schooner found wrecked on Sunk. Spars marked *Lady Nepean* brought in by RC *Scout*. **ES Jun 6**

Captain J Washington, RN, reports that following loss of the *Hero* on Landguard a lifeboat commissioned by the Admiralty and built at Rotherhithe is ready. 'The only other thing wanting is to place a low dark red warning light at the extreme end of Landguard Point in order to point out to strangers that the so called "Leading Lights" no longer lead to safety but will inevitably lead to destruction.' **ES Aug 15.**

Sarah of Gainsborough wrecked on Maplins. Crew saved by RC *Desmond*. Brig *Sceptre* (Shields to London) ashore on Middle and abandoned. Got off by RC *Scout* and brought in with seven feet of water in hold. Schooner *Hope* (Lynn to Bangor) ashore on Landguard. Cargo (rails and sleepers) unloaded and vessel dismantled. **ES Oct 10.**

Schooner *London* of Boston assisted off Andrews by RC *Desmond* and two smacks. **ES Nov 21.**

ss *City of London* on Gunfleet, assisted by RC *Scout* and smack *Fox*. Smack's owner and master, Mr Baldry, and one of crew killed in boat by steamer's paddle. **ES Nov 21.**

Brig *Dove* wrecked on Kentish Knock. Crew saved. **ES Nov 21.**

Clio of Newcastle (coal to Marseilles) wrecked on Longsand. Crew into Wivenhoe by *Unity* and *Louisa* 'who sustained serious damage at the wreck.' **ES Nov 21.**

Meeting debates whether to place Admiralty lifeboat, to be named Harwich and Ipswich lifeboat, at Landguard or at Harwich. Decided to approach Ordnance Board for use of boathouse at Harwich. **ES Nov 21.**

Schooner *Sally and Susannah* assisted off Felixstowe beach by RC *Royal Charlotte*. **ES Nov 21.**

Claim by thirty-eight salvors against *New Concord* (Sunderland to London, poles) brought in dismasted on June 28. Value £900. Claim £250. Admiralty Court regrets value so small. 'A meritorious service' but cannot award more than £90. **ES Dec 12.**

1846

Brig *Pomona* and schooner *Maria* assisted by *Endeavour* (Lewis). Schooner *Ashley* (80 tons) abandoned on Heaps. Crew saved by cod smack *Cobbold*, then schooner refloated and brought in by five smacks. Schooner *Lucy Ellen* towed in by cod smack *Swift*. (A few of many casualties over a black Christmas.) **ES Jan 2.**

Dredge came fast aboard *Seagull* dredging

cement stone on West Rocks. Wooden buoy weighing sixteen pounds jerked across deck, hit William Simpson's head and killed him. **ES Jan 23.**

Advertisement for sale of hull of schooner *Ashley* (see Jan 2), spars from *Clio* of Dundee (see Nov 21, 1845) and spars and cargo (railway lines and sleepers) from *Symmetry* wrecked on Gunfleet. **ES Jan 30.**

Schooner *Water Witch* of Jersey wrecked on Longsand. Crew in by RC *Scout*. **ES Feb 6.**

Schooner belonging to Boston wrecked on Shipwash. Crew saved. **ES Feb 13.**

Claim against *Endeavour*, salvaged in December 1845. Value £1,260. Tender £30 upheld as sufficient. **ES Mar 6.**

Caroline of Arundel assisted in off Longsand. **ES May 1.**

Thirty sail of foreign vessels in Harwich to load cement stone 'for the Continent, Mediterranean and elsewhere.' Upwards of 200 boats employed dredging. **ES May 1.**

Halcyon Trader (London to Newcastle) on Gunfleet. Got off by two smacks after slipping anchors which were recovered by smacks. **ES May 8.**

Alert of Whitby (133 tons, Oporto to London, wine and cork) on Longsand and 'early next morning upset.' Master, mate and three of crew took to boat and picked up by smack *William and Elizabeth* of Dartmouth, also one passenger floating on a spar. Wife of rescued passenger and his two children drowned, also another passenger, his wife and three children and one seaman. Cargo shipped into barges for London. 'No bodies found in the wreck as was expected.' **ES May 15.**

Seaman and apprentice of *Good Agreement* of Rowhedge drowned in boat in tow in Swin taking off pilot. **ES Jul 23** and **Aug 4.**

Smack *Ruby* of Woodbridge wrecked on West Rocks dredging stone. **ES Sept 11.**

French polacca brig *Pybeus* of Bayonne (Newcastle to Dunkirk, coals) wrecked on Longsand. Crew in by RC *Desmond*. **ES Oct 2.**

Stump of old Sheers beacon removed on Maplins after causing loss of eleven coasting vessels in nine years. 'Why this was not removed at once we are at a loss to understand.' **ES Nov 20.**

Brig *Dorothy* (of and from Sunderland) wrecked on Gunfleet. Crew saved. 'A number of stone boats have been to the wreck and brought in coals.' **ES Nov 20.**

1847

'Large Swedish barque' into Harwich after being on Cork, *Thomas* of Hartlepool after being on Gunfleet, brig *Spring* after being on Cutler. **ES Jan 29.**

William Lewis of *Tryal* charged with possessing anchor and chain picked up at sea. To pay £1 (double value) and 'the salvage forfeited.' **ES Apr 16.**

William Porrage, mariner and 'well-known diver in cases of wrecked vessels' charged with assault on member of crew of Revenue cutter *Scout*. **ES Apr 16.**

ss *Experiment* on fire off East Coast, sinks in Swin after eight-hour tow by ss *Clarence*, which brings in crew. **ES May 7.**

Claim by forty-five smacks and RC *Scout* following salvage of schooner *Ariel* (St Petersburgh to London, tallow and hemp) ashore on highest part of Gunfleet on October 25, 1846. Claims by three groups: *Tryal* with eight other smacks jointly totalling 282 tons with forty-nine hands; *Eagle* and eight others totalling 271 tons, forty-five hands; RC *Scout* and twenty-seven smacks totalling 300 tons, 132 hands. Value £11,371. Admiralty Court 'take time for consideration' and result not traced. **ES May 21.**

Schooner *Hopeful* lost on Gunfleet. Crew and some cargo landed at Wivenhoe. **ES May 21.**

Claim by smack *Brilliant* and yawl *Dart* against *Doncaster* (Middlesborough to London, coals). Smack, finding her leaky, is offered £60 to get her into Harwich with £10 extra if service lasts till following day. With leak increasing yawl engaged. Finally got into Yarmouth. Value £1,555. Joint tender £150 refused. Award £200. **ES May 21.**

Claim by cutter *Dolphin* and *Rose in June* against French ship *Juliette*, found abandoned after collision and taken into Harwich. Value £3,567. Award £500. **ES May 28.**

Brig *Osprey* (London to Sunderland) 'with old guns for ballast' ashore seven hours on West Rocks but gets off. **ES Aug 27.**

Loss of *Earl of Durham* 'with 17 keels of coals.' Crew reach Harwich in own boat. **ES Oct 1.**

Schooner *Regent* of Leith (Wemyss to Charente, coals) assisted in off Longsand by three smacks. **ES Nov 5.**

Charles Howlett, master of smack *Mischief* of Ipswich, charged with having 120 salt fish from wreck on Gunfleet. To pay £2 (double value) and £5 fine. **ES Nov 12.**

Favourite (London to Bremen) assisted in off Shipwash by smack *Endeavour*. **ES Nov 26.**

Barque *Victoria* assisted in by *Aurora's Increase* (Lewis) after parting from anchor off Orford Ness. **ES Dec 3.**

Brig *Mary Lyon* and *Earl of Vane* assisted in off Gunfleet by several smacks. **ES Dec 17 and 24.**

Prussian brig *Hugo* (Stettin to Bordeaux) assisted in by RC *Scout* and smack *Abeona* of Ipswich after losing rudder ashore on Kentish Knock. **ES Dec 31.**

Caroline (Wyburg to Bordeaux) assisted off Buxey and into Wivenhoe. **ES Dec 31.**

Sunken wreck on Whitaker, 'thought to be *Priscilla*' (Yarmouth to London). **ES Dec 31.**

Schooner *Earl Grey* (Yarmouth to London) abandoned in Swin and sinks the same night. **ES Dec 31.**

1848

Caroline (Wyburg to Bordeaux) assisted in off Buxey. **ES Jan 7.**

Sunken wreck 'on broadside on Whitaker, supposed to be *Priscilla* of and from Yarmouth.' **ES Jan 7.**

Earl Grey (Yarmouth to London), abandoned in Swin on December 24, sinks on same night. **ES Jan 7.**

Margaret of Liverpool (Danzig to Weymouth, wheat) wrecked on Longsand. Crew in by RC *Desmond*. **ES Jan 7.**

Ocean Bride (Newcastle to London) ashore on Middle and sinks in South West Reach. Crew in by RC *Desmond*. **ES Jan 14.**

Conrad of Bremen (Hartlepool to West Indies) wrecked on Longsand. Crew in by RC *Desmond*. **ES Jan 14.**

Claim by *Agenoria* and RC *Scout*, in all twenty-six men, against brig *Hugo* of Stettin. Struck Kentish Knock December 24, mistaking Knock light for Sunk. Came off and anchored with rudder disabled. Towed in by *Scout*, *Agenoria* astern steering, across east end of Longsand through Sledway. Claim £200 upheld. **ES Jan 28.**

Eliezer of Lynn wrecked on Gunfleet. Crew ashore at Clacton. 'The third shipwrecked crew in Harwich in past few weeks.' **ES Jan 28.**

Sunderland brig assisted off Sunk by five smacks and taken to Sheerness. **ES Mar 10.**

Brig *New Commerce* assisted into Colne by six smacks. Agreement £290. **ES Mar 10.**

Ripson of Scarborough (Newcastle to London) assisted into Colne off Gunfleet with loss of anchor and thirty tons of coal. *Lively* of South Shields and schooner *Gloria* both came off Gunfleet and resumed voyages. **ES Mar 31.**

Several vessels from Hamburg 'and other ports of Holland' in Harwich for cement stone. (Due to blockade of Continental ports by Danes, merchants refused to load and some went north to load coals.) **ES Apr 21.**

Brig *Jane* (of and from Newcastle) on Gunfleet. After *Aurora's Increase* and *Orwell* threw overboard seventy tons of coals brig broke up in gale. Crew landed. **ES Apr 28.**

Maria Ramiette (Sunderland to Brest) wrecked on Longsand. Crew saved. **ES Jul 7.**

John Lewis, master of *Endeavour*, with his diving apparatus removes wreck obstructing Spalding river, Lincs. **ES Jul 7.**

William Portuge (sic, but elsewhere Porrage), otherwise 'Don the Diver', using Lewis's apparatus walks under water from Harwich to Shotley, entering water twelve noon, emerging 1.20 pm. **ES Jul 14.**

Damaged wheat from *Hebe* of Lynn, 'lately wrecked on the Gunfleet,' sold at Harwich. **ES Aug 25.**

Brig *Adolphine* 'of Wismar' strikes Gunfleet, then making for Harwich sinks on Halliday and becomes total wreck. Crew and some cargo saved. **ES Sept 29.**

Schooner *Betty* of Port Madoc (for Woodbridge, slates) strikes Cork and fills. Crew and some cargo saved. **ES Sept 29.**

Eleanor of Hartlepool wrecked on Gunfleet. Crew and stores into Wivenhoe. **ES Oct 13.**

'Vessel sunk between Roughs and Sunk proves to be *Jane* of Sunderland, run down by brig *Dolphin*. Crew jumped aboard *Dolphin*.' **ES Oct 13.**

New light shown at Landguard, colours red, white and green. **ES Oct 13.**

'Fine barque *Scandia*, from Umea, deals, to Gibraltar for orders' found waterlogged on Sunk and assisted in by six smacks. **ES Oct 20.**

Cottingham of North Shields got off Shipwash by eight smacks with loss of rudder and anchored outside harbour. Later seen flying signal for further assistance and sank same night in three fathoms. Youth lost trying to render assistance. **ES Oct 20 and 27.**

Brig *Diligence* of Pwllelli lost on Kentish Knock. Crew in by RC *Scout*. **ES Oct 27.**

Two German emigrant ships wrecked in two days. *Burgundy* of Richmond, Virginia (800 tons, 300 passengers, Bremen to New Orleans) on Longsand. Ninety-nine passengers brought into Harwich, sixty-eight saved by *Tryal* (John Lewis.) *Atlantic* on Goodwins; four lost, rest saved by Deal and Ramsgate vessels. Award £41 to crew of Deal lugger *Prince of Wales* by Duke of Wellington as Chief Warden of Cinque Ports. **ES Nov 17 and 24.**

Hope, from London for Wivenhoe, wrecked 'here' (sic). Crew saved. **ES Nov 17.**

Claim by two smacks and two yawls (in all fifteen men) against *Harvey*, discovered on Maplins on Jan 13. Value £1,350. Tender £70. Award £120. **ES Dec 8.**

Brothers, of and from Shields, wrecked on Gunfleet. Crew and part cargo into Wivenhoe **ES Dec 8.**

Sloop *Speculateur* of Trouville (to Ipswich, paving stones) lost on Sunk. Crew saved. **ES Dec 8.**

Brig *Juventus* abandoned on Gunfleet, brought in by several Colchester smacks. **ES Dec 8.**

John Tye and Thomas Randall, apprenticed to Mr Groom, smack owner, charged with absconding. Previous convictions proved and sentenced to three months' hard labour. **ES Dec 8.**

Ocean of South Shields (Newcastle to Le Havre) wrecked on Kentish Knock. Crew saved. **ES Dec 22.**

Norfolk, of and from Southwold, ashore on Pye, and becomes total wreck. **ES Dec 22.**

Foreign schooner reported sunk off Shipwash. Cask marked *Phoenix* picked up. **ES Dec 22.**

Brig *Princess of Wales* of Sunderland (Hamburg to London) wrecked on Gunfleet. **ES Dec 22.**

Perseverance of Brussels (Nordenschluys to Jersey) assisted in off Maplins. **ES Dec 29.**

Mercury of Sunderland assisted off Gunfleet, leaky. 'A vessel struck soon after and became a wreck; no account of crew.' **ES Dec 29.**

Large foreign ship seen two or three days ago on Kentish Knock supposed from papers to be *Merker* of Sondeburg (Hamburg to China). 'Part of cargo landed in damaged state. Were (sic – ? crew) supposed to be lost.' (See also Jan 5, 1849.) **ES Dec 29.**

1849

Large vessel feared lost on Sunk with all hands. Signals answered by RC *Scout*. Proved to be

1849—cont.

Danish, 800–1,000 tons. Cargo, including eau-de-cologne and musical instruments, suggests Hamburg to Hong Kong. Much salvage taken to Wivenhoe. **ES Jan 5.**

Robert Barnard of 'lookout boat' *Violet* charged with having a cask of Geneva. Had been off to schooner wrecked on Gunfleet and brought in crew. Claimed twenty-four hours allowed to report, and Sunday intervened. Case dismissed. **ES Jan 5.**

Brig *Messenger* of Sunderland and brig *Hugo* of Stettin on Gunfleet. **ES Jan 5.**

Wheat landed from *Hugo*, spelter from *Skylark* on Gunfleet. (So there were at least three wrecks there.) **ES Jan 12.**

Two ships lost on night of Jan 15. 'One had been on fire.' Boat found marked *Express*, Hartlepool. **ES Jan 19.**

Sales at Southend of *Hebe* of North Shields (224 tons) 'lying on the flat', and gear from *Catherine* of South Shields (263 tons). **ES Feb 2.**

Sale at Brightlingsea from barque *Columbine* of Whitby (300 tons) wrecked on Maplins. **ES Feb 2.**

Long boat from Neopolitan brig seen rowing ashore at Landguard with five or six men. Drew knives 'with long blades' as Collector gave chase. Seeing Customs men were armed, threw over two casks of brandy. 'London pilot was steering boat but exclaimed when boarded that he had nothing to do with it and begged to be allowed to go about his business.' Master, mate and five crew each fined £100 or sentenced to Colchester House of Correction during Her Majesty's Pleasure. No mention of pilot. **ES Feb 2.**

Abraham of Yarmouth assisted in to 'Handfleet Water' after being ashore on Shipwash, followed by claim by *Agenoria* 'of Ipswich' (Adam Pinner) who said they had difficulty in keeping her afloat. Claim £80. Tender forty guineas refused. Award £50. **ES Feb 2 and 9.**

Cargo from *Angler* of Dundee (ashore on Gunfleet on December 27) is brought in. **ES Feb 2.**

John Salter, baker of Harwich, charged with having seventeen bushels of wheat from *Hugo* of Stettin. Fined £25 with request to Customs to review. **ES Feb 2.**

Daniel Day and George Minter of Brightlingsea charged with assaulting a Customs officer following fracas involving thirty to forty armed men. Case dismissed. **ES Feb 16.**

Wreck of emigrant ship *Floridian* and East India-man *Dyle* of Ostend on Longsand. **ES Feb 16, Mar 23, July 20.**

Claim against Danish schooner *Nicolene* (93 tons) wheat and butter for London. Mistook Nore light, grounded on Blacktail, December 20, 1848. Five smacks manned by twenty-four hands got her to West India Dock. Value £1,500. Tender £125 refused. Award £125. Lt Saxby of *Scout* said weather was 'worse than anything in his 23 years' experience.' **ES Apr 27.**

Nearly fifty cholera deaths in Harwich. **ES Aug 10, 17 and 24.**

Brig *Fleece* ashore on Gunfleet, got off by *Agenoria* and put ashore off Walton. Followed by pillage and prosecution of twenty-eight smacksmen. Also case by RC *Scout* and four smacks engaged claiming on salvage brought in by 'wreckers.' Award £300. **ES Oct 19, 26, Nov 2 and Apr 26, 1850.**

Action by smack *Providence* (40 tons) against ss *London Merchant* following collision near Mouse lightship. Steamer to blame for altering course. **ES Nov 23.**

Six vessels ashore on Gunfleet in one night. All hands (thirty men) saved – from schooner *William* and brigs *Rapid* and *Endeavour* by RC *Scout*; from brig *Beta* by *Petrel* of Colchester. **ES Dec 14.**

Swedish brig *Helena* wrecked on Cork. Crew saved. **ES Dec 14.**

W Barnes, S Barber, D Pittock, W Richardson, charged with having two gallons of gin from *Conqueror*, lost on Gunfleet with all hands. 'Small penalty' of 60s – (double value) and 40s fine. **ES Dec 28.**

1850

Schooner *Amaranthe* of North Shields wrecked on Gunfleet. Six hands left wreck in longboat, captain and two hands reach Mersea in jolly boat. **ES Jan 18.**

Claim by *Lalla Rookh*, *Five Brothers* and *George IV* against *Trident* (323 tons, Amsterdam to New York) on Cork with cargo and thirty-six German emigrants, September 22, 1849. £5,000 offered to *Lalla Rookh* which came out to seek vessels in distress. Others not engaged. But all towed and Admiralty court ruled 'if Master disapproved he should have cut tow ropes with an axe.' 'A simple service,' but in view of value £4,000, award £2,000. **ES Jan 25.**

Brig *Tigress* of South Shields founders in East Swin. Crew saved by *Henry and Mary* of Colchester. **ES Mar 20.**

Ann Catherina assisted in with loss of sails, rigging and topmasts, cut away during a gale off the Lemon Sand. **ES Mar 20.**

Smacks *Anna Maria*, with hams and lard, and *Good Intent*, with lard and female apparel, seized at Brightlingsea. Alleged to be from wreck of *Royal Adelaide* (Cork to London) lost with 200 passengers and crew off Margate. Many bodies washed ashore on Essex coast. **ES Apr 19.**

Johann Frederik (about 300 tons, of and from Bremen) on Gunfleet with 150 emigrants, mostly female. Thought he was off French coast. At dawn seen by *Louisa*, *Benevolence*, *Mary*, *Eagle* and *Elizabeth* of Colchester and smacks from Harwich. All saved after being dragged through surf. Forty landed at Wivenhoe by *Eagle*, rest at Harwich. Ship soon broke up. **ES Nov 1.**

1851

David Deeks and James Fielden of *Aurora's Increase* fined £15 15s (double value) for having sails and ropes from brig *Loyalty* salvaged off Whiting. SFMS awards £20 between the masters and crews of *Aurora's Increase* (William Lewis), *Tryal* (J Lewis) and *Wonder* (George Barratt). **ES Jan 3, 24 and Dec 12.**

Claim by *Maid of Kent* against *Ann Mitchell* (776 tons) assisted off Kentish Knock November 7, 1850. Value £8,445. Award £800. **ES Jan 24.**

Claim by four smacks against *Tino* on Cork, October 1, 1850. 'Only twelve men employed; the rest intruders.' Value £606. Tender £50. Award £150. (For loss of *Tino* see October 7, 1853). **ES Jan 24.**

Dutch galiot (Dordrecht to Belfast, flax) lost on Longsand. Captain, wife, infant and crew in own boat picked up by *Orwell* of Colchester. **ES Jan 24.**

Smack owned by Godfrey of Brightlingsea 'sunk a few weeks ago by steamer in Swin. Raised, brought in and repaired. On Monday nearly destroyed by fire. On Tuesday seized by County Court bailiff.' **ES Feb 21.**

Claim by *Saucy Lass* and *Tryal* against brig *Bure* on Pye, November 9, 1850. 'Only alongside sand and floated off with tide.' 'Slight service.' Award £5. **ES May 23.**

Captain Saxby of *Scout* finds 171 bales of contraband tobacco aboard *Fanny* of Rowhedge. Crew sentenced to Springfield Gaol for six months. **ES Jun 8.**

'To revive trade with Rotterdam' ss *Arab* (300 tons) placed at Harwich by Eastern Counties and Eastern Union Railways. 'London merchants will receive letters 12 hours earlier.' **ES Sept 5 and Dec 12.**

Wreck of *Etoile de la Mer* (Archangel to St Valery, hemp) on Longsand. SFMS award £5 and silver medal to crews of *Aurora's Increase*, *Tryal* and *Wonder*. **ES Nov 7 and Dec 12.**

1852

John Tye of *Good Agreement* of Colchester (William Gregory, master) fined £1 for smuggling Hollands gin, intended as his Christmas treat. **ES Jan 2.**

Schooner *Arrow* of Liverpool (Seaham to Bordeaux) on Longsand. Filled, fell over and abandoned. Crew in by *Aurora's Increase* (Lewis). Award £5 by Royal National Institution for Preservation of Life from Shipwreck. **ES Jan 2 and 16.**

Swedish schooner *Sabina* assisted in off Longsand by seven smacks with rudder gone. Hauled out and repaired. **ES Jan 2 and Feb 13.**

J Mills charged with possessing sails and rigging from wreck of schooner *York* of Goole, wrecked on Whiting on Jan 11. Adjourned, further hearing not traced. **ES Jan 23.**

Customs notice rope overboard from *Providence* and find mainsail weighted with stone. Master fined £5 and double value (£14 19s). **ES Jan 30**

Schooner *Ann and Elizabeth* of Caernarvon (Mogador to London) wrecked on Kentish Knock. Master and passenger lost, remaining crew and part cargo in by smack *Alpha* of Barking. **ES Jan 30.**

Schooner *Agenoria* of Lynn wrecked on Gunfleet. Crew reach Harwich in own boat. **ES Feb 6.**

Brig *Content* of Newcastle on Gunfleet after missing stays. Assisted off by *Tryal* and *Providence*. **ES Feb 6.**

Windbound fleet sailing from Harwich 'gives German ocean a regatta-like appearance.' **ES Feb 6.**

President of French Republic awards 500 francs to each member of crews of *Tryal* and *Aurora's Increase* for saving life from *Etoile de la Mer*. **ES Mar 12 and May 7.**

Brig *Endeavour* of Newcastle (for Maldon) abandoned on Shipwash. Crew in by *Providence* 'of Ipswich.' **ES Apr 30.**

Start of new Harwich Pier celebrated. **ES Jun 4.**

Maltese brig *Cerere* (Odessa to Ipswich) on Whiting. Crew of fourteen in by *Aurora's*

1852—cont.

Increase, which returns and with *Tryal*, *Mary* of Aldeburgh and tug *John and William* (employed on building Gunfleet lighthouse) gets brig in. **ES Aug 20.**

Schooner *Ocean Witch* and brig *Wanderer* ashore on Gunfleet same night. *Ocean Witch* brought in by tug *John and William*. Tender £70 refused. Award £100. *Wanderer* brought into Colne by six Brightlingsea smacks. **ES Oct 15** and **Mar 4, 1853.**

Brig *True Briton* of South Shields assisted in by *Rumley*. **ES Nov 5.**

Agenora of Jersey (Middlesborough to St Malo, coals) on Longsand. Got off but sinks in deep water. Crew in by *Eagle* of Colchester. **ES Nov 19.**

Russian barque *Emilie Elizabeth* (St Petersburgh to Liverpool, hemp and potash) on Sunk but beats over. Put ashore leaky on Gunfleet and breaks up. Charles Richardson and Alfred Jefferies of Brightlingsea charged with possessing hemp. Case dropped on payment of 10s. **ES Nov 19** and **Dec 10.**

Hanoverian sloop *Genius* found derelict and brought in by *Tryal* (Lewis). Value £514. Award £150. **ES Nov 19** and **Jan 28, 1853.**

French schooner *Aleyon* of Legne found by French lugger abandoned eight miles off Dungeness. Picked up by smacks *Lalla Rookh* and *Ranger*, and towed to Harwich by *Lalla Rookh*. **ES Nov 26.**

Bawdsey lifeboat station closed. **S from S.**

1853

Brig *W I Collingwood* assisted in off Cork by 'several smacks.' **ES Jan 7.**

Brig *Albion* of London assisted in off Gunfleet by smacks *Wide Awake* and *Fox*. Award £130. **ES Jan 14** and **21.**

Brig *Dervant* of Whitby 'beat over Whiting.' Picked up leaky by *Aurora's Increase* (Lewis) and run ashore at Orford Haven. Smack then fetched Cottingham pump from Harwich and successfully sailed brig to Lowestoft. **ES Feb 4.**

Claim by twenty 'yawls' manned by sixty men against *Peggy*, ashore on Leigh Middle with coal in July 1852. Tender £50 refused. Award £80. **ES Feb 4.**

Brig *Atlantic* of Hartlepool, riding between West Rocks and Gunfleet (wind SE, very dark), run down and sunk by ss *Hunwicke* of London. **ES Feb 18.**

Smack *Active* of London (Nash) ashore on

Hallidays. Kept afloat by Cottingham pump and got on to slip. **ES Feb 25.**

Strike by stone men for better price, and punitive raid on strike breakers. **ES Mar 18** and **25.**

Revenue cutter *Onyx* arrives at Harwich. **ES Apr 29.**

Galiot *Anna Gesa* of Blankanese assisted off Gunfleet by *Celerity*, *Agenoria* 'of Ipswich' and *Rumley* of Harwich. While under tow by *Agenoria*, galiot rolled over and sank in Rolling Grounds. **ES May 27.**

Swedish schooner *Alten* assisted in off Kentish Knock with rudder gone. **ES Aug 19.**

French lugger *Jeanne Emilie* (for Fécamp, coals) wrecked on Longsand. Crew in by *Tryal* (Lewis). **ES Oct 7.**

Schooner *Tino* of Sunderland (Peterson owner and master), leaky off Shipwash, runs up Black Deep. With water over cabin floor longboat is got out but schooner sinks too quickly. After night in rigging crew of five brought in by *Seagull* of Harwich. RNLI award £5 to five crew of *Seagull*. **ES Oct 7** and **Nov 4.**

Collier seamen of Manningtree strike demanding £4 per voyage and not to work out the coals. Present wages 14s a week and to unload, 'lower than at other ports.' **ES Oct 28.**

Brig *Elizabeth Laws* (of and from Dundee) assisted in by several smacks off Longsand or Shipwash (two accounts vary). Hauled out and repaired. **ES Nov 18** and **Dec 2.**

Two smacks in Harwich with coals from a wreck on Maplins. **ES Dec 16.**

Dutch ship '*Quereine Ann Anne*' wrecked on Gunfleet, Nov. 27. Smacks bringing salvage into Colne for a week. Charges of concealment against three Rowhedge smacks, *Benevolence* (D Collinson), *Industry* (A Walford), and *Martha* (J Lawrence.) Small fines, averaging £2–£5 a man, paid with thanks to magistrates 'after some conversation with friends in court.' Stated that none of them regularly engaged in salvaging and so 'not likely to be suspected.' But *Martha* attracted suspicion by anchoring unusually close to the shore. Yet when *Industry*'s crew failed to appear it was stated she was 'cruising in the Swin.' On finally appearing Walford said the first he heard was from the *Eagle* on December 23. **ES Dec 2, 16, 23, 30** and **Jan 6, 1854.**

Between 400 and 500 vessels of all sizes and rigs sheltering in Harwich from winter gales. Crowds of sailors ashore. 'Butchers, bakers, grocers and innkeepers can testify from the business they have done. A thousand letters were posted up to 4 pm on Thursday, mostly from the ships.' **ES Dec 30.**

1854

Rowhedge man lost rowing boatload of cement stone in Colne. **ES Mar 10.**

Month's hard labour for stealing cement stone from breakwater, using crome. **ES Mar 10.**

Partnership case between four Southend salvagers which agreed 'to be as one' in salvage of *Prince Albert* on Maplins. Adjourned. Resumed hearing not traced. **ES Mar 24.**

Swedish brig *Albertina* wrecked on Haisborough Sands. Seven took to boat, picked up by Jersey sloop *Liberty* and brought to Harwich. Captain, his wife and child, two mates and one man feared lost. **ES Apr 28.**

Partnership case between Rowhedge smacks *Gipsy*, *Prince of Orange* and *Blue-Eyed Maid* following salvage of *Hendrika Justina*. **ES Jun 23.**

Action by *Seagull* of Harwich, claiming share with eight smacks of £700 paid into court following salvage of Prussian brig *X June* on Gunfleet on March 11. **ES Jul 14.**

Schooner *Market Maid* towed in by *Aurora's Increase*. **ES Aug 4.**

Crew of brig *Isabella* sunk by unknown steamer near Shipwash, brought in by *Tryal*. **ES Oct 6.**

Conviction for stealing 'Wallet stone' found at Pattrick's Works. **ES Dec 29.**

1855

Stone men charged with stealing cement stone from John Watts. Claimed they 'could fetch tons from the Ordnance shore' and that the stone in question was green with weed. Acquitted at Assizes. **ES Jan 5.**

Schooner *Rose* of Dundee founders in Swin. Raised and brought in by Lewis's smacks. Cargo of potatoes sold. Schooner later sold for £200 to J Watts. **ES Jan 12 and Feb 9.**

Brig *Stanton* on Gunfleet. Six smacks could not get near. Next day William Lewis in *Tryal* again failed to reach crew in foretop. Following day *Tryal* joined by tug *Amazon* (employed on harbour works) towing 'paddle box life boat' belonging to HM steam sloop *Driver*. Saved four after two days and nights without nourishment. 'Paddle box lifeboat' lost. RNLI silver medals awarded to W and J Lewis of *Aurora's Increase* and *Tryal* and £3 to crew of tug. **ES Jan 16 and Feb 2.**

Salvage claims by smacks against sloop *Hebe* ashore outside Harwich. Award £70. **ES Feb 23.**

Newcastle brig *Woodman* wrecked on Shipwash. Crew of eleven saved by *Alfred* (William Newson). Awarded RNLI silver medal with £7 for boat's crew. **ES Mar 9.**

ss *Black Sea* (Sunderland to Crimea) off Aldeburgh with North Sea pilot asks local pilotage into Harwich from *Four Brothers* of Aldeburgh on fishing voyage. Smack leads into Harwich. Award £60. **ES Apr 13.**

Warships escorted by gunboats leave Sheerness Forced to anchor under Gunfleet. Gunfire heard by *Concord* of Colchester which slips anchor and seventy fathoms of cable. Skipper boards gunboat *Redwing* and pilots to Sheerness. **ES May 11.**

Brig *Tonbridge* of Rochester wrecked on Gunfleet. Mate charged at Rochester with neglect of duty in failing to call skipper when Sunk light sighted. Committed for trial. (Hearing not traced.) **ES Oct 5.**

Brig *James MacQueen* (Leith to Montanzas) on Longsand in May. Pulled off with rudder unshipped by tug *Commodore* after fourteen hours' work. Award £200 to tug and lugger *Secret*. **ES Nov 16.**

Brig *Eliza* of Amsterdam found abandoned on Sunk, brought in by *Aurora's Increase* (Lewis) and *Marco Polo* (Adams) and a lugger. 'A very handsome prize.' (See also May 9, 1856.) **ES Dec 21.**

1856

Smacksmen claim £75 for helping in Swedish schooner *Pandora*, found at anchor off the Platters with a pilot and not in distress. Offered £1 (per man presumably) and refused. Fifty shillings awarded. **ES May 9.**

Salvage claim by *Aurora's Increase* and *Marco Polo* against brig *Eliza*. Value £2,500. Offer of £850 refused. Court consider offer 'most liberal' and condemn salvors in costs. **ES May 9.**

Brig *Britannia* of Whitby, dismasted, towed from Southwold to Rolling Grounds by schooner *Alma*. Then boarded by galley *Champion* which found crew 'dispirited' by loss of the mate. Value £300. Four men claim £10 each. £30 awarded. **ES May 16.**

Salvage claim by smack *Wideawake* of Harwich against brig *Dalston*. Smacksmen claim they worked her in, denied by brig. Claim £75. Award £10. **ES May 23.**

Service by *Agenoria* to brig *Julia*, and RNLI award. **ES Jun 6 and Jul 4.**

1856—cont.

Meeting to form Harwich Mutual Marine Association. **ES Aug 29.**

RNLI present £1 and a second service clasp to William Lewis, master of *Tryal*, with £4 to his crew following service to brig *Maria* of Goole on Longsand. **ES Oct 10.**

Hope of Goole on Longsand on maiden voyage• assisted in by *Tryal* (W Lewis). **ES Nov 14.**

Salvage awards following wreck of *Clarissa* on Nov 15, 1855. **ES Jul 4.**

Ship *Pallas*, 500 tons, of London assisted into Harwich by smack *Jemima* 'of Aldeburgh'. **ES Nov 7.**

Crew of schooner *David* of Dundee landed at *Wivenhoe* by smack *Phoenix*. **ES Nov 14.**

Salvage claim by *Phoenix* against schooner *Vikin*. On June 9, cruising off Longsand, *Phoenix* warned *Vikin* which then went ashore on Longsand. *Phoenix* kedged her off and assisted into Harwich. Offer of £100 refused. Admiralty Court considered offer 'ample'. **ES Dec 5.**

1857

Harwich made headquarters of coastguard area. HMS *Southampton* to be guardship. **ES Jan 9.**

Philip Cook of *Blue-Eyed Maid* and George Cook of *Beulah* charged with concealing salvage. Colchester Receiver of Wreck 'compelled to bring case by Board of Trade, but no wish to be severe.' Fines of £5 on skippers, 2s 6d on members of crew. **ES Feb 6.**

John Carrington appointed Piermaster at Harwich. **ES Aug 7.**

Claim by Glover and smack *Increase* 'of Colchester' against French schooner *Frolic*, assisted off the Sunk. Value £575. Claim £100. Award £145. **ES Dec 19.**

1858

Southwold lifeboat launched in easterly wind, emptied water ballast and capsized. Ten saved by a yawl; seven lost. **ES Jan 8** and **S from S.**

Schooner (unnamed) wrecked on Barrow. Crew of five saved by *Magnet* of Colchester. **ES Jan 29.**

Crew of brig *Ocean*, on Pye with coal, brought in by *Tryal*. Coal brought in by other smacks. **ES Mar 5** and **12.**

Schooner *Lively* of Rye towed into Harwich by smack *Change* of Greenwich. **ES Mar 12.**

Barque *Annie Archibald* assisted in by a lugger and several smacks, having been on Longsand. Later advertised for sale 'for the benefit of owners, underwriters and salvors.' Later refitted and sailed after further damage by collision in harbour. **ES Mar 19, June 9** and **Oct 8.**

Crew of *Fidelity*, lost off Lowestoft, brought in smack *Adventure* of Harwich (Calver, master). **ES Mar 12.**

Crew of Dutch galliot brought in by smack *Alfred*. **ES Mar 12.**

Unity of Rye salvaged by smacks *Running Rein* of Colchester and *Celerity* of Harwich after nine hours on Sands. Bower and kedge anchors taken off, then slipped. Value £500–£600. Award £90. **ES Apr 30.**

J G Chamberlain, Lloyd's agent at Wivenhoe, charged with threatening R Raggett, Receiver of Admiralty Droits, following a quarrel over wreckage from *Wind's Bride*. Lloyd's agent had recently been deprived by Act of Parliament of rights to receive Droits. **ES May 7.**

Brig *Alciope* of Liverpool (Shields to Black Sea, coals) assisted off Longsand by *Marco Polo* and *Alfred*. Thomas Adams and William Newson charged with conspiring to put her ashore. Case dismissed. **ES May 28** and **Jun 11.**

Barque '*Robinsons*' (Cronstadt to London) assisted off Shipwash by *Jemima* and yawls *Assistance* and *Hand of Providence*. 'Evidence of the usual conflicting character.' Value £3,520. Award £200. **ES Jul 23.**

Marco Polo, *John and William* and *Aid*, going to Longsand to salvage from a Russian wreck, find French barque *Amiable Terese* ashore there. Despite objection by pilots from Dover and Queenstown, smacksmen engaged by captain and get ship off. Value of ship and cargo, £2,200. £200 claimed. £150 awarded. **ES Sept 17.**

Barque *Clydeside* on Sunk. Claim for salvage, 'vessel having been sold.' One-third awarded. **ES Sept 24.**

French lugger *Sophie* (Seaham to Bordeaux) assisted off Longsand. Award £120. **ES Oct 22.**

George Robinson, sailing from Harwich 'after extensive refit', wrecked on Gunfleet. Crew saved. (Presumably vessel previously described as *Robinsons*. See July 23.) **ES Oct 22.**

Aid 'of Harwich' and a Colchester smack bring in *Louise*, 'a very valuable brig of Amsterdam,' ashore on Longsand. **ES Oct 22** and **Oct 29.**

Russian schooner *Nelly*, damaged in collision, assisted in by *Agenoria* and *Jemima*. Award £70. **ES Dec 17.** (See also Jan 18, 1859.)

Reine des Anges assisted off Shipwash by *Aurora's Increase*, *Agenoria* and *Jessey* of Woodbridge, followed by case based on apparently forged agreement. **ES Dec 31.**

Brig *Esing Keit* of Swinemunde sent two hands in boat to put pilot aboard Sunk light vessel. Boat and hands then disappeared. 'It is feared they have perished.' **ES Dec 31.**

1859

Danish schooner *Margaretha Kristine* assisted off Shipwash by *Wonder*. **ES Jan 3.**

Brig *May* of Scarborough assisted in by *Tryal*, after collision with brig *Pete* of Hartlepool. **ES Jan 14.**

Brig *Schwan* of Rostock assisted in by *Jemima* of Aldeburgh. Brig claim £3 10s was agreed for pilotage, denied by smack. Award £35. **ES Feb 4.**

Schooner *Nelly* (Libau to Treguier, linseed) towed in by *Queen*. 'Left this port about a month since and it appears has been knocking about the seas endeavouring to make her voyage ever since and at last had to put back.' **ES Feb 18.**

Brig *Amelia* assisted off Cork. Had to be run ashore by Woodbridge Haven full of water. **ES Feb 18.**

Spanish brig *Anna* assisted off Longsand by *Celerity* and *Alfred* and Colchester smacks. **ES Feb 18.**

Admiralty Court action over charges for unsuccessful attempt to refloat brig *Helen* of Whitby, wrecked 'some time since' at Walton Naze. **ES Feb 25.**

Dutch ship *Australie* (Shields to Cadiz), a nearly new ship of 700 tons, wrecked on Shipwash. Seen moored near Middle Shipwash lightship at 9 pm in north-easterly gale. Later longboat and captain's gig seen adrift bottom up. Next day wreck seen but smacks could not get near her. Following day part of stern frame and broadside with painted ports picked up. Shipwash channel full of wreckage. Books and papers picked up by *Increase*. **ES May 13.**

Schooner *Hofflung* assisted in by *Adventure* of Harwich. **ES Jun 17.**

Claim by Henry Cook of *Qui Vive* against French schooner *Augustine* bound to Ipswich. Boarded off Galloper and sailed into Harwich. Claimed £3 3s. French captain said this should include passage to Ipswich. Award £3 3s and £2 for loss of time and costs. **ES Jul 1.**

Ipswich barque *Sarah* on Longsand. Claim by *Marco Polo*, *Alfred*, *John and William* and *Emma Jane*, all of Harwich. Award £50. **ES Jul 1.**

Dutch ship *Friesland* (700–800 tons) assisted in and hauled up Navy Yard slipway. Largest ship ever hauled up. Dutch crew manned capstans 'with four extra purchases below.' *Friesland* sailed the following month, but three months later a dispute over shares in the salvage between the *Emma Jane* and *Aid* of Harwich came to court. **ES Jul 22, Aug 12 and Nov 25.**

Brig *Fame* of Shields wrecked on Shipwash. Crew brought in by *John and William* of Harwich. **ES Sept 9.**

Schooner *Undine* of Harwich (owners Messrs Lewis) puts into Yarmouth with damage. **ES Nov 4.**

Dutch schooner *Margaretha Elizabeth* and barque *Asphalon* assisted in off Longsand. Swedish schooner *Egent* assisted in off Shipwash. **ES Nov 25.**

Claim by *Ranger* (John Crane) and *Violet*, 'both of Ipswich,' against *Karl Gustav* (Volgast to Mistley) assisted off Landguard. Award, after two-day hearing, £20. **ES Dec 9.**

Swedish barque *Hector* assisted in off Shipwash. **ES Dec 9.**

Brig *Nile* of Dundee (Riga to London) assisted off Maplins and brought in leaky. Sailed next day, got ashore on Cork and again assisted in. **ES Dec 9 and 16.**

Danish schooner *Valkyrian* sailed from Harwich and got on Andrews. Assisted in. **ES Dec 16.**

Barque *Eva*, of and from Dundee, assisted in off Shipwash. **ES Dec 23.**

Three Aldeburgh lifeboatman lost at launch. **ES Dec 30.**

1860

Salvage claim at Colchester by 'galley' *Aid* against brig *John and Mary*. £10 awarded. **ES Feb 10.**

Claim by *Pheasant*, *Prince of Orange* and *Scout* of Colchester for service to schooner *Margaretha Elizabeth* on Nov 20, 1860. Award £200. **ES Feb 24.**

Rescue from brigantine *Charity* of Goole by *Tryal* (John Tye). Part of hull later floated into Harwich. **ES Sept 7 and Nov 23.**

French chasse-maree *La Nymphe* (Blyth to Carentan, coals) assisted into Harwich by smacks and accuses them of 'conduct of a piratical nature'. **ES Nov 23.**

Salvage of Hanoverian brig *Commandeur*, ashore on Cork, by *Volunteer* of Harwich and

1860—*cont.*

Wonder of Woodbridge. Agreed payments £260 to *Volunteer*, £100 to *Wonder*. **ES Nov 23.**

Brig *Hanse* ashore on Longsand. Got off but so damaged she had to be run ashore again and became total loss. John Tye, master of *Tryal*, awarded £35 and silver medal from Hamburg. Divers worked on cargo including guns for Mexico. **ES Nov 20, Dec 14** and **Feb 15, 1861.**

1861

Claim by *Agenoria* and *Jemima* against koff *Wester Schouwen* of Zierickzee, ashore on Shipwash (Newcastle to Plymouth, coal). Award £60. **ES Feb 1.**

Claim against barque *Eudora* by crew of yawl *Star of Winterton* (thirteen hands). Ship had signed an agreement with yawlmen to take her into Lowestoft for £50. Then a pilot boarded her and she dismissed the yawl. £50 awarded. **ES Feb 22.**

French brig *Mariana* assisted off Longsand by *Volunteer* and *Celerity* and a lugger. **ES Mar 15.**

John Manning, master of smack *Celerity*, charged with concealing wreckage. Adjourned and resumed hearing not traced. **ES Apr 26.**

Claim against barque *Jane Cargill* (Hamburg to South America) by *Snowdrop, Increase, Qui Vive, New Unity* and *Concord*, all of Colchester, and *Alfred* of Harwich. Assisted off Longsand and piloted to Sheerness by James Cook of *Snowdrop*. Award £500 for a 'short but meritorious service'. **ES May 17.**

Lighthouse at Landguard lit for first time. Of low power to assist in entering Harwich harbour. 'A neat low building resembling a seaside cottage or villa – rather a pretty object on the beach.' **ES Jun 14.**

Claim by *Volunteer* against schooner *Thomas Edward* of London, assisted in leaky. Scropers had signed an agreement to 'lend a hand into the harbour for the sum of £1,' but claimed this was for piloting and did not include pumping. Award £4. **ES Aug 9.**

Brig *Cassandra* of Hartlepool wrecked on Gunfleet and burned out due to crew leaving tar barrel lit as distress signal. **ES Aug 9.**

Wreckage of Norwegian barque *Justitia*, wrecked on Corton on August 8, towed in by *Volunteer, Paragon, John and William* and *Agenoria*, followed by dispute with Gorleston lifeboat. **ES Sept 27, Nov 25** and **Feb 21, 1862.**

Wreck of schooner *General Cathcart* followed by Board of Trade awards. **ES Oct 15** and **Dec 25.**

Unidentified derelict timber barque towed in from Shipwash by *Aurora's Increase, Paragon, Wonder* and 'a fishing smack'. **ES Nov 22.**

Smack *John and William*, owned by H Baker and J Carrington, 'wilfully set on fire' in Harwich harbour. **ES Nov 1.**

Wreck of *Darius* on Longsand and awards to T Adams. **ES Nov 8** and **Jan 31, 1862.**

Salvage by smack *Orwell* of Colchester. **ES Nov 15.**

Harwich Steam Towing Co formed. Directors Mr Brett of London, Mr Watts, Mr Vaux, Mr Daniels, Mr Durrant, Mr Dorling, Mr Owen. **ES Nov 29.**

Wreck of *Regina* on Swin Middle. Seven Brightlingsea smacksmen, James Gould, George Oliver, Charles Cook, William Dove, William Rumble, James Bacon, James Fielding, fined £100 each for feloniously carrying away tallow. **ES Nov 29, Dec 6** and **Jan 3, 1862.**

1862

Bremen barque *Johanne* wrecked on Longsand. Fifteen lost, one saved by *Alfred*, followed by award of £10 by Senate of Bremen. **ES Mar 1** and **May 2.**

Claim by *Jemima, Industry, Lord Howe*, and *Louise* after assisting brig *Sirocco* off Gunfleet. Value £800. Award £25 to each smack. **ES Mar 28.**

Dutch barque *Vier Gezustus* wrecked on Longsand. Crew saved by *Queen Victoria* (John Tye), stores by *Alfred* and *Aurora's Increase*. **ES Apr 11.**

Aurora's Increase recovers by diving anchors and chain from Ipswich schooner *Princess Alice*, sunk under Sizewell Bank. **ES Apr 18.**

Guernsey schooner *Alexandra* in collision with French chasse-maree *Leonia*. Resumed voyage but struck Longsand and broke up. Crew saved by *Queen Victoria* which at same time assisted Whitby brig *Friends* off Longsand. **ES Apr 25.**

Norwegian brig *Phoenix* assisted off Longsand by *Aurora's Increase* (Lewis), *Volunteer* (Adams) and *Alfred* (Newson). **ES May 2.**

Launch of lifeboat *Ipswich*. **ES May 30.**

British Queen of Sunderland assisted off Shipwash by *Volunteer* and *Queen*. **ES Aug 9.**

William Inglis of Shields (Portugal to London) wrecked on Shipwash. Claim by *Qui Vive* settled and withdrawn. **ES Oct 10** and **31.**

Brig *CSM* of London, from Newcastle with coal, wrecked in Goldmers Gat. Ten men lost in salvage attempt. **Oct 14** and **31** and **July 31, 1863.**

Marco Polo brings in crew of *Elizabeth*, wrecked on Kentish Knock, 'one of many ships lost on October 10.' **ES Oct 31.**

Brig *Shepherd* on Gunfleet. Got off, founders in Wallet, raised by *Volunteer* with patent pump, got into Harwich by four smacks and a steam tug. **ES Oct 31.**

Schooner *Royalist* of London strikes Gunfleet running into Harwich for refuge. Assisted by *Queen* (Thomas Crane). Anchored off Cork due to ebb tide and foul wind. Parted from anchor and brought up to bower anchor and seventy-five fathoms of cable. Finally brought in. Value £798. Claim £200. Award £110. **ES Oct 24.**

Wreck of barque *Cresswell* on Longsand. **ES Nov 28.**

Barque *Elizabeth* of London on Longsand. Got off after jettisoning eighty tons of coffee, some of which sold at Harwich. **ES Dec 12.**

On same day schooner *Jason* (Whitby to Arundel, stone) on Shipwash. Claim by *Volunteer* and *Ranger* of Ipswich. Award £80. **ES Dec 12.**

Brig *Thomas Rusbridge* ashore. Three of crew taken off by *New Unity* (T Barnard.) Then floated, slipped cable and proceeded to London shorthanded. **ES Dec 18.**

Schooner *Thrifty* of Goole wrecked on Longsand, followed by awards to *Paragon*. **ES Oct 24, Dec 12** and **Feb 20, 1863.**

1863

Salvage of *August, Amy Louise, Prosperity, Johann Jacob, Marie Amelie* and *Danzig*. (See Introduction.) **ES Jan 9.**

Wreck of *Rosebud*, salvage of *Henrietta*, loss of Henry Holden from smack *Marco Polo*. (See Introduction.) **ES Jan 16.**

Maldon brig *Victoria* parts from anchor off Harwich. Anchors again off Aldeburgh and again parts cable. Crew leave skipper aboard. Burns tar barrel, twenty-three beach men assist her into Lowestoft. **ES Jan 16.**

Barque *Auxiliary* towed into Harwich by two Yarmouth tugs. Too deep to enter Yarmouth. **ES Jan 39.**

Salvage claim by tug *Robert Owen*, then of Yarmouth, against sloop *Anne* of Goole. Value £900. Award £120. **ES Jan 30.**

Schooner *Traveller* of Yarmouth assisted off Gunfleet. **ES Feb 13.**

Brig *Londonderry* assisted off Pye into Handford Creek by *John and William* of Harwich. **ES May 22.**

Crew of brig *Eliza* brought in by *Marco Polo*. **ES Oct 2.**

Brig *Leith* assisted off Shipwash by *Aurora's Increase*. **ES Oct 2.**

Claim by Edward Lewis of *Aurora's Increase* against galiot *Diana*. Boarded as pilot but claimed he found her without provisions and requiring assistance. Dismissed. **ES Oct 23.**

Claim by *Queen, Fox* and *William* against schooner *Mary* of Ramsgate, assisted off Beach End. Award £45. **ES Oct 23.**

Wreck of brig on Longsand with cargo of spirits, followed by prosecution of Benjamin Dale and of Captain Hezekiah Baker of *Agenoria* and death of member of crew of RC *Scout*. **ES Nov 13, Dec 4.**

1864

Five of crew of Russian brig *Elise* on Longsand saved by *Queen*. Captain, mate and three boys feared lost as masts fell. **ES Jan 8.**

Brig *Victory* assisted in by *Paragon*. Award £55. **ES Jan 29.**

Brig *Challenger*, after collision with brig *Ariel*, ashore abandoned on Barrow. Got off and put ashore on Gunfleet to avoid sinking. Became total wreck. **ES Feb 12.**

Schooner *Coronation* towed in dismasted after collision with Norwegian barque while at anchor off Sunk. **ES Feb 12.**

Harwich-Rotterdam passenger service established by ss *Avalon*. **ES May 12** and **Jun 17.**

Brig *Circassian* of Sunderland wrecked on Gunfleet. Crew into Brightlingsea by smack. **ES Sept 16.**

Schooner *Ellen* of Aberystwyth assisted off Longsand by *Increase* 'of Colchester'. **ES Sept 16.**

Brig *Torre del Ovo* of Bilbao (Hamburg to Havannah) wrecked on Kentish Knock. Crew saved by ten smacks. Four of Harwich, five of Colchester, one Ramsgate lugger. **ES Oct 28.**

Loss of ss *Ontario* at Haisborough on maiden voyage. Yarmouth beachmen refuse to launch lifeboat due to system of sharing rewards between companies and jealousy of steam tugs. **ES Nov 11.**

Brig *Juniatta* wrecked on Cork. Four lost, two saved by *Queen Victoria* and *Paragon*. **ES Nov 25.**

Claim by *Increase* and Ipswich tug *Amazon* against Norwegian barque *Falcon*, found waterlogged on East Barrow. Awards £40 to *Increase*, £20 to *Amazon*. **ES Dec 2.**

1864—cont.

Brig *Alliance* on Kentish Knock assisted by *Agenoria*. **ES Dec 9.**

Brig *Lima* of Rostock assisted off Longsand by *Wonder*. Agreement £250. **ES Dec 23.**

1865

Board of Trade award £5 to Mr Crane and crew of *Queen* for service to Danish brig *Thor* on Longsand, Dec 23, 1864. **ES Jan 13.**

Meeting at Harwich to promote J W Wood's lifesaving raft, following by test in Harwich harbour. **ES Jan 27 and May 28.**

Barque *Byzantium* (Shields to Alexandria, coal) wrecked on Gunfleet. Crew saved by *Marco Polo* and *Volunteer*. **ES Feb 17.**

Brig *Alcide* wrecked on Sunk. Crew saved by *Queen*. **ES Feb 24.**

Brig *William Pitt* assisted in leaky off Gunfleet. **ES Feb 24.**

Schooner *Formby* damaged in collision, assisted in by three smacks. **ES Feb 24.**

Hanoverian schooner *Erute* assisted off Barrow into Colne by Colchester smacks, and later towed to Harwich for discharge and repair. **ES Mar 24.**

William and S R Groom of Harwich charged with having in their possession certain wreck, to wit an anchor and chain. Case dismissed. **ES Jun 16.**

Hezekiah Baker and his son John charged with using abusive language to a policeman. **ES Aug 4.**

Stone men threaten strike and obtain extra shilling a ton. **ES Sept 29.**

Claim by *New Unity* and *Scout* of Colchester against Spanish brigantine *Villa de Luarco*, assisted off Sunk. Captain had already declined help from *Increase*. Award £30. **ES Sept 29.**

Claim by *Agenoria* and *Paragon* against brigantine *Fortuna* of Whitby, found with distress flag in rigging. Agreement of £250 rejected by owner as obtained by intimidation. But captain said he signed freely. Judgment reserved. **ES Nov 10.**

ss *Avalon*, crossing Brielle Bar, sees Norwegian barque *Forningen* go ashore. Anchored, took rope aboard, went full speed ahead, broke rope, took off captain and crew and proceeded to Harwich. **ES Nov 10.**

1866

Brigantine *Challenge* wrecked on Kentish

Knock. Crew saved by *Queen Victoria* which at same time saved crew of schooner *Roe* of Whitby, also on Kentish Knock. **ES Jan 5.**

Claim by smack *Violet* 'of Aldeburgh' for assisting brigantine *Aurora* of Ipswich, which claimed smacksmen were only aboard to help with pumps. Award £35 and £10 for damage to smack's boat. **ES Jan 26 and Feb 5.**

Gorleston volunteer lifeboat *Rescuer* (non-self-righting) capsizes crossing Bar with loss of twelve hands. **ES Jan 19.**

Presentation at Brightlingsea of telescope to John Salmon, who took his *Emily* to a wreck on the Barrow in February, and saved five out of six crew after sixteen hours' exposure to bitter weather. **ES Apr 13**

Brig *Queen* at anchor off Galloper rolls her mast out. Towed in by tugs. **ES Jun 22.**

Schooner *Mary Ann* assisted in off Longsand by *Aurora's Increase* and *Queen Victoria*. **ES Jun 22.**

Claim by John Tye and Edward Lewis, masters of *Queen* and *Aurora's Increase*, following salvage of *Mary Ann* of Barrow, on Longsand. Value £834. Award £130. **ES Jun 29.**

Sale at Brightlingsea of stores from Austrian barque *Venoge*, wrecked on Longsand on June 13. **ES Jul 6.**

J W Wood addresses Society of Arts on causes of shipwreck (published in society's Journal, July 9). **ES Jul 13.**

ss *Bruiser* sunk off Aldeburgh with loss of twelve passengers and three crew in collision with steam collier *Haswell*. Diving smacks *Aurora's Increase* and *Queen Victoria* employed. **ES Aug 13.**

First GER screw steamer at Harwich, ss *Great Yarmouth* (200 ft long, 800 tons). **ES Dec 21.**

1867

American brig *Moonlight* assisted off Shipwash. **ES Feb 8.**

Brig *Brotherly Love* of Shields assisted in by Greenwich cod smack *Hunter*. £180 claimed, £120 awarded. Brig had been built at Ipswich in 1764 and it was claimed that Captain Cook was apprenticed in her. **ES Mar 15 and 22.**

Russian ship *Dagmar* lost on Longsand. Jolly boat picked up and brought into Harwich; two other boats picked up by Bremen ship and transferred to *Jemima* which landed them at Brightlingsea. **ES Mar 22.**

Account of J W Wood's liferaft. **ES Jun 28.**

Full-rigged ship *Britannia* ashore on Corton

Sand, 'beat over', ran for Harwich, got on Pye Sand, towed off into Handford Water by tug *Robert Owen*. **ES Nov 22.**

ss *Sultana*, with horses and general cargo, sunk entering Antwerp in collision with ss *Harwich*. **ES Dec 13.**

Dutch brig *Minerva* assisted in by eight Colchester smacks. **ES Dec 27.**

ss *Smyrna*, abandoned off Norfolk, picked up by GER ss *Ravensbury* and towed into Brouwershaven, Holland. Ship insured for £40,000, cargo £32,000. 'Salvage will be very handsome.' **ES Dec 27.**

1868

Aurora's Increase and *Queen Victoria* (John and William Lewis) sail for Scheldt to salvage wreck of ss *Sultana*. **ES Jan 14.**

Barque *Walsoken* (owned by R Young, director of GER) towed in off Longsand by *Robert Owen* and 'a fleet of smacks.' **ES Mar 6.**

Claim by *Increase* (John Glover) against brig *Consort*. Smack with eleven hands sent four in boat across Longsand, then sailed round the end of sands. Boat took off two of her anchors with eighty-fathom warps while crews of brig and of smack *Elizabeth* hove 2,000 sleepers overboard. Brig came off just before next high water. Value £1,600. Award to two smacks, £250. **ES Mar 27.**

Norwegian brig *Anna Maria* wrecked on Gunfleet. Crew and some stores brought in by smack *Scout*. **ES Sept 25.**

After prolonged north-easterly gales 300 windbound ships sail from Harwich as wind veers. Several, damaged in collisions, have to put back for repairs. **ES Nov 13 and 27.**

Agenoria (Hezekiah Baker) falls in with ship's broadside adrift near Cork and tows it in. **ES Dec 19.**

1869

Two Sisters of Shields wrecked. Crew picked up by *Triune* of London, which also got ashore. Both crews brought in by *Volunteer*. Other casualties in this gale included brigantine *Nancy* lost on Longsand, schooner *Jane* and *Baltic* of Whitby on Gunfleet. **ES Jan 1.**

Brig *Trixie Wee* of Newport, Mon, salvaged by Rowhedgers. Alphonso Lay, Charles Crosby, Benjamin James, Thomas Barnard and Samuel Everett charged with conspiracy to defraud owner of £300. **ES Feb 12 and Mar 5.**

Barque *City of Carlisle* (Shields to Aden, 1,200 tons, coals and Government stores) lost on Kentish Knock. Crew of twenty-three landed by *Aurora's Increase* and *Ranger*. Life salvage awards £32 and £18 respectively. **ES Feb 19 and Aug 6.**

George Wyatt, master of *Alfred*, lost in saving crew of *Alvidia* on Longsand. **ES Feb 19.**

Barque *Eliza Caroline*, stranded on Yarmouth beach, towed to Harwich drawing twenty feet. Special sheers rigged on Vaux's slip to lift out guns in her cargo weighing twelve tons. Salvage award to Caister beachmen £1600. **ES Mar 26.**

Award £100 to *Volunteer* (W Redwood) and boat *Turtle* of Felixstowe. *Volunteer* saw brig *Diana* clew up topsail off Orford Ness, found her ashore, laid out kedge and 'pressed her off with this and a sail.' **ES Apr 2.**

Stone dredgers William Crosby and James Gardiner fined £5 for bringing ashore anchor and cable. **ES Apr 30.**

Crew of schooner sunk in collision in Swin landed by *Lizzie Mordue* of Colchester. (The only reference to this 21-ton smack, built at Rowhedge in 1866, and owned in 1893 at Kings Lynn). **ES Oct 15.**

William Wyatt of *Volunteer* fined £1 for piloting ss *Trident*. **ES Nov 19.**

Master of 'the late schooner *Margaret* of Weymouth' writes to *Essex Standard* thanking captain of *John and Jane* of Lynn who took crew aboard, and John Salmon of *Emily*, which landed them at Sheerness, after schooner foundered off Blacktail. **ES Nov 26.**

Claim by *Wonder* (Ablet Passiful) against brigantine *Empress* of Port Madoc at anchor in Hollesley Bay. Smacksmen pretended they were Harwich pilots and asked £100. Award £70. **ES Dec 17.**

Skipper and his sister saved by *Emblem* from barge *Rochford*. Five children lost. **ES Dec 24.**

1870

Crew of Greek ship *Trepaittus* on Longsand, brought in by *Ranger*. **ES Jan 21.**

Smack *Amy* (of and for London, coals) ashore on Heaps. Crew of seven reach Swin Middle lightship. *Amy* drifts off and sinks east of Barrow. Crew brought into Brightlingsea by *Alma* (Thrower). Finding that crew belonged to Maldon, *Alma* sailed them home where they 'shabbily gave the name of a person in Brightlingsea quite unconnected with the ship as the person they should recompense. This, if true, is very disgraceful and likely to have a bad effect

1870—*cont.*

when assistance is wanted at a future time from the smacksmen on this coast.' **ES Jan 28.**

Brig *Mystic* of Newport, Mon (West Indies to Ipswich), assisted in off Longsand by tug and nine smacks. Run on to mud to discharge cargo. **ES Feb 11.**

ss *Jacana* (Cork Steamship Company, 1,200 tons, with 900 tons coal for Cork gasworks) wrecked on Longsand on first voyage, Newcastle to Cork. **ES Feb 18.**

Severe frost and easterly gales stop Harwich Packet Service to Antwerp and Rotterdam. **ES Feb 25.**

Boston billyboy schooner *Blue Jacket* (Newcastle to Southampton) wrecked on Longsand. Crew first take to boat, then spend six hours in rigging before being taken off by *Celerity* (Roper), *Eudoxy* (Barnard) and *Kate* (Aldridge), 'after much hesitation due to the fearful sea. Clothes they had on were torn to pieces by the force of the gale.' Followed by claim and award £20. **ES Feb 25** and **Sept 16.**

ss *Ravensbury* (GER Harwich to Rotterdam packet) ashore near Brielle Bar and 'feared will become wreck'. **ES Mar 11.**

J W Wood's paper to Society of Arts on training schemes and liferafts. **ES Mar 20.**

Aurora's Increase run down and sunk by Norwegian barque. **ES Apr 1.**

Brig *Hope* of Rochester (Newcastle to Rochester, coal) ashore on Gunfleet in fog. Total wreck. **ES Apr 22.**

Barque *Christiana* of Hamburg, bound to Valparaiso with cargo and passengers, assisted into Harwich off Shipwash and unloaded for repairs. **ES Apr 22.**

Smuggling by *Two Brothers*. Three smacksmen unable to pay £100 fines sent to prison. **ES Nov 8.**

Brig *Macedonian* of Blyth (Lisbon, coals) assisted in off Longsand by several smacks. **ES Nov 18.**

Schooner *Escosa* (salt fish, Christiansand to Bilbao) wrecked on Longsand. Crew all night in rigging. Boy dies, remainder saved by *New Unity* (Barnard). **ES Dec 2.** (See also Aug 8, 1873.)

Member of crew of *Paragon* charged with attempting to stab another of crew following dispute as to which should take charge of a wreck. **ES Dec 15.**

Italian barque *Argos* (Odessa to Ipswich) wrecked on Longsand. Crew in boat picked up by *Faith*. **ES Dec 16.**

Brig *Blyth* of Blyth wrecked on Longsand. **ES Dec 23.**

1871

ss *Battalion* wrecked on Longsand. William Youngs, William Roper and lad Sadler of Harwich drowned. **ES Feb 3, 10** and **Mar 31.**

Suicide of William Lewis. **ES Jun 9.**

Schooner *Caernarvon* wrecked on Longsand. Crew saved by *Snowdrop* (J Cook). **ES Jun 9.**

Barque *Augusta May* wrecked on Longsand. Crew saved by *Increase* and *Deerhound*. **ES Sept 8** and **15.**

Brigantine *Ava* wrecked on Longsand. **ES Oct 6.**

French brig *Anna Marie* on Sunk. Crew saved by *Marco Polo* (W Wyatt). **ES Nov 10.**

Application to dredge cement stone in River Stour. **ES Nov 24.**

Barque *Thomas Knox* (Shields to Sebastopol) wrecked on Longsand. One lost, six saved by *Deerhound*. **ES Dec 8.**

Brig *Ceres* on Shipwash assisted off by *Wonder* and *Reaper*. **ES Dec 8.**

1872

Brig *Ruby* wrecked on Platters. Crew in by *Volunteer*. **ES Jan 19.**

Schooner *Anne* of Haugesand on Longsand. Tug *Robert Owen* responds to flares, takes off crew, schooner then 'knocks off' sand and is towed in. **ES Jan 16.**

Sloop *Isabel* sunk on Longsand. Crew saved. **ES Oct 13.**

French schooner assisted off Longsand by six smacks. **ES Nov 8.**

Ship *Australia* abandoned on Shipwash. **ES Nov 22.**

Charlotte of Colchester got off Longsand but sinks in deep water. Crew saved by *Tryal*. **ES Dec 20.**

Death of Captain Isaac Saxby, formerly commander of RC *Scout*, aged 80. **ES Dec 27.**

Charges of concealing wreck against George Death, Mrs Giles and others. **ES Dec 27.**

1873

Closing months of 1872 'among most disastrous on record. In one month nearly 400 vessels wrecked round coast. No colliers in (London) river. All gone down.' **ES Jan 24.**

Sloop *Rose* hits wreck on Sunk, sinks in deep water. Crew in by smack. **ES Jan 24.**

Dutch schooner *Sophia* (St Petersburg to Bordeaux, hemp) stranded on Pye. Cargo unloaded and schooner towed in two weeks later by tug *Gleaner*. **ES Feb 7** and **21**.

ss *Kate* of Middlesborough taking water off Orford Ness. *Perseverance* of Harwich (Britton) attempts tow but breaks boom. Steamer sinks. Crew in by *Perseverance* and *Vigilant* of Harwich (Thomas Smith). **ES Feb 14**.

John Eade and William Scarlett of Brightlingsea and W Bartholomew, W P Cheek and John Brown of Rowhedge charged with possessing salt beef, alleged to be from a wreck. Prosecution referred to two wrecks on Kentish Knock 'on or before June 7' *Empress of India*, 'a very fine vessel,' and *Stornoway*, a smaller vessel. Bartholomew, owner and master of the *Alexander*, claimed they had not been within twenty miles of the wrecks but were given the beef by Ramsgate smacks while fishing. Case against him and Cheek dismissed. Eade and Scarlett to pay £4 (double value) and 10s fine; Brown £10 and £1 15s. **ES Jul 16**.

Presentations of silver medals from Spanish government to Turner Barnard, John Barnard, Harry Warren and John Raynor of *New Unity* for rescues from *Escosa* on Longsand in November 1870. (See December 2 1870.) Turner Barnard said the boy died only half an hour before they reached him after eleven hours in the rigging and that he took his body to Harwich and buried it. **ES Aug 8**.

ss *Black Duck* of London wrecked on Gunfleet. Crew row into Harwich in own two boats. **ES Sept 12**.

Ephraim Dennis, Robert Cook and Walter Austin fined for smuggling tobacco aboard *Snowdrop*. **ES Oct 29**.

Dutch schooner *Goud Visen* of Veendam (Russia to Schiedam, barley) knocked down by squall off Dutch coast, reaches Harwich with bulwarks and sails gone. **ES Nov 14**.

Thousands of planks and deals and a large mast strewn for miles on beach at Clacton. Foredeck with body of man lashed to ring bolt ashore near pier. Thought to be French brig. 'Very rotten.' Few days later scaffold poles picked up at St Osyth thought to be from another wreck, and a vessel seen on Gunfleet. **ES Nov 19**.

Complaint that 'the Essex coast does not possess a single lifeboat station.' **ES Nov 21**.

1874
Death of John Vaux, senior. **ES May 29**.

Prussian barque *Nereide*, dismasted, holed and derelict, brought in by 'a fleet of smacks'. **ES Aug 22**.

Sophia and Isabella of London, on Clacton beach to discharge coal, refuses help to get off as wind freshens and breaks up. **ES Oct 30**.

Barquentine *Grace Millie* ashore on Shipwash. Crew, in boat all night, picked up by *Violet* of Woodbridge (Passiful). Next morning nothing to be seen of ship. Life salvage claim rejected. **ES Nov 20** and **JG/LB**.

Crew of Italian barque on Longsand brought in by Colchester smack. **ES Dec 4**.

Claim by Ablet Passiful, master and owner of *Violet*, against brig *Famileus Horab*, on Suffolk coast on October 14. Value of brig £90, of cargo £670. Award £120. **ES Dec 4**.

1875
Sale of stores from ship *Lion* of Dunkirk (817 tons), barque *Maria Borzone* of Genoa (424 tons), brigantine *Millie* of Dundee (116 tons) and other vessels. **ES Jan 1**.

ss *Eclair* on Shipwash. Crew brought in by smack *Mystle* **ES Jan 8**.

Schooner *Deborah* on West Rocks, refloated by two smacks. **ES Jan 15**.

Harwich church bells to ring 'fog chimes', as call to prayer in bad weather. **ES Feb 9**.

Swedish brig *Cleopatra* assisted in by tug *Liverpool*. **ES Sept 17**.

Brig *George Smith* of Sunderland lost on Gunfleet. Crew brought in by steamer which had attempted to tow her. Hundreds of vessels in Harwich for shelter. **ES Nov 26**.

Wreck of ss *Deutschland*. **ES Dec 10** and **17**.

Mary Jane of Exeter on The Heaps. Crew of seven brought into Brightlingsea by smack *Mary Ann*. **ES Dec 13**.

1876
Service to barque *Hunter* on Shipwash by *Jemima* and tug *Liverpool*. **ECS Jan 28** and **Feb 4**, also **JG** and **SWSC**.

Smack *Moonshine* of Burnham (Lewis Nethercoat) sunk between Mouse and Nore. Crew saved. **ES Jan 28**.

Gunboat *Cherub* to be stationed at Harwich. 'Will no doubt proceed to vessels in distress.' **ES Feb 4**.

Smack *Isabella* of Burnham lost on Nore. Crew saved. **ES Mar 31**.

1876—*cant.*

Claim against barque *Orto* by *Albatross* and tug *Liverpool*. Award £1,046. **ES Apr 14.**

German emigrant ship *Humboldt* ashore off Winterton. 'Thought he was off France.' Iron ship, compass blamed. **ES Apr 21.**

Atlantic towed off Kentish Knock and into Ramsgate by tug *Liverpool*. £800 agreed. **ES May 19.**

Lifeboat *Springwell I* at Harwich. **ES Jun 30.**

Brig *Glencairn* on Platters assisted by *Argo* and tug *Liverpool*. **ES Oct 6.**

Board of Trade inquiry into stranding on West Rocks of ship *Lapwing*, bound from Rotterdam to Africa. Captain had been twenty-six years in South Sea trade and was 'quite lost'. Certificate suspended for three months. **ES Nov 24.**

Advertisement for sale of salvage from *Gustav Fretwurst* (wrecked on Longsand), and from *Henry, Drammersen, Hope* 'and other vessels.' **ES Dec 1.**

Life salvage claim by A Passiful rejected. Brought in crew of *Aspendus* of Falmouth. **JG/LB**

Three-masted schooner *Zephyr* on Longsand. Six lost, two saved by *Concord* of Colchester. **ES Dec 23** and **JG/LB.** (See also Mar 30, 1877.)

1877

New Unity's boat lost going to pilot ss *Tiger*. Daniel Barnard (32), James Harris (28), and John Raynor drowned. **ES Jan 19.**

Claim by *Aquiline* against barque *Amalie* of Uldstadt, assisted off Longsand. Claimed 'only wanted pilot.' Claim £360. Award £100. **ES Feb 2.**

Claim by *New Blossom* (C Crosby), *Qui Vive* and *Emily*, all of Rowhedge, against brig *Emma*, assisted off Buxey Sand. 'Would have been lost but for salvage.' Claim £700. Award £425. **ES Feb 2.**

Eighteen smacks from Lowestoft and Yarmouth given up as lost with all hands, 116 men and boys, leaving fifty widows, eleven aged parents, 115 orphans. **ES Feb 23** and **Mar 26.**

Claim by W Wyatt and Walter Watts, owners of *Volunteer* and tug *Promise*, against brigantine *Roma* of Londonderry, assisted off Landguard. Claim for £275 rejected as 'monstrous'. £50 (already paid into court) awarded. Watts said he would appeal but was told the sum was too small to permit this. **ES Feb 13.**

Bankruptcy of W J Watts of Harwich. **ES Mar 9, 24** and **Apr 27.**

Board of Trade awards £14 to *Concord* of Rowhedge for rescue of two of crew of *Zephyr* of Liverpool lost on Longsand with rest of crew, December 14, 1876. **ES Mar 30.**

Henry Cook of Rowhedge (master of *Aquiline*) charged with assault. **ES Apr 27.**

Pigeons put aboard Sunk and Cork lightships. **ES Apr 20.**

Tug *Harwich* arrives at Harwich. **ES May 25.**

Martha Lavana of Stavanger lost on Shipwash. Crew reach light vessel and brought in by *Albatross*. **ES Jun 1.**

Sixth sale of cargo from ss *Deutschland*. Silks, satins, velvets, skins, embroidery, wines, musical instruments. 'Silks and velvets look quite new.' Enough left to keep divers busy for months. **ES Aug 17.**

Ketch *Brilliant* of Goole assisted off Barrow into Colne by *New Unity*, followed by salvage case. **ES Nov 30** and **Dec 21.**

Norwegian barque *Franklin* (Riga to Le Havre) on Longsand. Captain and crew of twelve brought into Harwich by Brightlingsea smacks. **ES Dec 7.** (See also April 13, 1878.)

Small barque *Jacob Landstrom* of Gothenburg wrecked. Crew saved by *Springwell*. *Harwich* fails to refloat her. (She was, however, ultimately brought in and rebuilt by Vaux as his three-masted schooner *Clacton*.) **ES Dec 7.**

James Cook and crew of *Concord* fined for concealing wreckage, including seventy-two bottles of Geneva, twenty-two decanters and six wine glasses, from *Francesco Ferrara* (Rotterdam to Buenos Aires). Severe penalties might have been demanded under Customs Consolidation Act (1876). **ES Dec 14.**

1878

Claim by *Phoenix* of Rowhedge (Samuel Everitt) against brigantine *Portia* of Hartlepool, assisted off Buxey on December 6, 1877. Claim £250. £40 paid into court. Defendant at sea so case adjourned. Further hearing not traced. **ES Jan 7.**

Collision off Bawdsey between ss *CM Palmer* and ss *Ludworth*, followed by prosecution of smacksmen. **HD Feb 23** and **Mar 30.**

George Orman, smack owner of Brightlingsea, and wife and son, charged with smuggling two gallons of Geneva. Fined £100 under Customs Consolidation Act (1876), with recommendation to Customs to reduce to £25. **ES Mar 8.**

German barque *Auguste Loescher* wrecked on

Longsand close to place of *Deutschland* wreck. Charges of concealing wreckage against smacksmen and divers, F Buston, J Wheeler, J Smith, John Glover, Henry and Charles Jutson and Edward Jones, of *Ann* of Whistable, *Increase* of Colchester and *Cupid* of Harwich. Glover and Jutsons acquitted, others fined 40s. **ES Mar 29.**

Claim by tug *Harwich* and Colchester smacks *Concord*, *Snowdrop* and *Faith* against Norwegian barque *Franklin*. **HD Apr 13.**

Board of Trade awards £10 to Frederick Salmon of *Emily* for saving crew of smack *Beverley* of Hull on Barrow, November 25, 1877. **ES Apr 25.**

Brightlingsea cement stone dredgers sentenced to two months' hard labour for dredging Ipswich Oyster Company's oysters. **ES Apr 25.**

ss *Chicago* of Hartlepool wrecked on Longsand on maiden voyage. Crew of twenty-three brought in by pilot cutter *Stella*. Swedish sailor sentenced to four months for stealing a watch. **ES May 17 and 23.**

Lifeboat *Albert Edward I* at Clacton. **HD Jul 6.**

Claim against brig *Phoebus* by *Volunteer* (A1.10s Catt), *Cupid* (S Walters), *Paul* of Colchester (S Springett), tug *Harwich* (R Keeble and J H Vaux). Claim £300. Award, £2 'per standard of the cargo' plus £32 paid into court. **ES Dec 21.**

1879

Norwegian barque *Hebe* wrecked near Swin Middle lightship. Crew brought in by Clacton lifeboat. **ES Feb 1.**

Barque *Lina* wrecked. Crew reach Swin Middle lightship and taken to London by passing steamer. **ES Mar 29.**

Barque *Pasithea* of Liverpool (587 tons, Hamburg to Cardiff) on Kentish Knock. Crew spent night in *Springwell*, then towed in by *Harwich* which returned and towed in barque. Salvage claim by *Harwich*, *Springwell*, *Agenoria* (A Baggott, owner and master), *Aquiline* and *Prince of Wales* of Ramsgate. Value £2,600. Awards £600 to tug, smacks and lifeboat, £50 to *Prince of Wales*. **ES May 31.**

Barque *Nef* of Arandal (New York, railway iron) on Longsand. First wreck reported by pigeons from lightships. Found abandoned. **ES Sept 27.**

1880

Smack *Care* of Colchester abandoned ashore off Thorpeness. Refloated and taken into Harwich

by pilot cutter undamaged. **HD May 22.** (See also Aug, 1884.)

Claim by *Volunteer* (Amos Catt, master) for assistance to brig *Bertha* of Guernsey. Award £110. **HD Aug 28.**

Crew of three-masted schooner *Ann Lucy* saved by *Ripple* of Colchester. **HD Oct 9 and Nov 20.** (See also Mar 17, 1883.)

Skipper of schooner *Arrival* (Goole to Plymouth) hanged in cabin after salvage by *Dawn* of Woodbridge. **HD Dec 11.**

1881

Wreck of *Indian Chief* and ss *Nymphaea*. **HD Jan 8 and 15.** Inquest Feb 19. B.O.T. inquiry Mar 5 and 19 and Aug 20.

Wreck of *Rosita* (Hamburg to Puerto Rica.) **HD Jan 15.** Application to remove wreck. Hughes: *History of Harwich Harbour.*

Wreck of *New Unity*. **ES Jan** (reprinted in **LSS**).

Capsize of *Springwell*. **HD Jan 22.**

Wreck of ss *Ingerid*. **HD Jan 29 and Apr 16.**

Wreck of ss *Clytie*. **HD Feb 26.**

Norwegian barque *Facina* on Gunfleet. **HD Sept 17.**

Lugger *Madeline* of Boulogne on Gunfleet. sixteen saved. **HD Oct 2 and Sept 9, 1882.**

Swedish barque *Iris* on Cork. Crew saved by lifeboat which was not allowed to return next day for salvage and as a result refused to launch in response to later signals from Cork. *Iris* later salvaged by *Reindeer*, *Volunteer* and tug *Harwich*. **HD Oct 29.**

Claim by John Emeny of Aldeburgh for smacks and lifeboat against schooner *Equity* in Aldeburgh Bay. Award £75. **HD Dec 3.**

Barge *Olive Branch* on Longsand. Claim for £85 by lifeboat. Award £50. **HD Dec 24 and Feb 4, 1882.**

1882

Service by *Volunteer* and tug *Harwich* to Italian barque. **HD Jan 7.**

Service by *Volunteer* and tug *Harwich* to *Lucy* of Whitby, wrecked on Gunfleet. **HD Mar 4.**

Barque *Lois* of Nova Scotia on Shipwash stripped by smacks. **HD Mar 4.**

Barque *John Barfield* got off Shipwash by two smacks. Agreement £200. **HD Mar 18.**

Lifeboat *Springwell II* at Harwich. **HD Apr 29 and Jul 29.**

1882—cont.

First service by *Springwell II* to *Henrietta* on Cork. **HD Apr 29.**

ss *Claud Hamilton* tows barque *George Bewley* into Flushing. **HD Oct 28.**

ss *Richard Young* abandons ss *Ben Avon*. **HD Nov 4 and 18.**

ss *Adelaide* tows barque *Kong Sverre* into Harwich. **HD Dec 9.**

Duke of Edinburgh avoids wreck on Gunfleet. **HD Nov 18 and Dec 2.**

Service by *Cupid* and *Volunteer* and tugs *Harwich* and *Robert Owen* to barque *Scottish Chief* of Liverpool on Gunfleet. **HD Dec 23.**

Service by *Queen Victoria* (now of Brightlingsea) to *Sagar* of Holbeach on the Middle. Mr Major, owner of *Queen Victoria*, hurt in accident. **BPM Dec.**

1883

ss *Polymnia* of Stavanger found by *Volunteer* ashore abandoned. **HD Feb 3 and 10.**

ss *Adelaide*'s service to ss *Carl Woerman*. **HD Mar 24.**

Claim by *Wonder* against brigantine *Ann Lucy*. Award £30. **HD Mar 17.** (See also October, 1880.)

Russian schooner mistakes Orford Ness for Spurn Head. **HD May 5.**

Smacksman from *Albatross* fined £5 for piloting. Claimed to be salvor and bargained for £50. **HD May 12.**

Vaux's towage offer refused by RNLI. **HD July 21.**

Service by *Albert Edward* to Norwegian barque *Roma* on Gunfleet. (*Springwell* on slip.) **HD Sept 8.**

1884

Brig *Arabian* of Colchester at anchor near Kentish Knock 'rude to the lifeboat'. **HD Jan 26.**

Capsize of lifeboat *Albert Edward*. **HD Jan 26.**

Service by *Albert Edward* to ss *Hawthorn* on Gunfleet. **HD Feb 2.**

Service by *Faith* and tug *Harwich* to ship *Lathom* of Liverpool on Longsand. Six of crew saved by *Faith*. Became total wreck. **HD Feb 2.**

Emblem 'still at work on ship on Longsand, getting out turmeric and jute.' (Presumably *Lathom*.) **BPM Aug.**

Crew of brig *Ellide* landed by *Faith*. **HD Feb 9.**

Lifeboat *Albert Edward* saves eight from brig *Thorly* in Middle Deep. **HD Apr 19.**

Death of John Carrington, piermaster, former master of tug *Liverpool*. **HD Apr 19.**

Barque *Niord* total wreck on West Rocks. Crew landed. **HD Apr 26.**

ss *Harwich* (railway packet) converted from paddle to twin screw. **HD Jul 19.**

Care rebuilt as *Lady Olive*. **BPM Aug.**

Gospel ship *Mystery* (Calais to Southampton) assisted off Gunfleet by *Albert Edward*. **HD Sept 13.**

Brigantine *William* wrecked on Shipwash. Boat with captain and two men broke adrift and reached Yarmouth. Four others found on raft and taken to Dover. **HD Sept 13.**

Wreck of barque *Mirford and Trubey*. **HD Oct 18.**

Lifeboat *Honourable Artillery Company* at Walton. **HD Nov 22.**

Iron barque *Berengaria* of Greenock wrecked on Shipwash. Crew of thirteen landed at Aldeburgh. **HD Dec 6.**

Smack *Energy* of Colchester run down. **HD Dec 20.**

Smack *Greyhound* of Colchester run down. **BPM Oct.**

Service by *Honourable Artillery Company* and *Reindeer* to barque *Dieke Rickmers* on Longsand. **HD Dec 27.**

1885

Wreck of Liverpool barque *Canossa* on Kentish Knock. Crew of twelve saved by Ramsgate smack *Nelson*. **HD Jan 17.**

ss *Ashfield* (Aarhus to Tyne) on Kentish Knock. Assisted off by tug *Harwich*, smacks and lifeboat. **HD Jan 31.**

Three-masted schooner *Akyub* of Genoa assisted into Harwich by tug and beachmen. **HD Mar 14.**

ss *Bedder* assisted off Shipwash. Claim by owners and fourteen-man crews of yawls *Jane* of Orford Haven and *Deben* of Woodbridge Haven, Caister lifeboat and tugs *Harwich* and *Robert Owen*. Award £1,900 including £900 to tugs. **HD Mar 14 and May 9.**

Three-masted screw steamer *Enrique de Calvet* on Shipwash. Claim by *Wentworth* yawl from Aldeburgh, Langmaid's yawl from Orford Haven and Percival's yawl from Woodbridge

Haven. Insured for £12,000. Agreement for one-third of the value. **HD May 9.**

Lifeboat *Albert Edward II*, with centreboard, at Clacton. **HD May 2.**

Caister yawl *Zephyr* hits wreckage and sinks, near Cockle lightship. Eight of crew of fifteen lost. **HD Jul 25.**

ss *Crystal* on Gunfleet. **HD Aug 22** and **BPM Sept.**

Albert Edward II meets ss *Hawthorn*. **HD Oct 10.**

Russian timber barque *Delphin*, found water-logged, dismasted and abandoned off Cork after being ashore, towed in by *Harwich* and *Robert Owen*. **HD Nov 7.**

Smack *Energy* run down. **BPM Jan.**

Smack *Orion* run down. **BPM Feb.**

1886

Barquentine *Victoria* of Shoreham found abandoned and waterlogged on Maplins by Clacton lifeboat which left Lloyd's agent from *Brightlingsea* aboard. **HD Jan 9.**

Claim by lifeboat *Ipswich* (stationed at Thorpeness, Harling cox'n, fourteen hands, value £400) against collier ss *Agnes and Louise*. Cox'n sent lifeboat home and went to London in the collier. Offered £50. Award £150. **HD Jan 30.**

Carrier pigeon service from lightships (established 1877) abandoned during 1885. **HD Feb 13.**

Schooner *Success* of Boston run down by steamer off Gunfleet. Crew saved by *Reindeer*. **HD Feb 13** and **20.**

Yacht salvages sb *Pride of the Colne*. **BPM Apr.**

Aldeburgh pilot cutter *Maiden* run down and sunk by ss *Carl Rathkens* 'of Middlesborough, owned by Germans,' flying flag for pilot. Crew saved. **HD Jul 31.**

Wreck of three-masted schooner *Ocean Pride* of Guernsey on West Sunk. Mistook Gunfleet for Varne. Crew saved by Clacton lifeboat, wreckage including masts brought in by *Queen Victoria*, *Emily*, *Emblem*, *Ella* and *Thought*. **BPM Nov.**

Smack *Weigh* run down. **HD Aug 17.**

ss *Swift*, first steam barge, at Ipswich. **HD Sept 11.**

Kentish Knock lightship sunk by barque. **HD Dec 4.**

Constanze of Hamburg on Longsand. Crew taken off by Walton lifeboat. ss *Harwich* overtook lifeboat and took her in tow. **HD Dec 4.**

1887

Wreckage of *Trixie Wee* sold for £16 at Thorpeness following great gale of December 1886. **HD Jan 1.**

Barque *Isabel* (petroleum) on Galloper, assisted by cod smacks *Gipsy* and *Zealous*. Then got on Shipwash. Towed in by tug *Harwich*, summoned by *Zealous*, 'the smack steering.' Master's certificate suspended for three months. **HD Jan 15** and **Feb 5.**

Inquiry as to whether cable to Sunk lightship has justified cost. **HD Feb 26** and **BPM Jan.**

ss *Swift* tows in *Antonia* ashore on Gunfleet. **HD Mar 12.**

Reindeer (C Forster owner, Thomas Daniels master) wrecked on Gunfleet. Crew take nine hours to row ashore at Felixstowe in a gale. **HD Mar 26.**

Trinity House cutters to cruise at Sunk and take off 'down' pilots. **HD May 28.**

Brigantine *Eliza and Emma* assisted off Shipwash by *Increase*. **HD May 28.**

Norwegian ice vessel *Henry Parr* wrecked on Shipwash. Crew saved by ss *Nerissa*. Gear salvaged by *Countess*, *Hilda* and *Test* of Brightlingsea. **BPM Apr.**

Yawl *Queen of the Ocean* (Henry Britton) assists ketch *Sylphide* of Maldon, ashore at Holland Low. Six men took off anchor. Agreed £60, reduced to £30. **HD Sept 3.**

John Hannah ashore at Felixstowe. 'If the vessel breaks up it is expected the beach will be littered with coal from Landguard to Bawdsey Ferry.' **HD Oct 22.**

ss *Capri* of Liverpool wrecked on Kentish Knock. Crew taken off by Walton lifeboat and transferred to tug *Harwich* with one Ramsgate smacksman. **HD Dec 3.**

1888

Award by Netherlands vice-consul at Harwich of £12 6s 9d to Captain W Wheeler of *Excellent*. On 'Skilling' voyage rescued master and crew of waterlogged *Anna* off Texel in gale in September 1887. Aneroid also awarded by SFMS. **HD Feb 4** and **BPM Oct 1887.**

Norwegian ice brig *Ipselen* (312 tons) wrecked on Whitaker. Crew taken to Clacton by lifeboat, and returned next day for their possessions. **HD Feb 25.**

Schooner *Dorothea* of Riga with crew of four on Maplins towed off to London. Clacton lifeboat reports crew drunk, riotous and 'attempting to use their knives rather freely.' **HD Feb 20.**

1888—cont.

Brig *William and Anthony* of Folkestone at anchor off Platters after damage in collision with GER ss *Peterborough*. Lifeboat responds to rockets and flares in south-east gale with snow. Cox'n Tyrell injured in fall from ladder trying to board. Award £45. **HD Mar 17** and **Apr 14.**

Italian barque *Raffaele Ligure* on Longsand. Refused lifeboat. Next day crew taken off by *Increase* and barque a wreck. **HD May 9.**

Spanish ss *Ciscar* on 'west edge opposite Bradwell.' Refuses and threatens smack *Topaz*. **BPM Oct.**

Lifeboat summoned by telegram from Sunk lightship. Towed by Trinity House ss *Satellite* to Gunfleet. Found Russian Finn barque *Carl Gustaf* total wreck with only foremast standing. Took off crew of ten. **HD Nov 10.**

Norwegian barque *Cromwell* (Baltic to Barcelona, timber) on Shipwash. Refused *Gipsy*. Came off, wind fair for Harwich but drifted on to Cork. Then accepted *Gipsy*. Deck cargo thrown overboard but too late. After night's gale tug *Harwich* could not shift. But came off and towed in week later. **HD Nov 10** and **17.**

Cod smack *Mary* of Aldeburgh awarded £104 for services to Norwegian barque *Arundel*. **HD Nov 17.**

Two Sisters of Brightlingsea sunk in Woolwich Reach by ss *Olivia*. Captain Sawyer and two apprentices saved, two men lost. **HD Dec 1** and **Jan 23, 1889.**

ss *Akaba* (new ship worth, with cargo and freight, £90,000) stranded off Yarmouth. Awards: £2,000 to tugs *Yare* and *United Services* and lifeboats *Mark Lane* and *Refuge* (a volunteer boat which capsized towing in after the service with loss of four lives, for which £300 awarded), tug *Cambria* £1,600, ss *Ouse* £200, ss *Richard Moxon* £600, tug *Meteor* £300, trawler *Preceptor* £130, tug *Gleaner* £100, trawler *Try Again* £70. **HD Nov 17** and **Dec 8.**

Master (W Wheeler) and crew of *Excellent* charged with concealing part salvage from *Explorer* sunk near Mouse. Liable to forfeit salvage claim, pay double value and fine up to £100. Fined one shilling each and to pay double value (£4 10s) and costs. **HD Dec 29.**

Faith's boat holed rowing to abandoned brig on Whitaker. Smacksmen took brig's boat to return. **BPM Mar.**

Norwegian timber barque *Albatross* hit by steamer, drifts first on to Longsand, then on to Sunk. Got off abandoned by *Emily, Aid* and *Express* of Brightlingsea and *Pearl* of Tollesbury. Crew saved by Margate lifeboat which returned to find ship claimed by smacksmen. **BPM Dec.**

1889

Sale of salvage from brigantine *Parrot*, of Haugesund, on Barrow. 360 bales hemp, 80,000 oak staves. **HD Jan 8.**

Newcastle brig *Ismyr* assisted off Cutler by yawl *Pride of the Deben* (Ablet Passiful). Used yawl's 5 cwt anchor. Value of brig £200, of cargo (348 tons gas coal) £192. Offered £5, then £10. Award £50. **HD Feb 8.**

ss *Albacore* of Glasgow sunk on Gunfleet. 'Must have struck wreck to sink so soon.' **HD Apr 13.**

Smack *Vanduara* ashore in Scheldt with dynamite for Antwerp. **BPM Sept.**

Norwegian schooner *Edward* on Longsand brought in by Walton lifeboat and 'Mr Vaux's tug'. **HD Nov 16.**

ss *Speedwell* runs out of coal due to towing brigantine *Georgia* of Nova Scotia, London to Ipswich. Both found in fog at anchor in East Swin and towed in by ss *Swift*. **HD Dec 14.**

1890

ss *Speedwell* salvages sb *Formosa*. **HD Apr 12.**

Aldeburgh yawl *Wentworth* awarded £10 against Norwegian barque *Passepartout* for showing flag for pilot and then not employing her. **HD May 24.**

Pilot cutter *Rapid*, on Sunk station, sees Norwegian timber barque flying flag for assistance, puts seven men on board and assists in, tug *Harwich* towing. **HD May 24.**

Cable to Sunk lightship taken up by ss *Sedgemoor*. **HD Jun 7.**

Yawl *Jane* salvages *Winifred* on Shipwash. Underwriters offer £80. £250 claimed. £100 paid into court. 'Not enough for seventeen hours' hard work by ten men.' Award £200. **HD Jun 21** and **Aug 9.**

ss *Barniston* assisted by Old Company of Beachmen, Lowestoft, with yawls *Success* and *Jenny Lind*. Award £600 between company and three GER tugs. **HD Jun 28.**

Smack *Osprey* of Burnham sunk in Long Reach. Pilot of steamer acquitted of manslaughter. £1,260 damages to relatives of two men lost. **HD May 17, Jun 28** and **Dec 2.**

Norwegian ice brig *Alice* towed in off Shipwash by tug *Harwich*. **HD Jul 12.**

Duke of Northumberland steam lifeboat at Harwich. **HD Jul 26** and **Jan 17, 1891.**

ss *Blanche* arrives at Ipswich. 'Is 28 years old and has been sunk in collision four times in Thames Estuary.' **HD Aug 9.**

Tug *Merrimac* arrives at Ipswich. **HD Sept 13.**

Coal brig *Larissa* on Gunfleet. Lifeboat towed by fish carrier *Albatross*. Took off crew of eight. **HD Oct 11.**

ss *Dunelm* on Gunfleet. Got off by boats and tug *Harwich*. **HD Oct 11.**

Brigantine *Ada* of Faversham towed in. Agreement £40 with smacksmen, who agreed £20 with tug *Harwich*. **HD Oct 11.**

ss *Achilles* on Shipwash. Reserve Number Three lifeboat leaves under sail, overtaken and towed by *Duke of Northumberland*. Ship accepts two lifeboats and tug *Harwich*. Threw overboard 300 tons of sleepers and towed in by tug and *Duke of Northumberland*. Awards £560 to *Harwich* and lifeboats. Tug *Merrimac* had £50 agreement. **HD Oct 25** and **Dec 13.**

Aldeburgh lifeboat fires 'usual green signal' on return from service. Taken for distress signal and yawl *Anna Maria* launched. **HD Nov 1.**

Schooner *Sensation* of Dover got off Shipwash by Aldeburgh smack *Alpha* and yawl *Jane*. Shipwash lightship fired twice but did not show flag, so lifeboat secretary awaited return of cox'n from fishing before launching. **HD Nov 8.** (See also March 7, 1891.)

Schooner *Christine Elizabeth* of Haugesund (Rotterdam to East Indies) on Longsand. Crew picked up by pilot cutter. *Duke of Northunberland* towed out, Reserve Number Three pumped out schooner, refloated. Towed in by *Harwich* and *Duke of Northumberland*. **HD Nov 15.**

ss *Adelaide* disabled by broken piston, salvaged by ss *Brandon*. **HD Dec 13.**

1891

Billyboy *Days* of Goole wrecked on Cork. *Duke of Northumberland* tows out Reserve Number Three, saves two men, leaves boy dead in rigging. **HD Jan 16.**

Three-masted schooner *Mercury* (Grangemouth to Buenos Ayres, coals) wrecked on Longsand. After twenty-six hours' delay in receiving call *Duke of Northumberland* saves all crew of twelve. **HD Mar 7.**

Claim by yawl *Jane* (which was damaged), smack *Alpha* of Harwich and cutter *Sheldrake* of Woodbridge Haven against brigantine *Sensation*

on Shipwash on November 1, 1890. Award £150. **HD Mar 7.**

Schooner *J W Bebell* of Beumaris on Gunfleet. Mate in boat washed ashore at Holland Gap. Clacton lifeboat, towed off by passing steamer, finds two dead, one alive. **HD Mar 14.**

Duke of Northumberland launched in response to misunderstood signals from lightships. **HD Mar 21** and **Jun 18.**

Robert Legerton, cox'n of Clacton lifeboat since its institution, retires. **HD May 23.**

ss *Speedwell* II at Ipswich. **HD Jun 18.**

Wreck of barque *Oliver Cromwell* of Oland on Whitaker. **BPM November.**

Smack *Aid* run down off Greenwich. **BPM Apr.**

1892

Ship *Enterkin* wrecked on Galloper with loss of twenty-eight lives. Scandal over lack of communication. **HD Jan 2.**

ss *Violet*, disabled off Shipwash, assisted to London by tug *Harwich*. **ES Jan 16.**

Schooner *Trio*, damaged by steamer off Aldeburgh, refuses assistance of cod smack *Ocean Wave* and is towed into Harwich by 'another schooner of the same firm.' **HD Jan 30.**

Experiments to find 'distinguishable rocket signals.' **HD Feb 6.**

Claim by tugs *Jubilee*, *Harwich*, *Shamrock* and *Thistle* against *Vega*, disabled near Gunfleet on Feb 16. Defendants tendered £1,500, awarded as £300 to *Jubilee* and £1,200 between *Harwich*, *Shamrock* and *Thistle*. **HD Apr 9.**

Miss Williams (Bangor to Ipswich, slates) assisted off Cork by tug *Merrimac* for £90. **HD Apr 23.**

Barque *Ephrussi* of Brevig, with 500 tons of ice, on Shipwash. Towed in by tug *Harwich*. **HD Jun 11.**

Salvage awards for ss *Brighton* on Gunfleet. £200 to *Harwich*, £175 to *Merrimac*, £150 to *Robert Owen*, £50 to *Cormorant* of Grimsby, £150 to crews of lifeboat *Honourable Artillery Company* and yawl *Dogger Bank*. **HD Jun 25.**

Brigantine *Berthold* of Maldon (Riga to Maldon, timber) on West Rocks. Refuses *Springwell* but pays £70 to bawley crews to throw timber overboard. Followed by dispute between bawleys. **HD Sept 24** and **Jan 21, 1893.**

Schooner *James Taylor* wrecked on Kentish Knock. Crew saved by Aldeburgh lifeboat. **HD Oct 29.**

1892—*cont.*

Springwell and *Merrimac*, called to Longsand, find sunken ss *Dilsberg* and schooner under water on Kentish Knock. Six of crew of *Dilsberg* drowned, captain died later. 'A remarkable illustration of the lack of electric communication.' **HD Dec 17** and **Jan 28, 1893.**

1893

Royal Commission on Coast Communication recommends telegraphs to five lightships and some lighthouses. But Parliamentary grant already expended. **HD Jan 7** and **BPM Jan** and **Mar.**

Danish ss *Helsingor* (Ghent to Dundee and Buenos Ayres) on Galloper. Crew row to Longsand lightship and taken off by *Springwell* and *Merrimac*. **HD Jan 21.**

Claim against iron four-masted barque *Glencairn* of Glasgow (1,564 tons) ashore in fog at Thorpeness, November 25, 1892. Got off and taken to Gravesend. Value £9,000, cargo £7,410. Awards: £450 to GER tugs, £400 to beachmen, £650 to *Iona* and *Mercie*, £225 to *Merrimac*, £150 to *Gleaner*, £125 to *Yare* and *Meteor*, £175 to *United Services* – total £2,175. **HD Feb 4.**

Royal Commission (see Jan 7) recommends 'proposed Gunfleet lighthouse' be connected with Walton, and Shipwash light vessel with Aldeburgh. **HD Mar 11.**

Schooner *Agnes Cairns* of Fowey on Gunfleet in fog 'close to the submerged *Darenth*.' Crew taken off by Walton and Clacton lifeboats, schooner refloated by tug *Harwich*. **HD Apr 15.**

Russian Finn barque *St Olaf* on Longsand after parting from anchor. Crew of twelve saved by *Springwell* and *Merrimac*. Imperial Senate of Finland rewards *Springwell* cox'n W Tyrell with silver cup, second cox'n Benjamin Dale with diamond ring, thirteen others of crew with seventy-five marks (£2 19s 2d). Barque later refloated and towed in by Trinity House tender *Irene*, dismasted and with six-inch freeboard. **HD Nov 11, 18, Dec 2** and **Oct 26, 1895.**

German barque *Martha Brockelmann* on Gunfleet. Crew saved by ss *Resolute* of Leith. Walton lifeboat finds only dog aboard. **HD Nov 18.**

Guernsey schooner *Reward* on Gunfleet refuses tug *Harwich*. Later brought in by Clacton beachmen. **HD Sept 23.**

Cable laid to Gunfleet lighthouse. Telephone lines to be laid to Walton, Harwich and Clacton coastguards. **HD Sept 30.**

ss *Rockcliff* on Longsand, refloated by tug *Harwich* and Ramsgate smack *Annie*. First call by new Gunfleet lighthouse phone. *Springwell* towed out by tug *Harwich*, Walton lifeboat by *Merrimac*. Awards: £750 to *Harwich*, £150 to *Annie*, £50 to *Springwell*. **HD Nov 11** and **Feb 17, 1894.**

Danish barque *Anna* assisted off Gunfleet by *Merrimac*. **HD Dec 2** and **9.**

Barque *Venscapen* drives on to Sizewell Bank. Crew saved by Aldeburgh lifeboat just before she hit. RNLI awards £96. Imperial Senate of Finland awards silver cup to cox'n Cable and seventy-five marks to seventeen sailors. **HD Nov 25, Dec 9** and **Oct 26, 1895.**

Tug *Harwich* tows in timber barque drawing twenty feet, only kept afloat by cargo. **HD Nov 25.**

Volunteer (now of Brightlingsea) assists kb *Alice Watts* adrift in Colne. **HD Nov 25** and **BPM Dec.**

Service of *Emily* to *Winifred* and ship *Fiery Cross* of Glasgow (1,399 tons). **BPM Dec.**

Emblem and *Thought* sold to Iceland. **BPM July.**

'Another Norwegian barque' found on Heaps by *Matchless*, *Vestal* and *Queen of Brightlingsea*. Taken to Sheerness by tug. **BPM Dec.**

Samuel Whyard lost at sea. **SWSC**

1894

Three-masted schooner *Rosendale*, of Barrow, ashore on Maplins after losing anchor, assisted by *Welcome*. **BPM Jan.**

Steam lifeboat *City of Glasgow* I at Harwich. **HD Feb 10** and **Jun 9.**

Volunteer lifeboat *True to the Core* at Walton. **WR**

Barquentine *Eboe* of Liverpool (Rotterdam to West Africa) on Sunk having mistaken lights. *Harwich* tows out *Springwell*, *Merrimac* tows out Walton lifeboat, then two tugs tow in barque and two lifeboats. **HD Feb 24.**

sb *Isabella* sinks on 'the Holidays.' Crew picked up by *Tyro* and barge raised by diving boat *Invicta* of Faversham (Rigden, master). **HD Mar 2** and **24.**

Death of J H Vaux. **HD Jul 7.**

ss *Wickham* fined for not taking a pilot into Felixstowe. **HD Oct 6.**

Barque *Guiste* of Trieste (Sundsvall to Cape Town, deals) on Gabbard. 'Cut away masts and beat off sands.' Towed in by *Merrimac* drawing twenty-four feet, grounding several times on entering. **HD Oct 27.**

Receiver of Wreck permitted to sell marked anchors and cables without warranty. **JG/LB.**

Royal Humane Society testimonial to Captain Tovee of *Merrimac* for life-saving at Slaughden. **HD Dec 1.**

1895

Barque *Picton Castle* of Swansea on Shipwash. Crew brought in by cod smack *Volo* and pilot cutter *Bittern*. Barque refloated and picked up by French fishermen who tried to get her into Calais but drove into pier-head. **HD Jan 26.**

Loss of German liner *Elbe*. **HD Feb 16.**

Assault by Walton RNLI man (A Lee) on volunteer lifeboat man (F Collins). **HD Feb 23.**

RNLI Silver Medal to A Simmons, chief engineer of *Duke of Northumberland*. First award to an engineer. **HD Mar 9.**

Norwegian ice schooner *Fingal* on Longsand. Crew in boat picked up by *Merrimac*. **HD Apr 6.**

German schooner *Hanse* (Hamburg to Colchester, oil cake) found on West Rocks with rudder gone. Towed in by *City of Glasgow*. **HD Jun 8.**

ss *Express* (one of three United Steamship Company passenger and cargo ships, trading Esbjerg to Parkeston) blows to *Merrimac* off Shipwash to tell her of ship in trouble nearby. Tug hits *Express* holing her and flooding engine room. Eleven passengers put aboard tug. *Robert Owen* arrives and two tugs tow ship in. **HD Nov 16.**

'Dutch' barque *Gustav Omar* of Bremen (1,350 tons) on Shipwash. Towed in by *Harwich*, *Merrimac* and *Cambria*. **HD Nov 23.**

Atalanta of Hamburg (for South America) ashore five miles east of Black Deeps. *City of Glasgow* and *Merrimac* failed to find; Margate lifeboat *Quiver* and two tugs stood by. **HD Dec 28.**

North Goodwin lightship to have 'phone cable to Ramsgate. Authorities look for an answer to 'chafing which has caused continual breakages, an exception being the last cable from Aldeburgh to the Shipwash.' **HD Jun 29.**

1896

ss *Harwich* (railway packet) turns back towing derelict. **HD Jan 18.**

Death of Thomas Barnard of Rowhedge. **HD Feb 22.**

ss *Tellus* on Gunfleet. Refuses two boats from Walton (*Edith*, belonging to Skylark Company and Mr Polley's *Volunteer*). Offers small sum to *Merrimac*, which declines. Got off next tide. **HD Mar 12.**

Springwell towed out by steam pinnace of HMS *Mersey* in response to signals from Cork. Trinity House steamer *Satellite* then took over tow. On arrival vessel (*Coraline* of Whitby) had taken down distress signals. **HD Sept 26.**

Barque *Ebenezer* of West Hartlepool on Kentish Knock. Crew rowed to Sunk lightship and brought ashore by pilot cutter *Cynthia*. **HD Oct 3.**

Tug *Harwich* sold to the Tyne. **HD Oct 17.**

Claim by *Merrimac* against schooner *Aire* for £300 for getting off dangerous position off Aldeburgh. Counter claim £40–£50 for negligently slipping chains and preventing crew returning aboard. Award £50; £30 to owners, £15 to three men who jumped aboard ship and £5 to rest of crew. **HD Mar 21.**

Yawl *Druid* of London (46 tons) on Buxey. *Antelope* and *Norman* of Brightlingsea and two Mersea smacks take out ballast, and ss *Gem* of Colchester tows off. Agreement £200. **BPM Nov.**

1897

Trinity House proposes inward and outward traffic lanes at Swin Middle. **HD Jan 2.**

Claim by *Merrimac* and Walton lifeboat against Guernsey brigantine *Lord Strangford* (164 tons) assisted off Gunfleet on Dec 3, 1879. Built in 1825 at Cowes as yacht and lengthened. Value only £140 due to age. Award £35. **HD Jan 23.**

Faversham schooner *Sancho Panza* driven across harbour mouth and ashore at Dovercourt. Crew of six and boat's crew from cod smack *Zealous*, assisting, saved by *Springwell*. Wreck sold for £18 17s. **HD Jan 30.**

Sunk lightship seen flying flag and ball. *Springwell* towed out by *Harwich* and *Spray*. Lightship 'had seen barque heel over.' Nothing found. **HD Apr 17.**

New Walton volunteer lifeboat *True to the Core II* ordered from Houston of Rowhedge 'entirely on the lines of the Aldeburgh lifeboat.' **HD Jul 3.**

Death of Alderman John Watts, aged seventy-seven. **HD Jul 17.**

German barque *Triton* (Raumo to Port Natal) on Cork. Brought in by *City of Glasgow* and

1897—*cont.*

True to the Core. Underwriters award each boat £145. **HD Oct 30.**

Barque *Charlotte* on Gunfleet, towed in by tug *Spray*. **HD Oct 30.**

City of Glasgow leaves for six months' trials at Gorleston. Returned after one unsatisfactory trial. **HD Nov 27 and Feb 5, 1898.**

Springwell towed out by *Spray* in 'worst weather for 15 years.' Three men washed overboard but got back. Nothing found. **HD Dec 4.**

1898

GSN Co's ss *Seamew* sinks Goole billyboy *Rose* in June. Owner's son and two others lost. **HD Mar 26, Apr 2, Apr 30.**

New steel German barque *Pampa* on Gunfleet. *City of Glasgow*, *True to the Core* and Aldeburgh lifeboat (in Harwich with a shipwrecked crew) help throw 300 tons of cement overboard. Refloated and towed to London. On return voyage Aldeburgh lifeboat finds Norwegian ice barque *Magdimenta* on Heaps, and saves crew of ten. RNLI rewards crew for rescue from *Magdimenta*. *Pampa* treated as salvage. Awards: £550 to tug *Cambria*, £300 to tug *Spray*, £450 between three lifeboats. **HD Apr 2 and 9, and Feb 25, 1899.**

'King's pipe' lit at Parkeston (for burning contraband.) **HD May 7.**

G W Newson, Trinity pilot at Felixstowe, fined 10s for piloting ship into Harwich. **HD Sept 3.**

Swedish barque *Inga* flares for pilot at Sunk. Then anchors and drags on to Gunfleet. *Springwell* towed out by *Satellite* followed by *Spray*. Ship lightened and towed to London by London tug and *Spray*. **HD Oct 22.**

Smack *Faith* wrecked on Cork. **HD Nov 4.**

Schooner *Ornan* of Osthammer on Gunfleet. Mistook lights. Crew taken off by Clacton lifeboat and *Volunteer* and *Varuna* of Brightlingsea. Smacks returned with *Emily*, refloated and towed schooner into Colne. **BPM Dec.**

1899

Full-rigged ship *Hawksdale* of Liverpool (1,723 tons, Hamburg to Melbourne) on Longsand. Believed pilot mistook Kentish Knock for lights of France. Clacton lifeboat saves eighteen, Margate lifeboat seven. Pilot and two men lost in capsize of boat. *Emily* brings in furniture, including chairs, lamps and pianos 'of which there were said to be 500 on board.' **BPM Feb and Mar.**

ss *Admiral Aube* of Le Havre assisted off Sunk by three lifeboats and six tugs – *Warrior, Burmah, Cambria, Columbia, Spray, Merrimac.* 'Claim expected to be close on £2,000.' **HD Jan 21.**

Tug *Spray* reports schooner *John Anderson* on Swin Middle due to steering gear failure. Crew of five into Clacton by lifeboat and received by John H Harman, local agent of Shipwrecked Mariners Society. **HD Jan 28.**

Pilots at Southwold and Yarmouth ordered to move to Harwich. **HD May 13 and Jun 10.**

Contract for daily conveyance of mails between Harwich and Hook of Holland approved in Parliament. **HD Jul 29.**

Barque *Pactolus* of London on West Rocks 'to the North of Cork lightship.' Abandoned and next day full of water. Crew brought in by *Springwell* and *Spray*. **HD Nov 4.**

ss *Lambeth* run down and sunk by unknown steamer. Harwich steam lifeboat, called by phone from Walton, brings in eight men. **HD Dec 9.**

RNLI 'intends replacing steam lifeboat *City of Glasgow* by a boat built by White of Cowes as at Padstow and Grimsby. To have protected screw instead of turbine which has not been found a success.' **HD Dec 23.**

Swedish brig *Lyn* damaged when coal cargo explodes near Outer Gabbard. Crew board lightship and then return to brig which is taken in tow by Trinity House ss *Vestal* but sinks near Shipwash. **HD Dec 30.**

1900

'Year 1899 like its predecessor unusually fine. Months without any bad weather.' **HD Jan 6.**

Claim by tug *Spray* against ss *Bellarden* of Glasgow assisted off Shipwash. Value £22,916. Award £1,000. **HD May 5.**

Schooner *Saxon Maid* of Goole ashore on Gunfleet. *City of Glasgow* finds Walton lifeboat alongside. John Cook (19), his brother David and John Jenner also launch their boat at Frinton but capsize sailing off. Walton lifeboatmen save David Cook and Jenner but John Cook, a bathing machine attendant and native of Lowestoft, drowned. **HD Jul 7 and 21.**

New Walton lifeboat *James Stevens*, 43 ft × 12½ft. Two drop keels, twelve oars. 'Cost of a lifeboat station exceeds £100 a year.' **HD Jul 7.**

Barque *Argo* ashore on Gunfleet June 28–29 in fine weather, towed by tug *Privateer*. Towed off by *Merrimac* and *Privateer*. Engaged smacks

Queen Victoria and *Secret* at £8 to jettison deck cargo. Awards £250 to *Merrimac*, £50 to (? other) plaintiffs. **HD Aug 4.**

1901
ss *Swallow* loses lighter *Lily* in tow. One man lost. **HD Jan 5** and **26.**

Coastguard cutter *Hind*, tender to Harwich guardship *Severn*, wrecked on Shipwash November 27, 1900. At court martial chief officer dismissed ship and to lose six months' seniority. Second mate to lose six months' seniority. Crew saved by *Satellite* and pilot cutter *Alpha*. **HD Jan 12** and **BPM Feb.**

Ipswich schooner *Rose* blown ashore on Felixstowe beach. **HD Apr 6.** Awards May 4 and Jun 15.

Lifeboat *City of Glasgow* II at Harwich. **HD May 11** and **18.**

Lifeboat *Sailors' Friend* at Frinton. **WR**

Schooner *Harriet* of Goole on Cork. Race between *City of Glasgow* and Felixstowe ferry yawl, won by yawl which gets schooner off and into harbour. **HD May 25.**

Crew of *Satellite* fined for smuggling. **HD Jun 22.**

Barque *Lendfield* (Melbourne to Frederickstadt) on Gunfleet. Refuses lifeboat. Towed to Downs by three tugs. **HD Jul 20.**

Ramsgate smack *Isabella* wrecked on Gunfleet. **HD Sept 7.**

E Cattermole and 'The Darker the Night the Better the Deed.' **HD Sept 17, Dec 14** and **Jan 4, 1902.** Also **JG.**

Death of Captain John Glover. **HD Sept 28.**

1903
HMS *Mersey* to replace HMS *Severn* as coastguard ship at Harwich. **HD Feb 7.**

1904
ss *Norham* of Sunderland (1,131 tons) wrecked in fog on Longsand. Captain and crew of eight brought in by French tug *Atlas*. **HD Jan 16.**

Walton lifeboats race to schooner *Lief* ashore in Gatway and towed in by *Spray*. 'The sailing of the lifeboats was a treat to witness.' *James Stevens* had a minute's start and kept ahead of *True to the Core.* **HD Mar 5.**

Ernest Tovee charged with being drunk in charge of horse and cart. 'Not in charge, only driving.' **HD Mar 12.**

Lifeboat *Ann Fawcett* for Harwich. 43 ft × 12½ ft.

Two drop keels, ten oars, 'double backed.' **HD Mar 26.**

Brig *Remembrance* of Whitby sinks near Whiting. Crew of six in by *Gipsy* of Aldeburgh. **HD Apr 9.**

Steel screw tug *Foam* for Paul's of Ipswich launched at Paisely. To do ten knots. **HD Oct 1.**

ss *Tyne* on Shipwash. Assisted off by *City of Glasgow*. **HD Nov 26.**

1907
Wreck of ss *Berlin*. **HD Mar 2, 9, 16, 23.** BOT inquiry **Apr 20, 27.**

City of Glasgow launched to ss *Ariadne* on Shipwash. Refused assistance and proceeded. **HD Jun 22.**

New Frinton lifeboat *Sailors' Friend*, 40 ft × 12½ ft, centreboard, non-self-righting, launched by Cann to replace surf boat of the same name. **HD Aug 10** and **17.**

1908
GER ss *Vienna* (sister of *Berlin*) ashore at Hook of Holland in fog. Passengers taken in in boats. *Vienna* soon came afloat and passed her own boats to arrive before them. In same week, GER ss *Amsterdam* damaged in collision entering Hook. **HD Jan 25.**

Three-masted schooner *Notre Dame de Toutes Aides* of Nantes wrecked on Kentish Knock. Eight of crew of eleven saved by *City of Glasgow*. Crew awarded £1 each and certificates by RNLI. **HD Apr 11, May 16, Sept 17.**

City of Glasgow out to signals north of West Rocks. Returned without finding vessel in distress. 'It has since transpired that a large liner burned a flare for a pilot through the Swin and the pilot responded by also burning a flare.' **HD Jun 27.**

'GER have decided to fit their steamers with a system of wireless telegraphy. The turbine ss *Copenhagen* and the twin screw ss *Dresden* have already been so equipped.' **HD Jul 4.**

City of Glasgow tows in Dutch vessel *San Pedro* (for Brazil with coal and pig iron) in distress off North Foreland. 'Launch was made in eighteen minutes, which is extremely good.' **HD Sept 12.**

True to the Core to be fitted with 'motor apparatus.' **HD Oct 10.**

GER cargo steamer *Yarmouth* (805 tons) founders on passage Hook of Holland to Parkeston with twenty-one crew and one passenger. Seen by Gabbard lightship circling on beam ends but 'not thought to be in distress.' **HD Oct 31, Nov**

1908—cont.

7 and **14**. **BOT** inquiry **Feb 27, 1909**. '**GER** not guilty of fault.' **July 24, 1909**.

Death of Oliver J Williams, aged 84. **HD Dec 5**.

1909

Harwich, Clacton, Walton and Frinton lifeboats out all night in snowstorm on fruitless errand. Frinton boat damaged in collision with Harwich boat. **HD Jan 2**.

'Submarine signalling', already installed in Dutch lighthouse at mouth of the Maas, to be installed in Gabbard lightship and in GER steamers working to Hook of Holland and Antwerp. **HD Feb 6** and **Apr 24**.

Death of Ben Dale, former cox'n of Harwich sailing lifeboats. **HD May 8**.

1910

Ramsgate smack *Valiant* ashore on West Rocks, brought in by fourteen Walton beachmen. **HD Jul 11**.

Index of Wrecks and Casualties

These vessels were all at the receiving end of the salvagers' attentions, though not all were wrecked. This index does not attempt to include every incident listed in Book Three, but as far as possible connects references in Books One and Two with their dates and sources in Book Three. References from page 165 onwards are noted *a* or *b*, denoting first or second column of the page.

Index of Smacks

Some details, including place and date of building and dimensions, are included when I happen to know these. Alternatives are given when more than one smack of the name was registered.

Index of Other Vessels

kb – ketch barge   sb – sailing barge   ss – steamship   lb – lifeboat   RC – revenue cutter

Index of Persons

Index of Subjects and Places

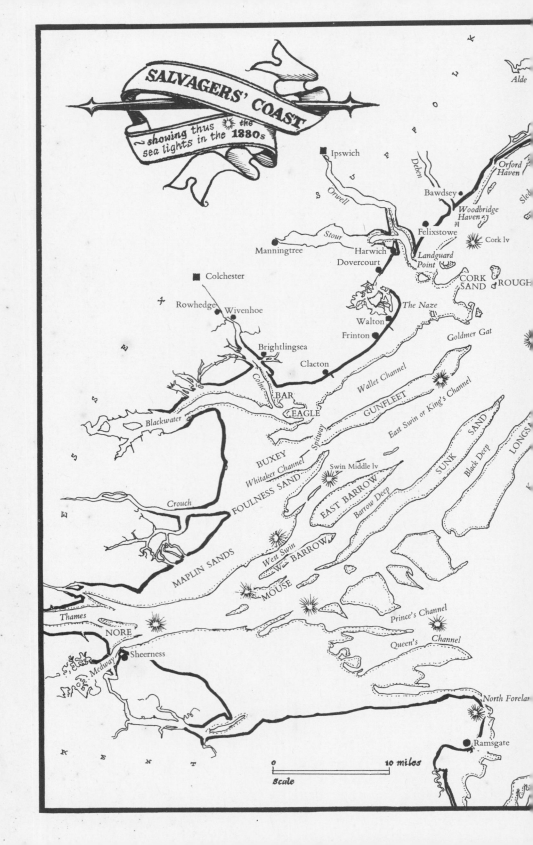

SALVAGERS' COAST

showing thus ✳ the
sea lights in the 1880s

Alde

■ Ipswich

Orford
Haven

Debben

Slebb

Bawdsey

Woodbridge
Haven

Felixstowe

✳ Cork lv

Orwell

Stour

Manningtree

Harwich

Dovercourt

Landguard
Point

CORK
SAND   ROUGH

■ Colchester

Rowhedge

Wivenhoe

The Naze

Walton

Frinton

Goldmer Gat

Brightlingsea

Clacton

Colne

BAR
EAGLE

Wallet Channel

GUNFLEET

East Swin or King's Channel

Blackwater

Spitway

BUXEY

Whitaker Channel

Swin Middle lv

SUNK
SAND

Black Deep

LONGS

Crouch

FOULNESS SAND

EAST BARROW

Barrow Deep

West Swin

W. BARROW

BARROW

MAPLIN SANDS

MOUSE

Prince's Channel

Thames

NORE

Queen's   Channel

Sheerness

Medway

North Forelan

10 miles

0

Scale

Ramsgate

K   E   N   T